The Happiness of the Pursuit

Felicitous Episodes Along the Way

The Happiness of the Pursuit

Felicitous Episodes Along the Way

Ted Lamont

publishers name TK

Hamilton Books CONFIRM NAME ▪ ADDRESS TK ▪ WEB TK?
First Edition ▪ All rights reserved
Design by Inger Gibb ▪ Printed by Hamilton Books CONFIRM
Library of Congress Control Number : NUMBER TK ▪ ISBN NUMBER TK

In memory of my brother, Tommy Lamont

Contents

continued

Introduction

While Thomas Jefferson believed in "the pursuit of happiness," a wise friend once observed that what life was really all about was "the happiness of the pursuit," and he made a good point. Writing an account of your life for your progeny and friends is a popular pastime for senior citizens, and it's time to take pen in hand when the number of funerals that you attend is greater than the number of weddings, and young men and women offer you their seat on the subway. Private recollections often tend to be boring chronological records of the journey from womb to tomb, and I will try not to subject readers to this form of tedium. An alert traveler will observe some pretty funny happenings as he strides down the road of life, enjoying "the happiness of the pursuit." Of course, some did not seem so funny at the time, and some may strike the author as amusing but leave others nonplussed.

Autobiographies are good reading and reliable history only when the author is frank enough to tell it like it was – the good and the bad, the heroics and the blunders. Senator John McCain, Thomas J. Watson, Jr. and Katherine Graham each wrote autobiographies with these attributes – all great stories. But to polish one's image and gloss over one's failures and shortcomings à la Richard Nixon is a very human temptation. I'll try to be forthright, but I'm not going to tell in graphic detail about the times when I stayed too late at the party. Not even George W. Bush would do that; nor should he. Of course, the aforementioned authors all had fascinating lives, wheeling and dealing at a history-making level.

If you want to read a really good biography about a man who for decades *was* engaged at the cutting edge of history with leading players from J.P. Morgan to Charles Lindbergh to Franklin D. Roosevelt, read *The Ambassador From Wall Street – The Story of Thomas W. Lamont, J.P. Morgan's Chief Executive*. I am the author and Thomas W. Lamont was my grandfather. However, *The Happiness of the Pursuit* is a different kind of book – simply a story about my family and events in my life as I tried to keep the faith and get the job done while enjoying some fun along the way. I am very grateful to my good friend E. S. Yntema for her editorial suggestions and insights. Peggy is a real pro and a pleasure to work with, and so is Terry Walton, who managed the production of my book. My wife Buz designed the book's cover and was a big help throughout.

I once was invited by the Cowles family to go duck shooting at their *Minneapolis Star and Tribune* shooting lodge in the Minnesota lake country, where the regular evening drill called for bridge games after dinner. I knew nothing about bidding conventions and had never played serious bridge – just the infrequent family game in Maine on a rainy day. On the other hand, the other Cowles guests, mainly corporate executives, were avid bridge players. So a friend and I elected to sit out the bridge action, which worked out fine because they had several full tables without us. One evening a player retired early, however, and I was drafted to replace him. My partner was Paul Hoffman, the former chief of the Marshall Plan and widely admired as a distinguished American statesman. I was somewhat nervous to be playing in such fast company. I warned Paul that while I knew the game, I was a bit rusty and would not be a speedy player. I never got to be "dummy," as I had hoped, for, as it turned out, I was the one who ended up playing the hands for our team. Slowly and surely I won them all. I basked in my partner's congratulations as we collected our financial winnings at the end of the evening. In fact, it was an easy victory because we had held such great cards that not even a rank amateur like me could blow it.

In life, as in card games, the luck of the draw is important. You play the hand you are dealt, and I have always been grateful for the super cards that came my way – my forebears and Buz, my wonderful wife and partner.

My Boyhood
on Park Avenue

Grandfather Lamont, the son of a small-town Methodist parson, was a self-made man who worked his way through Exeter and Harvard and with great ability and ambition rose to become the chief executive of J.P. Morgan & Co., the most powerful investment bank in the world at the time. He made a fortune during the Roaring Twenties and enjoyed the good life to the fullest. Grandfather Miner, son of a doctor in Winchester, Illinois, was another self-made man. He rose to become the chairman of the Pfaudler Company of Rochester, makers of glass-lined tanks for dairies and breweries. Sagacious and courtly mannered, he served on numerous boards and was for many years the leading citizen of his home town. At Harvard there stands the Lamont Library for undergraduates; at the University of Rochester there stands the Edward G. Miner Library at the Medical School. That says it all. I am grateful to them and their wives for their contributions to my own gene pool.

Mother and Dad fell in love at North Haven, Maine, where both families were summering, and were married in 1923. Elinor Miner from Rochester, who had attended Miss Porter's School at Farmington, was pretty and vivacious, a real charmer. Thomas S. Lamont had followed in his father's giant footsteps to Exeter and Harvard and J.P. Morgan, where he became a partner in 1929 and later vice-chairman of the board. So a comfortable life was assured for Tommy and Ellie and their children. The first arrival in 1924 was Thomas W. Lamont II, brother Tommy, whose promising life was cut short at the age of twenty when his U.S. Navy submarine was lost in action in World War II.

My vintage was 1926 (December 10). In that year Gertrude Ederle became the first woman to swim the English Channel; heavyweight champ Gene Tunney defeated Jack Dempsey in ten rounds, President Calvin Coolidge governed silently, and Jimmy Walker became the playboy mayor of New York. It was the heyday of the Roaring Twenties, notorious for flappers, jazz music, and the Great Gatsby, and perhaps the timing was prophetic: I have always enjoyed a good party. My parents named me Edward Miner Lamont after Grandfather Miner. I started life off with the nickname of "Teddy," and later switched to "Ted" when I had something to say about it, and joined my family in a spacious Manhattan apartment on the eleventh floor of a new building on the northeast corner of 72nd Street and Park Avenue – 101 East 72nd Street.

My earliest memory is playing with my soldiers and cowboys and Indians on the floor of the big double bedroom that I shared with my brother. Tommy became my big brother mentor, early on and throughout my teenage years. When he first explained to me how babies were conceived, I was astounded. Tommy and I used to have some grand fights, sometimes with pillows but mainly verbal. He had a sharp wit and was adept at needling a slower-thinking adversary like myself. I was a pudgy lad and he soon dubbed me "jelly-belly."

I had a valid reason for being a chubby youngster. The household was staffed with an Irish cook and an Irish maid who made it their practice to heap our plates with food – including mounds of mashed potatoes. There would be no dessert, some delicious concoction, until I had completely cleaned my plate. No hiding spinach under the knife. At breakfast the staple was huge portions of hot oatmeal, or sometimes Cream of Wheat, often lumpy; I have never touched the stuff since. The country was in the midst of the Great Depression, and we were constantly reminded that there were many Americans going to bed hungry. Wasting food was almost sinful, and the experience of going hungry was certainly a real one for many poor Irish families as well. Nowadays stuffing little kids with food is out. In this era of junk food and TV watching, childhood obesity has become a serious health problem.

My younger siblings, Lansing and Elinor, arrived on the scene during the thirties, and so did Rose Quinn, our Irish nanny. Rose was plump and rosy-cheeked and blessed with a happy smile and disposition. She was a loving caretaker during those early years. Mother was not exactly hands-on in her devotion for her little tots and infants.

I attended Buckley, my elementary school, for nine years – the same number of years I spent at prep school, college, and graduate school combined. Sometimes in the surging flow of communications we all receive from these institutions, soliciting donations or announcing upcoming alumni events, we forget how much we owe our old grammar school in the learning process. After a tour of kindergarten duty, I entered Mrs. Stoddard's first grade at Buckley School in September 1932. Each school day for the next nine years I donned my dark blue cap with the little white B over the visor, and walked to school, two blocks away on 74th Street. My first report card gave me good marks in Music, Playground Activities, and Social Conduct in which I rated well as both a "leader" and a "good follower" – a sign of uncommon flexibility. In music the comment was "Very good – sings well and has rhythm." I've been singing away at parties, in the shower, and even on stage ever since.

The marking system at Buckley was exceedingly friendly, designed to keep the children's morale high and their parents pleased. Let kids enjoy a happy childhood. Everyone knows how tough the marking system becomes later in life. From time to time I received the honor roll award of carrying the American flag at morning assembly. In fifth grade I received fourteen A's and a B in art – a gift, remembering some of my creations. The inflated marks were accompanied by glowing comments, such as in Crafts: "Grand worker." Who was kidding whom? I remember constructing one beat-up wooden chest after considerable frustrating effort. Years later I saw our granddaughter Emily's report card from Greenwich Country Day School – six A's and one B, in Graphic Arts. Some things never change.

The real fun was outside the classroom. On fall and spring afternoons we were bussed across the Queensborough Bridge to a playing field in Astoria, Long Island, to play football and baseball. In the winter we played basketball in the school gym and once a week ice hockey at the Madison Square skating club. I also liked performing in the school plays put on in the gymnasium – playing a rollicking British tar in "H.M.S. Pinafore," and poor Bob Cratchit in "Christmas Carol."

At the Buckley graduation ceremony in 1941 I received the Best English Composition Award for seniors. My favorite composition was my story of an all-star band's slide downhill to its eventual breakup, based on the theme that practice and teamwork were just as essential for a band as for a sports team. At the time the big swing bands like those of the Dorsey brothers, Harry James, and Glenn Miller were very popular, playing a new style of dance music that was sweeping the country.

One teacher stands out above all others at Buckley in his contribution to my education – Ben Long, who taught grammar, punctuation, and composition. But for Ben I would never have appreciated the sage advice of a Harvard commencement speaker who said, "Always remember, as you go out into the world to pursue your destiny, that it's not who you know that counts, but whom." Ben Long was a very nice man with a twinkle in his eye. One time he caught me sneaking a look at my watch during English class and dead-panned, "By the way, Ted, what time is it?"

At the graduation ceremony I was also given another award – the cup for The Best Citizen. My Miner grandparents had driven from Rochester to attend the ceremony, and I hoped Grandfather Miner would be proud of his namesake. Every other Christmas we boarded the Pullman train for the overnight journey to Rochester to spend the holidays with the Miners at 2 Argyle Street – a massive, homely three-story brick house just off East Avenue. I happily recall playing with our second cousins the Macomber boys; mountains of snow for snowball fights; the jovial presence of Mother's redheaded brother, Uncle Ranny Miner; Grandfather's special panache in carving the turkey at Christmas dinner; Grandmother's electric car; and Grandfather smoking his cigar in the library surrounded by his beloved books. The aroma of cigar smoke clung to the drapes and upholstery down through the years, a reminder on each visit that a well-loved old man was still enjoying a favorite diversion right up until he passed away at the ripe old age of ninety-one.

I remember Grandfather Miner as a kindly, courteous, and distinguished elderly gentleman. He had an old-fashioned air about him: I never saw him without a coat and tie – usually a double-breasted dark blue suit, his tie adorned with a pearl stickpin. Everyone treated him with tremendous respect, from the doorman at the Genesee Valley Club to the CEO of Eastman Kodak. He was wise, and he was erudite. When Grandfather Miner was appointed chairman of the board of the University of Rochester, a local businessman said, "Ned Miner makes me mad. No matter what subject I bring up, he knows more about it than I do." President Alan Valentine of the University, in awarding an honorary degree to Miner, stated, "You brought with you out of the plains of Illinois a little of Lincoln, much of Mark Twain, and just a suspicion of Paul Bunyan, and staid Rochester has profited from all three."

Edward G. Miner, born in Waverly, Illinois, in 1863, had left Illinois for Rochester at age nineteen to become secretary of the Pfaudler Company, founded by a cousin. In time he rose to lead the company, which he transformed into an international operation and the world's largest manufacturer of glass-lined containers.

Grandfather Miner never went to college, but he had a tremendous curiosity about a variety of subjects – from medicine to history – and he was a voracious reader. He also collected rare books, many of which he purchased on his business trips abroad. He donated his excellent collection of books on yellow fever, purchased after a trip to South America, to the University of Rochester medical library – later named after him. He had a keen interest in American history and left me several books on the origin of Mormonism in upstate New York, as well as a collection of articles and letters about Abraham Lincoln, who had been a friend of his grandfather's in Winchester, Illinois. Grandfather contributed greatly to the welfare and progress of his city, and Rochester honored him with civic awards for his many good works. The following letter, written to my brother Tommy on his eighteenth birthday, tells more about Grandfather Miner than could any words of mine. Tommy had recently given the Senior Class Oration at his Exeter commencement exercises.

> *You were my first grandchild, and your birth meant a great deal to all of us. I was in the Milwaukee Club, Milwaukee, Wisconsin, when the telegram came telling of your arrival. I was sitting talking with Governor Frank L. Lowden, and he suggested that we have a small bottle of champagne and drink a toast to the young man, which we did. . . . Time has gone so fast since that day that I have not realized that all of a sudden, my grandson has grown to man's estate. . . . I have loved you all through the years, as only a grandfather can, and I tried to tell you this in my awkward way when I saw you last at Exeter.*

Your Class oration that day made me proud beyond words. . . .
I know that you will make your life worthwhile and that all of us will
be proud of your work. Whatever you do, wherever you go, you will
always carry with you the love and hopes and prayers of us all.

You will have your periods of doubt as to the future; you will
have your disappointments that men will not rise to the best that is
in them, and are content to live among the husks and swine. But if
you keep your faith in ultimate truth, decency and goodness, you will
come out in the end strengthened for the conflict which runs through
a man's experience.

Be true to yourself, and at the same time have infinite charity
for your fellow man who does not see the light, as God gives you to
see it. Be honest and charitable with those men who hold mistaken
views, and scorn deceit as you would the plague; a man who is hon-
est with himself and has charity in his heart for his fellow man will
never lack friends. You will have disappointments, sorrow, doubts of
yourself, and some suspicion of your fellow man at times – all the
miseries which every man of honor has had since the beginning of
history, but you can overcome these. A smile, a kind word, a gracious
deed, no matter how small it seems to you, bulks large with others.
Be charitable, and forgiving – it does not pay to hate. In other words,
be a man, and God go with you.

There was indeed "a little of Lincoln" in that message as we recall the
words of his second inaugural address: "With malice toward none; with
charity for all." Nowadays such wise and virtuous advice from our elders,
commencement speakers, or ministers sounds old-fashioned and is rare.
It's a pity.

Today my daughter Camille Burlingham lives in Stonington,
Connecticut, not far from where Grandfather's forebear Thomas Minor
lived on his farm in the 1600s. Thomas, born in 1608 in Somerset County,
England, had been the first of my Miner ancestors to come to the New
World. After leaving the Massachusetts Bay Colony he settled in the present day Stonington in 1653; today, an imposing granite monument in the
town honors Minor as a founder of the small frontier community. Minor
was a farmer, militia officer, and active public official of Stonington for
many years. He sometimes hired Indians from the local Pequot tribe to
work on his farm – the same tribe that now owns the highly successful
Foxwoods Casino nearby. I don't know if Thomas gambled, but he did
enjoy a glass of wine. An entry in his diary in August 1656 – a non sequitur,
I trust – states, "Bought wine and broke my scythe."

My tenth birthday, December 10, 1936, fell on the same day that the
king of England, Edward VIII, renounced the throne to marry the woman
he loved, Wallis Warfield Simpson, an American divorcée. The advocates

of duty and romance in the Lamont family and around the world had a splendid time debating the king's momentous decision. The king and Mrs. Simpson had been guests the previous June at a dinner in London which my Lamont grandparents had also attended. They reported that the king had indeed appeared smitten with Mrs. Simpson. Some noted that when Edward was Prince of Wales before the death of his father, King George V, he was something of a playboy with an eye for pretty girls. Some years later an elderly Locust Valley dowager told me a story about the young prince's behavior during one of his visits to Long Island's Gold Coast during the spring social season in the twenties. At a gala "coming-out" party, at which young ladies were officially introduced to society, he swept one lovely young debutante off her feet and, without a word to anyone, they slipped away together into the night, not to reappear until late the following day. The prince's aide, a British naval lieutenant, was beside himself with anxiety; part of his assignment was to keep the prince out of trouble.

"Did the girl's parents call the police to report that their daughter was missing?" I asked.

"Don't be silly," was the reply. "What self-respecting mother would want to break up her daughter's liaison with the future king of England?"

When I was twelve I started taking piano lessons once a week from Joe Kruger, who taught his worshipful students to play popular music by ear. An earlier mandated effort at conventional piano lessons with a Mrs. Perfield had left me cold. Joe was a wonderful teacher and a good friend who gave our family piano lessons for many years. The first two songs I learned to play were "Oh, Johnny, Oh!" (the Bonnie Baker vocal with Orrin Tucker's orchestra was a hit record) and "Over the Rainbow" (from "The Wizard of Oz" starring Judy Garland, which became an all-time movie classic).

Joe's teaching and style took hold, and I am still playing away, usually at dinner parties. Nothing formal: After cocktails and a good dinner and wine there are often some guests eager to go public with their vocalizing, and my vintage repertoire appeals to our age group. In these sing-alongs it is important for the piano player to know the lyrics – because the would-be Sinatras and Streisands usually do not. The high point of my piano playing career was playing twin pianos with bandleader Bill Harrington, at a Piping Rock Club party. Just a few numbers; I was wise enough to know when to quit, especially when he suggested that we switch out of the key of C.

Town and Country

We spent weekends and holidays during the school year at the country estate of my Lamont grandparents at Palisades, so named because of its site near the brim of the great cliffs overlooking the Hudson River. Palisades was about an hour's drive from our city apartment – over the George Washington Bridge and then about fifteen miles north on Route 9W. The house was large and comfortable – plenty of room for children, grandchildren, and house guests – and well staffed. There were rolling lawns, gardens, a tennis court, and an indoor pool, all surrounded by woods crisscrossed with hiking trails. In the winter we went sledding on the big hill in back of the house and skating on a frozen pond in the woods.

Grandmother Lamont was always ready to play or read aloud with her grandchildren, and we adored her. Grandfather was most kindly, but I knew that he was a busy and important man (especially after President Roosevelt telephoned him one Sunday) so kept a respectful distance until called on. He favored sporty waistcoats, and even in casual attire looked smoothly elegant. He seemed to go everywhere worth going and know everyone worth knowing. My uncle Corliss Lamont and his family also spent weekends there, and Tommy and I often invited Buckley pals to keep us company. To escape from the bustling city each weekend to an idyllic spot in the country, where almost every conceivable need and amusement was sumptuously provided, was every city kid's dream, wasn't it? Well, not exactly.

I did not always welcome the mandatory limousine trip to the country every Friday afternoon. During the 1930s and 1940s the American movie truly came of age. People flocked to movie theatres, in many cases to enjoy a few hours' respite from the grim Depression realities of everyday life. Surely everyone's spirits were lifted in watching Fred Astaire in white tie and tails and Ginger Rogers in a shimmering gown twirl and glide gracefully about some elegant penthouse salon. In the city the extravagantly glamorous theatres themselves were part of the attraction – the gloriously Art Deco design of Radio City Music Hall, the Roxy with its huge neon-lit marquee on Broadway, and the exciting Paramount where the big bands and Sinatra performed. My favorite neighborhood theatres were Loew's 72nd Street with its pharaonic décor (and a Schrafft's soda fountain next door), and RKO 86th Street with its special added feature for kids on Saturday afternoons, such as the serial adventures of Flash Gordon.

The parents of my Buckley buddies in the city organized weekend movie parties for their kids, and I wanted to join them. My parents said "Sorry, we're going to Palisades!" and that was that. They followed quite an active social schedule during the week with dinner parties, benefits, and the occasional Broadway show or opera. Accordingly, they were delighted to head for the country over the weekends to relax in lovely surroundings and luxurious lodging offering all the amenities from tennis to fine dining and room service.

Furthermore, my elders had a poor opinion of most movies, considering them low-brow trash produced by a Hollywood culture that they disdained. It wasn't a question of sex and violence in films; industry censorship (the Hays Office) was operating, and movies were pure and innocent compared to current offerings. It was rather that in their view the plots, characters, and language were poor models for impressionable children and simply a misuse of time better spent in more worthwhile pursuits like reading good books.

For the same reasons my parents also frowned on radio dramas (even "The Shadow" played by Orson Wells, an avenging character whose real name in the serial was Lamont Cranston) and radio comedians such as Jack Benny. I also listened regularly to radio serials for kids like Buck Rogers and the 21st Century, Jack Armstrong, The All-American Boy, and Little Orphan Annie. On Sundays I would stealthily sneak off to the estate superintendent's house at Palisades to read the comic strip section of his copy of the *Journal American*, a New York tabloid scorned by my elders. Dick Tracy, the very cool big-city detective, was my favorite character. During my early years the cultural divide between my parents and me was wide indeed.

My keen interest in the sports section of the daily newspaper was additional vexation for my father, who felt that reading about sports was a waste of time that would serve no useful purpose. Many years later I still turn to the sports section in the morning paper. I have found that sports talk constitutes a common language among men, a real ice-breaker that can trigger friendly conversation – whether at a formal business dinner or a Lions Club picnic on the beach. It is a far safer topic for strangers to discuss than presidential politics.

At Sunday lunches around the big dining room table at Palisades we did not talk sports. If we had, I might have had more to say. In fact Grandmother Lamont had never heard of Babe Ruth! Instead the family discussed politics and other big issues of the day – war and peace in Europe, socialism versus capitalism, FDR versus Wall Street – vigorously, and sometimes heatedly. The usual line-up was the Morgan partners, father and son, debating the Socialist Lamonts, Corliss and his wife Margaret. The exchange was similar to CNN's "Crossfire" today, except the bankers TWL and TSL were more moderate in their Republican views than television's Robert Novak, representing the right. In those good old days the moderate wing of the party led by the Eastern establishment still dominated the G.O.P. During these exchanges we all noted the intellectual prowess and maturity of brother Tommy, as, well informed and articulate, he waded into the heady discussions with his elders. His siblings and cousins held him in awe.

I engaged in political activity two times as a boy. In 1936 I passed out Alf Landon sunflower buttons and pamphlets, mainly to Park Avenue doormen, who were nonplussed to receive propaganda about the Republican candidate for president.

Four years later Mother and I attended the Republican presidential convention in Philadelphia for a day. Grandfather was an ardent supporter of Wendell L.Willkie, a fast-rising dark horse candidate for the nomination, and had purchased two tickets in the visitors' gallery of Convention Hall. However, newspapers opposing Willkie were charging that he was a captive of Wall Street. So TWL thought it best to stay away, and Mother and I went instead.

The Willkie partisans at his Benjamin Franklin Hotel suite and in the visitors' gallery at Convention Hall were enthusiastic and vocal in supporting their candidate, and the upper tier gallery was packed with them. I had heard my elders state that he had been rapidly gaining ground against his rival candidates, New York Governor Thomas E. Dewey and Ohio's Senator Robert A. Taft.

Outside the hotel headquarters of Senator Taft a live elephant led a parade of his supporters. Taft was the son of a former president, but the pachyderm and pedigree didn't get the job done for him. Charisma is a vital ingredient for success in modern politics, and Wendell Willkie, a Wall Street utility executive from Indiana, was loaded with it; he won his party's presidential nomination on the sixth ballot. On November 2 my friend Kelly Simpson, whose father was a Republican Party official, invited me to attend a monster rally for Willkie at Madison Square Garden. It was an exciting spectacle for a thirteen-year-old boy: Bands blared away, the crowds chanted "We want Willkie," and finally the great man appeared on center stage, bathed in the focus of beaming spotlights. His rousing speech evoked even greater tumultuous cheering. The crowd loved his unpretentious, dynamic, and wisecracking style. In the general election Willkie polled more votes than any Republican before him, but he still lost to the champ, FDR.

I enjoyed sports as a boy, although my athletic talents were no better than average. I played first base and rooted for the New York Giants baseball team. The great southpaw pitcher Carl Hubbell and home run slugger Mel Ott were my heroes, and I stood and cheered as Mel trotted around the bases after hitting one over the short right-field wall at the Polo Grounds, the old Manhattan ballpark by the Harlem River. Some twenty years later I was cheering the incomparable Willie Mays, the greatest Giants player of them all. The Giants were usually underdogs to the powerhouse Yankees in World Series match-ups, which is one reason I backed them. No other team has dominated its sport over a long span of years like the Yankees.

My favorite spectator sport, however, has always been football. I have spent many a Sunday afternoon watching NFL games on the tube, often just the second half when it can really get exciting. (You can also read the Sunday *New York Times*, probably the most voluminous Sunday paper in the world, during commercial breaks.) The physical action is fast paced; a close game in the fourth quarter becomes high drama, and guessing the plays that coaches will call – run or pass, punt or go for it, and all the other strategies – gives the viewer an added sense of participation. For me the completion of a long downfield pass from a beleaguered quarterback to a leaping, sure-handed receiver is as graceful as Swan Lake and far more exciting. Once again I chose the New York Giants and have remained a loyal fan through thick and thin, and there has been a lot of the latter.

My enthusiasm for football games was first sparked by watching Yale teams battle their opponents in the Bowl, thanks to my Buckley pals and their Eli fathers who invited me to the games. Ivy League football was big-time then, and Yale was a powerhouse with two Heisman Trophy winners in the late thirties.

Driving up the Merritt Parkway from the city, we joined a scene that has changed little over the years – tailgating station wagons; picnic hampers loaded with roast beef sandwiches and stuffed eggs; ruddy-faced old grads in double-breasted polo coats and green Tyrolean hats pouring Bloody Marys from silver cocktail shakers; the spirited Yale marching band spelling out some illegible attempt at wit; and the excitement of the game itself. I've been back to the Yale Bowl many times since those days, once for an NFL game between the Giants and the Jets before Giants Stadium was built. The Bowl was filled to the brim with 80,000 raucous fans, many hoping to watch Joe Namath, the Jets' star quarterback, do a job on the Giants in a game of high-powered intra-city rivalry. It was not an Ivy League crowd. To reach our seats we had to squeeze by a very large man who had set up a small bar in front of his seat. As he struggled to stand up to give Buz room to pass, she inquired, "Can you make it all right, sir?," and he replied, "I can make it any time you want to, honey."

It is simply a myth that everything becomes more efficient with the passage of time. Consider the parking arrangements at the Yale Bowl. Years later a visit to the Bowl for a Harvard-Yale game would end up in a near disaster. After the game we found our car, along with hundreds of others, trapped in a stadium parking lot surrounded by a high chain link fence, anchored in concrete, with one single-car exit gate. A disorganized mass of drivers converged on this gate with much horn-blowing and fighting for position every inch of the way. The road from the exit then merged into another glacially slow stream of cars. It was the Mother of all Traffic Jams. Furthermore it was cold, darkness was falling, and there was not a single cop or Yale official in sight.

I passed a man in a car telling his wife on his cellphone that he was imprisoned by Yale and probably would not reach home until well after dinner. We all faced the same grim prospect. Then I had a brainstorm, and said to the caller, "Why don't you call 911 and tell them the situation here and that they should send some officers immediately to open up additional exits?" I called in the same message on our cellphone, and soon had twenty other frustrated drivers bombarding 911. I told the police operator that the crowd was angry and getting ugly. Fifteen minutes later three patrol cars arrived, opened up gates directly onto the avenue, and we all got out of there in a hurry. I had previously looked askance at people walking around with cellphones glued to their ears. Not anymore.

Roller-skating around town with my pals was another Fun City sport in my boyhood years. We buckled and clamped the four-wheeled skates onto our shoes, tightened the clamps with a skate key, and off we went. My friend Curtis Cushman and I covered every nook and cranny of Central Park from the Reservoir to the Zoo to the twisting and hilly little concrete paths of the wooded Rambles. Another dazzling attraction was the New York World's Fair, the 1939 model with the Trylon and Perisphere as its signature landmark. At Futurama, the General Motors exhibit, I boarded a train of little cars for an imaginative trip into the future. But the Midway, the amusement park with its parachute jump and weird freak exhibits, was my favorite place.

One evening, strolling down the Midway with my father and visiting friends, we stopped in front of a show called "Salvador Dali's Dream of Venus." The out-of-towners were eager to see the exhibition, so we bought our tickets and went on in. To my delight and my father's surprise the show featured bare-breasted girls with painted bodies and mermaid tails, swimming in a big tank of water with a Daliesque background. Dad mumbled something about "modern art," and we were soon on our way. My father clearly felt that I was too young and innocent to be ogling naked girls in the flesh. Naturally, I had not told him about the stack of nudist camp magazines, well illustrated, that we kids had found in the house of an old hermit in Maine, or the collection of French girlie postcards that a friend kept safely hidden in a closet at his house. These materials were not nearly as illustrative as *Playboy* magazine decades later, which just goes to show that life gets better for each generation.

The best times I spent with my father as a boy were our ski trips to the Green and White mountains of Vermont and New Hampshire. During the late thirties and early forties, the two of us and a horde of other skiers would board the night train in Grand Central Station bound for Woodstock or North Conway, via Portland. As soon as the train left the station the party began, and I would drop off to sleep in the upper berth to the sounds of tinkling ice and laughter.

Holding on to the primitive rope tows at Bunny's and Suicide Six in Woodstock, or Catamount in the Berkshires, was a formidable challenge when the rope was wet and icy. One time my dad bought me a special pair of rubber mittens to grip the rope at Bunny's. They did more than grip: They froze right onto the rope, and at the top of the tow this twelve-year-old boy was hoisted bodily into the air. I finally wrenched my hands free and fell into the snow, while my mittens and ski poles were carried up into the big wheel that clattered to a stop – leaving scores of angry skiers stranded on the hillside.

On our trips to North Conway we stayed at the large, rambling Eastern Slopes Inn, where I sipped Cokes when my dad and I joined the merry après-ski crowd in the Pink Elephant Bar. Mt. Cranmore featured a multi-colored "ski-mobile" tramway and the legendary Hannes Schneider as head of the ski school. The sport was still in its infancy in America, and Schneider, a famous Austrian ski-meister, made sure that the novices under his tutelage had a full complement of lessons as they advanced deliberately from class to class – walking, climbing, snow plough, stem christie, and so forth – before they were permitted to ski down from the summit. The snow bunnies, led by bronzed and handsome Austrian instructors, followed this drill unswervingly. I was soon cutting class to head for the top of the mountain.

Those were the days of wooden skis and loose bindings – and long before the introduction of artificial snow that has virtually saved New England ski resorts from extinction. The slopes and trails, worn thin by the weekend crowds, were often washboard hard, with patches of ice and granular snow here and there. With lots of slipping, sliding, and hard-edging I navigated tough mountain trails such as the Nose Dive at Stowe's Mt. Mansfield, disdaining the easygoing Toll Road as a route for mothers and little kids. I also recall my first experience skiing in deep snow, two feet of fresh powder on Cannon Mountain's narrow Taft racing trail – no walk in the park either.

Then when spring arrived, there were new hazards awaiting the unwary. I was skiing with my father one day in late March when he broke his ankle on the S 53 trail at Mt. Mansfield; the warm sun had made skiing tricky on the melting stop-and-go surfaces of slush and sugar. Years later I realized that trail skiing in New England, under all conditions, had readied me for tackling any other mountains with confidence – from the Rockies to the Alps.

Lowell Thomas, the celebrated radio news reporter and an avid skier, invited my father and me to join his ski parties several times. He always performed his seven o'clock evening news broadcast from wherever we were. I have a photograph of his broadcast from the base lodge at Cannon Mountain with my dad holding up the time cards for him. My father asked Lowell if he couldn't skip a broadcast every now and then when he was on the road, to avoid the extra expense and effort of putting on the show away from the studio. Lowell replied that he would never do such a thing. Some of his listeners might turn the dial to another station and desert his program; he wouldn't run the risk of losing them to the competition. As a youngster I was very impressed by Lowell's style: He was gregarious, self-confident, and masterful at bringing people of different backgrounds together for a good time. Our party at Cannon Mountain included my father the banker, a judge, and the New York State boxing commissioner.

Some twenty-five years later I would meet Lowell Thomas again at Stratton Mountain, and he introduced me to the owner of Mt. Snow. "Meet Ted Lamont of J.P. Morgan. You guys should get along well. Mt. Snow is planning a big expansion and Morgan is loaded with capital!" said Lowell breezily, as he pushed off down the trail in a series of well-carved turns.

In the summers the Lamont clan spent almost every vacation in North Haven – the island in Penobscot Bay, Maine, where my grandfather had bought land and built a big, rambling yellow summer home in 1920. My family lived in a smaller house on the same property overlooking the bay. Sky Farm lived up to its name in those days, with an operating dairy and a couple of dozen sheep, which we enjoyed chasing through the spacious pasture.

The Lamont boys swam in the frigid bay water off the rocky beach below our house where there was a rowboat and a swimming raft anchored just offshore. Plunges into bone-chilling water lost their appeal when I was older, although I came to recognize the therapeutic shock value of diving in after partying late the night before. Some evenings, friends and family gathered for picnics on the beach where we feasted on lobsters and corn. When we were well fed and sitting around a roaring driftwood fire, we broke into song – "You Can Roll a Silver Dollar on the Ground," "You Are My Sunshine," and other sing-along favorites. The legal ban on campfires in recent years has dampened enthusiasm for evening beach picnics, and that's a pity. Sometimes with the best of intentions society goes too far – overkill.

We did a lot of sailing in the small and fragile North Haven dinghies and twenty-one-foot knockabouts, often in the races organized by the yacht club quaintly known as the Casino. The inability to set a spinnaker smoothly was apparently a genetic family defect. Each year Mother recruited a highly presentable clean-cut junior or senior from Harvard to look after her three boys; they were called "tutors" and looked forward to spending their evenings off duty with the pretty teenage daughters of other summer residents. Brad Simmons, who stroked the Harvard crew, Austie Harding, the hockey captain, and the others were all great guys.

The most famous celebrity I encountered as a boy was as modest and laconic as Lowell Thomas was outgoing and convivial. Charles A. Lindbergh, a true American hero, sometimes visited the summer home of his in-laws, the Dwight Morrows, in North Haven, where I met him in 1936. Dwight Morrow and Grandfather Lamont were fellow partners at J.P. Morgan and good friends. Colonel Lindbergh, slim and boyishly handsome, offered to take a few of the local kids up in his two-seater single-engine plane for short flights over the bay. When my turn came I climbed into the little plane, and we took off from the big lawn running down to the shore that served as Lindbergh's air strip. There was no steering yoke; a "joy stick" controlled the plane's flight. After a few minutes flying over the bay, Colonel Lindbergh put my hand on the stick and told me that I could steer the plane. I pushed the stick a little too far and the plane's nose started to head down toward the blue waters below. "I think I'll take over now, son," said Colonel Lindbergh, removing my hand.

My father's family is descended from the ancient Lamont clan of Argyllshire in western Scotland. I have long been proud of my Scottish heritage and even occasionally sport a pair of dark green Lamont tartan trousers at dinner parties. It has been said of the Scots that the world is their pillow, and the current Clan Lamont chieftain is Father Peter Lamont, a Catholic priest in Australia. I talked with him when Buz and I visited there in 1990. His grandfather had emigrated to Australia from Scotland, and his father had married a French Catholic girl. The title of clan chieftain is passed down from one generation to the next, following the same family bloodline. I asked Father Peter how the succession would proceed in that he was a priest. "Not to worry. My brother is prolific," was the reply.

I am a member of the Clan Lamont Societies of North America and Scotland and have returned to the homeland of my forebears several times. My ancestors later joined the many Scots who migrated to Northern Ireland in the seventeenth century before coming to America. On a trip to Ireland a few years ago Buz and I drove north to Coleraine in County Antrim, where the Lamonts had settled, and walked about the port. It was around 1745, the story goes, that young Archibald Lamont was enticed aboard a ship in the harbor by the captain, and then kidnapped to serve as a cabin boy on the vessel, which was bound for New York. He settled upstate and was joined by his mother and two brothers. I am a direct descendant of brother Robert. They are all buried in the cemetery of the old Methodist Church in North Hillsdale, New York.

They were in fact part of a huge migration. Perhaps a quarter of a million Ulster Scots came to America during the sixty-year period leading up to the Revolutionary War. The Scots-Irish in America, unlike so many Tory Highlanders, were strong supporters of the Revolutionary cause, and Robert's son William served in the Continental Army and witnessed British General Burgoyne's surrender at Saratoga in 1777. There have been other Lamont descendants whose forebears followed the same route to America, including Senator John McCain, as he records in his autobiography.

It was a family trip to Scotland in 1937 that first sparked my interest in our Scottish background. Grandfather Lamont had rented the ancestral home of Sir Ian Colquhoun, named Rossdhu, on the western shore of Loch Lomond for the summer, and invited his children, grandchildren, and a stream of guests to join him.

We made the crossing on the German passenger liner *Europa*. For a ten-year-old boy this was endless excitement and fun – steaming out of New York Harbor past the Statue of Liberty, betting on the horse race games in the main salon, and taking the Captain's tour of the bridge. After a tourist stopover in London to see the sights (Madame Tussaud's waxworks scenes of blood and gore were my favorite), we boarded the night train for Glasgow and Rossdhu, a stately stone manor in the woodlands by the loch.

We bicycled to the little thatched-roofed village of Luss to buy postcards, attended clan games with burly caber throwers and kilt-clad bagpiper marching bands, and watched sheep dog trials on the heather-covered highland slopes. We also learned that Scots pronounce our name with the accent on the first syllable. Any other pronunciation is considered pretentious. Buz and I would return to Scotland sixty-some years later and visit Rossdhu. It is now the clubhouse for an exclusive golf club with eighteen holes along the "bonny banks" of Loch Lomond and is owned by a Scottsdale resort developer. The beautiful loch, celebrated in song, is a major tourist attraction.

For me the high point of my first trip had been visiting the ruins of Toward Castle, once the principal seat of the Clan Lamont. Mary, Queen of Scots, reportedly visited the castle in 1563. As with George Washington in America, many castles and houses in Scotland claim that the ill-fated young queen once slept there.

Toward Castle was also the scene of the greatest tragedy in Lamont clan history, later known as the Dunoon Massacre. The castle ruins are located near Dunoon, across the Firth of Clyde from Glasgow, and my brother Tommy and I had a grand time climbing about the fallen ramparts and dungeons. Sir Norman Lamont, the local clan leader and our guide, recounted the events leading up to the appalling massacre. The belligerent Campbells and Lamonts had been feuding for years when in 1646 a large number of Lamonts with their families became trapped in the castle surrounded by the Campbell warriors. Facing a long siege the Lamonts, with a promise of safe passage from the Campbells, agreed to surrender Toward Castle and Ascog, another Lamont castle. The Campbells, ignoring their pledge, then proceeded to slaughter close to two hundred Lamont men, women, and children in cold blood – some at the castle and some later in Dunoon.

A contemporary account describes the scene. The Campbells took their prisoners to Dunoon and "there in the churchyard they most cruelly murthered . . . by shotts, by durks, by cutting their throats, as they do with beasts, above one hundreth, and lastly they hanged on one tree thirty and six at one time of the cheifs and speciall gentlemen of that name, and before they were half hanged they cutt them downe and threw them in by the dozens in pitts prepared for the same; and many of them striveing to ryse upon their feet were violently holden down untill that by throwing the earth in great quantity upon them they were stifled to death."

At Dunoon we somberly gazed at the gray granite shaft, carved with a Celtic cross, and its bronze plaque commemorating the fallen Lamonts. For me the ruins and town were filled with the ghosts of our doomed clansmen of long ago, and you could almost hear the mournful dirge of the bagpipers lamenting their cruel fate.

Sixteen years after the slaughter Sir Colin Campbell, its ringleader, was brought to justice and beheaded. Yet "Time heals all wounds." In 1773 John Lamont of Lamont, the eighteenth Chief of the clan, married Helen Campbell. The couple had five children and lived happily for twenty years in an elegant Georgian house in Charlotte Square in Edinburgh, which we visited on our last trip.

Sir James Lamont, the chief of the clan in 1646, was tortured and imprisoned in a dungeon for five years by his victorious enemies after the fall of the castle. His descendant, U.S. Navy pilot John McCain, suffered the same fate during the Vietnam War. I know several Campbell families, and the members all seem to be gentle souls. Do adversaries in these modern times treat each other with greater mercy and respect? We all know the episodes of genocide and brutality in our own lifetimes. Christians ignore the teachings of the Bible, and Muslims ignore the teachings of the Koran. Technology races forward with the speed of light, but human relations crawl forward at a snail's pace. When I take the subway in New York I ride with many people whose skin color and language are different from mine. But we are all fellow passengers on this planet, and hope springs eternal that our common humanity will bind us together.

The Preppy Years

Grandfather Lamont had gone to Phillips Exeter Academy and was president of the board of trustees; my father had gone to Exeter and was a trustee before he joined the Army Air Force in 1942; two uncles had gone to Exeter, and brother Tommy was a member of the senior class. No need to discuss where I would go to boarding school. In the summer of 1941 I was far more interested in the riveting baseball season that was unfolding. Joe DiMaggio, the Yankee Clipper, hit safely in fifty-six straight games, a new record, and Red Sox slugger Ted Williams was on his way to producing a batting average of .406 for the season, a feat never since equaled. Each morning I raced to the newspaper sports section to see if Joe had kept his streak alive.

Since my birthday fell in December, my parents and Exeter felt I was ready to enter the Lower Middle Class when I was still fourteen. The rest of my Buckley classmates heading for Exeter joined the Prep Class and would remain for four years. I would attend P.E.A. for three years, and be one of the younger members of my class.

There were pluses and minuses to this arrangement. On the one hand three years of confinement in a boarding school in rural New Hampshire far from the bright lights of the city seemed quite long enough. The cold and snowy winters followed by weeks of dampness and mud seemed endless. On the other hand, Exeter was a marvelous place to be when the warmth and greenery of spring finally arrived – guys sunbathing on the lawns outside the dormitories, baseball and lacrosse games on the vast playing fields, and the winding little river beckoning canoes and swimmers. By staying another year I would have engaged more in extracurricular activities and moved up to playing on varsity teams, something I was eager to do. Then on December 7, 1941, the Japanese bombed Pearl Harbor, America went to war, and everyone's future plans became murky.

Wartime conditions shaped the school in new and different ways. There were more older teachers, from Principal Lewis Perry on down, who might have retired were it not for the war; some twenty-five younger teachers left to join the military. Complaints about the food served in the dining halls drew the quick retort, "Don't you know there's a war on?" and I had to remind my mother to send me my sugar ration coupons. Gas rationing dictated the mode of travel in seeking a respite from Exeter – by railroad on the Boston and Maine to Boston's North Station; we tended to stick around the campus more during the war years.

Each fall we students picked and crated apples on neighboring farms;

the regular pickers had gone to war. In the winter we shoveled snow off the tracks of the Boston and Maine to keep the trains running. I took a course in first aid and was appointed to serve as an Air Raid Warden, charged with spotting enemy planes and sounding the alarm; an official protective helmet went with the job. Not a single Luftwaffe plane got through to bomb Exeter on my watch.

As we approached our eighteenth birthdays we each weighed the various military options facing us – Army, Navy, Marines, or Air Force. Should we apply for one of the officer's training programs – V-12, V-5, or ASTP? Should we enlist early or wait to be drafted? Would it be necessary to attend summer school and graduate early? Certainly the war had aroused our patriotic instincts; we listened to war news on the radio and rejoiced over the American and British victories in battle. In 1942, brother Tommy and the other seniors and older brothers everywhere went off to war, and before long we learned firsthand about the perils and hardships they faced in military life. Sometimes the news was very bad.

None of us had serious gripes about life at Exeter during the war years – just the traditional complaints about the mandatory daily morning chapel and the dress code requiring coats and ties. Of course, there were a few Holden Caulfields, vulnerable kids who fell through the cracks, but not many. We know that today's P.E.A. has created a warmer and more nurturing environment for its students, now a thousand boys and girls. The presence of girls on the campus has civilized and smoothed the coarse grain of the old boys' school, and the kids can e-mail Mom and Dad every night. Nothing wrong with that, but we didn't need it. Our esprit was high in the early forties. We felt lucky to be there before we were called off to war ourselves.

I thought that the Exeter faculty, depleted as it was, was outstanding – fine teachers and for the most part true gentlemen, who served as excellent role models for a student body of teenage boys with plenty of rough edges. Lest you think that I am merely overcome with nostalgia, I point to the respect and pleasure with which returning alumni greet their old teachers at reunions. They know that these good men did well by them.

Among the teachers that I especially liked and admired were P. C. Rogers, a French teacher, tennis coach, and a very funny man; Harold Gross, a wise and kindly English teacher who left to become a naval officer; and a host of Exonians have called Hamilton Bissell, the sophisticated admissions officer and crew coach, a good friend. Hammy was short, bald, and overflowing with good humor.

Dr. Perry, who had been Exeter's principal since 1914, was now no longer an active, hands-on administrator of the school's affairs. He was often off campus in Boston, and mildly forgetful of names and identities. (I can now sympathize completely.) Portly and jowly, he was still a very impressive figure when he appeared at morning chapel from time to time

Fifteen years later I joined the Navy.

Elinor, Lansing, Tommy, Ted, Mother, and Dad at Sky Farm, 1941. The island home in North Haven, Maine, has been a summer mecca for five generations of Lamonts.

Major Thomas S. Lamont, U.S. Air Force, in London 1942.

The Exeter years, 1941-1944.

Thomas W. Lamont and grandson Tommy (T.W.L. II), who liked to discuss world affairs with his grandfather.

to address the students. He was the soul of geniality and wit and masterful at public speaking – a superb exemplar of the worth of good delivery in making a speech or reading out loud. Exeter alumni fondly remember Dr. Perry's annual reading of *The Devil and Daniel Webster* and passages from *Huckleberry Finn*. Furthermore, Dr. Perry was an ardent Red Sox fan and by chatting baseball with his young charges, helped put them at ease in the presence of their elderly and distinguished headmaster.

From the students' point of view, the man who actually ran Exeter was Dean Edwin Silas Wells Kerr. My fiftieth reunion class report said about the dean: "Feared by all, beloved by many, the figure of Edwin Silas Wells Kerr, Dean of Phillips Exeter Academy, overshadows even Principal Lewis Perry in 1944's memory. . . . Tweedy, pipe smoking, he dispensed good advice to the homesick in his dorm. And in his office in Jeremiah Smith he dispensed justice." The dean was in charge of student discipline, and a "Dicky Slip" was a summons to his office to answer for your crime. I received two.

One mild spring evening there was a rumble – a large and noisy gathering of high-spirited Exeter students at the downtown park along the banks of the river. It had been a long winter and I joined the crowd. Unfortunately, some of the boys got carried away and vandalized a few park benches. The authorities were clueless for a few days, and then Charlie Commings received a Dicky Slip in his post office box.

A day later about twenty-five of us received summonses to the dean's office, and later to the town police station. Charlie, in a fit of exuberance, so the story goes, had described the raucous get-together on the back of a postcard to a friend, and the card had mysteriously found its way to the dean's office. Dean Kerr handed Charlie a piece of paper and a pencil, stating, "Give me the names of at least twenty boys who were there or you'll be out of here on the first train tomorrow morning." Charlie's pencil flew across the page, and mine was one of the names he wrote down. The punishment was "probation" – in your room by eight o'clock and confinement to Exeter for several months. If you screwed up when you were on "pro," you were in big trouble; expulsion from Exeter for disciplinary reasons was not all that rare, as my classmate George Plimpton later found out to his sorrow.

About a week before graduation in 1944 I collected my second Dicky Slip. Sunday morning church attendance was mandatory at that time; occasionally a late afternoon vespers service was substituted for the morning service. I had biked over to Hampton Beach for a day of fun and sun and was having such a fine time that I decided to cut the vespers service and stay on at the beach.

"You knew we wouldn't punish you because it was so close to graduation, and so you took advantage and broke the rules. I'm ashamed of you," said Dean Kerr. He was absolutely right, and I felt like two cents.

The formative period of adolescence significantly shapes everybody's life, and with parents' control waning it is our peers – our friends at home and at school – who increasingly influence our conduct. By today's standards the student body at Exeter in my time was hardly diverse. There were no girls or African-American students. It was a boys' school, as it had been since 1781, and we were all white, although not all WASPS. The boys came from all over the country and a variety of backgrounds. Some had been educated at big city private schools, others at small town public schools in the Midwest and New England. Some of us had Rogers Peet tweed jackets hanging in our closets; others had white waiters' jackets for their dining room duty to qualify for scholarship grants. Some boys were big and athletic and manned the varsity teams, while struggling with their academic grades; others were shy and scrawny and played in the woodwind section of the school orchestra, while making A's and B's. The Exeter student body, seven hundred and fifty strong, contained diverse personalities, cultures, tastes, and talents. We learned a lot from each other.

The boys brought their own brand of social democracy to the school and were adroit in piercing inflated egos. They did not put up with phonies and snobs, who learned quickly to mend their ways; pomposity and hypocrisy were shunned. The Exeter campus itself was a great social equalizer. The "butt room" in each dormitory was the smoking room where the boys gathered for bull sessions (and where such attitudes were sharply disparaged). During the 1940s, tobacco-stained fingers and lipstick-smeared cigarette butts on prom weekends were a sign of the times.

The dingy, smoke-filled butt room in the basement of Amen Hall during my Upper Middle year was our center of fun and games thanks to a merry band of inmates. There were some very funny guys, such as Bill Murray, noted for his hilarious accounts of exploits with girls during vacations. Most of us were given nicknames, some quite weird. The king of comedy was Edgar Pope. My hairy legs led him to dub me "Booker" after the famous black leader Booker T. Washington, about whom he had been reading in history class. I much preferred another nickname – "Champ" – that he gave me after some modest success at lightweight boxing. Prep school nicknames can be long-lasting. I know three aging preppies who still answer respectively to "Tish," "Squish," and "Squeaky." When you heard the Amen butt room exploding with laughter, you knew that Edge Pope was imparting his observations on life.

I roomed with Farwell Smith for two years, an imaginative guy in planning all sorts of wild pranks – like smearing himself with blood-red ketchup and staggering down the trail under the liftline at Mt. Mansfield. Jake Underhill, the band leader and drummer of the Royal Exonians, has been a congenial golfing and traveling companion on trips to Ireland and China. Drummer Jake, Buzz Merritt, George Plimpton, and I formed the heart of the percussion section in the P.E.A. marching band, which performed at football games, rallies, and parades. Buzz played the cymbals, George beat the huge bass drum emblazoned with a large red E, and I carried it, a pleasant task requiring a strong back and no skill whatsoever. In a memoir about his days at Exeter George later wrote, "Ted Lamont carried the drum, as I recall, on his back like a mammoth papoose, while I went along behind him, whacking it with a felt-covered hammer."

Unfortunately, George was expelled from Exeter late in his senior year for an accumulation of minor disciplinary offenses. One time he removed a stuffed rhinoceros head from Phillips Hall, where it was mounted on a wall with the heads of other jungle beasts in a room called the "Zoo." However, he was nabbed by a teacher before being able to place it on the Academy Building stage to greet students at morning assembly. George's creative juices were flowing at an early age. He would progress to fame and fortune in his writing and public speaking career.

Other old Exeter friends include Angus McIntyre, an Oyster Bay neighbor; Al Williams, no longer with us, who did a superb job in editing *The Ambassador From Wall Street*; Harry Cobb, a world class architect and boyhood chum from North Haven; and former soccer captain Phil Potter, a New York trial lawyer. I sold my purple bicycle to John Knowles, P.E.A. '45, when I graduated. His book *A Separate Peace*, set in wartime Exeter, became a best-selling classic and was made into a fine movie by Paramount Pictures.

That I was the grandson of a Wall Street tycoon who was also the president of the board of trustees of P.E.A. was pretty well known to my fellow students, especially after Thomas W. Lamont spoke to them in chapel one morning. There was also the Lamont Infirmary, donated by Grandfather, to remind them of my pedigree. Naturally, I hoped to avoid being considered by my peers as a rich kid with "pull"; I wanted simply to be "one of the boys." Bill Clark, the not-very-sensitive mathematics teacher and football coach, did not help my situation. One day after Grandfather's talk I was walking across the yard with some buddies when Clark approached. "Well, Ted," he asked, "what are you going to do with your first million dollars?" Everybody laughed, but I was embarrassed and had no witty reply. However, I never received any flak from the boys about my Park Avenue background and grandfather. There were many other kids from affluent families, and the style and tradition of New England boarding schools precluded luxurious living anyway. Even well-to-do fathers who had worked their way through the tough Depression years were far stricter about their children's allowances and spending habits than nowadays, and with the country at war extravagance was out of place. The boys judged their fellow students on their merits and what they contributed to campus life. Star athletes were the high-profile figures on campus. Bill Jackson, captain of the football team and a respected leader, was elected president of the student council. As for "pull," at the time Exeter expelled George Plimpton his father was a trustee of the school. So much for pull.

In my studies I was by no means the sharpest, nor the dullest, knife in the drawer. I had to work hard to achieve my C's and rarer B's. I would not become a rocket scientist. Mathematics did not come easily for me. (However, the basic math that I had learned at Buckley was enough for being a banker.) I did well in English and wrote my father that Boswell's *Life of Johnson* was "the most boring book I have ever read." However, I thought Sinclair Lewis's *Arrowsmith* was great. Latin was tedious, but I really enjoyed American history. The Harkness system of seating a dozen or so boys and the teacher around an oblong table was designed to promote free and easy discussion of course material. It was fine if you were well prepared and had something to say; otherwise there was no place to hide. Homework assignments at Exeter often kept me busy well into the night.

In extracurricular activities I became a member of the Golden Branch debating society and the Christian Fraternity Council, which organized fund drives for the Red Cross and performed other good works. I sang second bass in the Glee Club, whose main allure was to visit Dana Hall and other girls' schools for concerts, a happy respite from the all-male campus life. I was an actor in two Dramatic Association plays, hardly starring roles but good fun.

As one of the newsmen in "The Front Page," I had the opening line in the show. A group of reporters are sitting around a table in the state prison playing poker while awaiting an execution. After the cards are dealt, I take a drag on my cigarette and open the bidding: "Crack it for a dime!" In his review of the play for *The Exonian* Tommy Lamont stated, "The reporters were good. But we might add that those parts would be meat for anyone with butt room experience. All the bum has to do is act and talk on the stage as he does in the butt room."

"Outward Bound" was a hilarious musical revue about life at Exeter written entirely by the students, and the rehearsals were high-spirited affairs. As a member of the chorus I sang a solo entitled "Boogie Woogie Letter" about a love letter I had received from my girlfriend back home. Just a great acting job on my part. There was no sweetheart pining away for me that I knew of, or vice versa.

My brother Tommy, a four-year boy at Exeter, graduated in June 1942 and went on to Harvard where he had a very good time for a few months. He reported in his diary about a coming-out party he had attended: "Everyone was there. . . . Swell party. Champagne, women, wow! Mighty glad I went." Tommy enlisted in the U.S. Navy when he turned eighteen in October.

At Exeter Tommy had been a star member of the Academy Debating Team, which won all its contests against other schools including its traditional rival, Andover. Before Pearl Harbor the boys had often debated the role of the U.S. in the spreading war against Nazi Germany. Tommy was a strong advocate of aiding Great Britain and Russia in their desperate struggle, while Gore Vidal, another Exeter student, led the America First group at Exeter forcefully backing the isolationist cause. Sometimes the sparks flew. After the U.S. had gone to war we debated our military strategy, such as the need for opening up a second front in Europe.

Tommy was also president of *The Review*, P.E.A.'s literary magazine, and Feature Editor of *The Exonian*; he was prolific in writing entertaining and thoughtful stories, articles, and play reviews. At the commencement exercises he gave the Senior Class Oration, an address that deeply impressed the audience of parents, faculty, and boys. At the close of his talk Tommy stated, "We will fight primarily to save the homes and soil of America but also for the peace and freedom to create something really better. . . . It is a rotten thing to die in vain."

When Tommy was reported missing in action three years later, the mother of an Exeter student who had heard his talk wrote my parents: "Our hearts and eyes were filled when he had finished, and we felt that America's destiny was quite safe if boys brought up like yours could express sentiments so common to the heart of man." In the senior class ballot Tommy was chosen as "Best Speaker." I thought my older brother was a terrific guy.

I was on a different and slower track. My classmates voted me number one "Playboy." Why they did so was a mystery to me; I imported dates for the Exeter dances just as many others did. The popularity of the big swing bands went hand in hand with a renewed craze for dancing, and high school and college kids led the way. Exonians joyfully joined in. The Exeter dances, black tie and evening dresses, were held in the Thompson Gymnasium – foxtrots, jitterbugging, the occasional waltz, and slow dancing by the romantic types in the darker corners of the gym. Walking your girl back to the Exeter Inn after the dance was the time for amorous advances if the stars were aligned properly.

Big band swing was the music favored by a whole generation of American youth, resounding from radios, juke boxes, and phonographs everywhere. On a warm spring day you could hear the big band sounds wafting through dozens of open dormitory windows around the campus. I had a phonograph and a prized stack of records – ten-inch 78 rpm's – from the peak of the Swing Era, including the Glenn Miller recordings of "String of Pearls," "Chattanooga Choo-Choo," and "American Patrol"; Artie Shaw's "Dancing In the Dark" and "Beyond the Blue Horizon"; Harry James's "Flight of the Bumblebee" and Benny Goodman's "Jersey Bounce."

I made the preppy dance scene in New York during the vacations – the Junior Holidays, Get Togethers, and the like – and checked out Broadway where the swing bands were performing at the big movie theatres. It was a grand moment when the stage curtains parted to reveal Tommy Dorsey, baton in hand, leading his orchestra in "I'll Never Smile Again," golden trumpets, trombones, and silver saxophones gleaming in the stagelights. I also went to Broadway shows like "The Boys From Syracuse," "Knickerbocker Holiday," and" Oklahoma," the 1943 pace-setting pioneer of the modern Broadway musical.

Another time I dined and danced on a double date at the Rainbow Room, which my mother thought was pushing the envelope for age seventeen. Fortunately, she never learned of the party one night at a friend's East Side apartment where we partook liberally of his father's Scotch. Edge Pope dubbed me the "White Horse Kid" for weeks afterwards.

After vacations these Manhattan adventures were reported to the butt room crowd, naturally with some embellishment. Maybe my classmates associated me with the glamorous party-going scenes of Manhattan social life depicted in magazines and movies, but I've never considered that my deeds justified the dubious honor of being elected class "Playboy."

During the summer of 1942 my father, now Major Thomas S. Lamont of the U.S. Eighth Air Force, was stationed in London, my brother Tommy was at Harvard, and I headed west to a cattle ranch that took in paying guests at Encampment, Wyoming. Rick Humphrey from Exeter, who became our ringleader, and three boys from Milton were the other Eastern dudes at Paul Holmes's 1 Bar 11 ranch that summer.

It was my first trip out West, and we enjoyed all the fun and wholesome activities plus a few others. We did a lot of riding, including an eight-day pack trip into the snow-peaked mountain scenery of the Continental Divide. We helped the cowboys in the summer roundup, tagging and branding the hog-tied bawling calves. We swam and fly-fished for rainbow trout in the Platte River; we shot gophers and prairie dogs, rabbits and crows; we played poker and horseshoes and chopped a lot of firewood. We also kicked up our heels with the local folks in nearby towns.

Saturday night was party time in Encampment, a small two-saloon town with boardwalk sidewalks and false front buildings right out of a Western movie. The guys and girls came into town from the surrounding ranches to have a good time, and the local lasses taught the Eastern dudes to swing at the town dance hall. At the rollicking Cheyenne Frontier Days celebration the rodeo was the big show with the full range of events from riding bucking broncos and steers to roping and hog-tying calves. At the Laramie Jubilee celebration, the ranch hands and local gentry meandered from bar to bar down the main drag, which had been transformed into a huge street carnival. There was a colorful parade with old-fashioned stagecoaches, and the song of the day, "I've Got Spurs That Jingle, Jangle, Jingle, as I Go Riding Merrily Along," blared from loudspeakers in the small amusement park.

I have long been known to have a glass of spirits on festive occasions, and it all began at the Laramie Jubilee where Rick and the ranch foreman first introduced me, at the age of fifteen, to the pleasing diversion. After a couple of Tom Collinses at the "Silver Dollar" bar I sauntered through the carnival and with my newly liberated charm enticed a pretty young thing to join me for a ride on the Ferris wheel. The rotating motion of the wheel plus the fact that my innocent digestive system was unaccustomed to two quick belts of gin did me in at the top of the giant wheel's cycle. I threw up, or barfed, in the vernacular of the time, and I can still hear the shouts of those beneath us, first querulous and then quite unkind. The girl was very understanding as she beat a hasty retreat at the end of the ride. I wrote my father in England that it had been a terrific summer and noted the difference in personality that I had observed between the easygoing friendly Westerners and the more buttoned-down Easterners that I knew.

For me, the symbols of fall in Exeter were leaves in autumn colors, tawny jugs of cider cooling and fermenting outside dormitory windows, and hundreds of boys and faculty families turning out to cheer on the P.E.A. football team on Saturday afternoons. All week long I looked forward to Saturday's contest when my buddies and I would cross the little bridge over the Exeter River to the pocket-sized Plimpton Stadium to watch our crimson-jerseyed pigskin heroes take on the Harvard Freshmen, Hebron Academy, and other worthies – all leading up to the climactic game against our traditional rival, Andover. At halftime I carried the big bass drum as the marching band took to the field trumpeting Exeter's vintage fight song, whose final line was "Cheer now for Exeter, Cheer for old P.E.A."

And cheer we did, led by our frenzied cheerleaders with their bright red microphones, and with the enthusiasm of a Madison Square crowd at a Knicks playoff game. "Give me an E! . . . Give me an X!" and so forth. Some twenty years later I attended an Exeter–Andover football game with the other members of Exeter's board of trustees and their wives. This time the favorite chant from the Exeter cheering section, over and over, was "Screw the Blue!" Principal Dick Day smiled sheepishly and shrugged his shoulders. In the forties the cheerleaders would have considered this rallying cry far too crude to include in their repertoire; Dean Wells Kerr would have quickly made their lives miserable. Different times, different mores.

I am especially glad that the good dean never learned about the dumb stunt that I pulled after one Exeter game at Andover. To avoid paying the fare on the train trip back from Andover I hid in the toilet of the last car on the train. Unfortunately, the car was dropped off in Haverhill. After a while I stealthily opened the door a crack to see why we weren't moving, and there was the rest of the train pulling away in the distance. I hitchhiked back to school, having learned the hard way that crime doesn't pay.

The Exeter–Andover game with its attendant activities was always a huge event in student life at Exeter. First came the exhortations to "Beat Andover" by old grads at morning chapel, then the pre-game rally and exchanging raucous cheers with the Andover student body on the quadrangle before Dr. Perry's house.

In saluting Exeter's headmaster the Andover boys, well coached by their cheerleaders, gave three Perry-sounding cheers of "Fairy, Fairy, Fairy!" The Exonians' less mischievous reply pronounced the name of Andover Principal Fuess by stringing out the s's in a long hiss, the same sound with which an audience greets a stage villain.

Then came the parade to the football field led by the marching band and cheerleaders carrying the giant Exeter banner strung between two bamboo poles, and the excitement of the game itself. Again, the times and mores have changed. Football games at Exeter (and Harvard, my next stop) no longer excite school spirit and morale as in these earlier times. But in my senior year at Exeter, when Exeter beat Andover 12-6, we sang and cheered the team lustily at the victory bonfire that evening.

I eagerly looked forward to weekends then, as I have ever since. On Saturday afternoons Exeter teams played their games against other schools. Football, basketball, and baseball were my favorite spectator sports, and in my senior year I joined the action in hockey and soccer games against outside opponents. On Saturday nights we abandoned the dining hall to indulge in a steak sandwich, French fries, and a malted at the P.E.A. grill before heading on to the main event of the evening – movies in the Thompson Gymnasium. When the MGM lion roared on the big silver screen, the whole student body roared back.

Sundays were good fun too, once the mandatory church service was out of the way. My religious beliefs and faith would come later in life. The little Exeter River was the scene of many happy outings. In winter when it was frozen, two or three of us, armed with hockey sticks and puck, would skate up its smooth black ice for miles. Exeter did not have its current superb rinks of artificial ice in those days; we had to rely on Mother Nature for skating and hockey.

In the spring we navigated the river in canoes as it wound gently through the woods. We ate our sandwiches on its grassy banks and swam in its murky waters. There were daring leaps into the river from overhanging branches (like the key incident in *A Separate Peace*) and naval battles and mud fights between rival canoes. I once caught a mud ball in the eye, which sent me to the infirmary for two days, but I was soon back up the river again.

Other weekend adventures were bicycle rides to Hampton Beach, where the ocean was frigid in May, and excursions to nearby ski areas. One time an Academy teacher drove a bunch of us over to North Conway, where we skied Mt. Cranmore from dawn until dusk. We then crowded into the cheapest lodgings that we could find, a skimpy summer cottage, cooked our dinner over an open fire in the fireplace, drank beer and smoked cigarettes, had a lot of laughs, and retired, two to a bed. It was a glorious weekend.

By the summer of 1943 Exeter was fully into its wartime footing. Many teachers had departed for military service. Sixty-four boys attended summer school so that they could graduate before being drafted. Most of them worked on nearby farms in the afternoons at forty cents an hour, replacing farm workers who had joined the armed forces. I worked on a farm too – Grandfather's Sky Farm in North Haven – from 8 a.m. until 4:30 p.m. each afternoon, along with a handful of local farm hands, older men beyond draft age. Haying and working in the vegetable garden were good clean work, but I detested the task of plucking newly killed chickens covered with lice. For social life that summer I biked several miles to the village to hang out with the other teenagers.

During my senior year at Exeter I lived in Williams House, a private house with about a dozen students supervised by a very popular Exeter couple, French teacher Harris Thomas and his wife. Academically I was getting ready for the College Board examinations in the spring. In athletics I played some sport every afternoon, changing with the season, and still harbored the hope that I could raise my skill level enough to make a varsity team.

However, I was also realistic. My performance in club baseball had been weak, fully confirmed by the observations of two friends in messages accompanying the class photographs we exchanged at year-end. Buzz Merritt: "You're the worst damn first hassock man that I ever hope to see." Edge Pope was slightly kinder: "Unfortunately you were no longer the sensational performer of past years around the initial bag. I also noted with sorrow that you failed to belabor the nugget as in previous seasons." Damon Runyan sports talk was in vogue with the butt room crowd. It has been said that jazz, the U.S. Constitution, and baseball are the unique American creations most perfectly designed for their place in the American culture. I agree. My appreciation of jazz and its pop music derivatives and my understanding of American history blossomed at Exeter. My performance on the baseball diamond clearly did not.

However, I did make the varsity soccer squad, but not the first team. Said Pope: "Your deeds on the soccer field will no doubt be remembered (by you) for years to come. Particularly your rise to sensational heights in the Governor Dummer game." Substitutions in soccer games (usually low scoring and close) are infrequent, and I became exceedingly anxious as I rode the bench in the Andover game. Would Coach Arthur Weeks ever call on me? Weeks was a feisty Scottish mathematics teacher who sometimes threw erasers at his slow-thinking students to get their attention. I assumed that he did not hold my classroom achievement against me on the playing field and kept sneaking glances down the bench at him. He finally did put me in the game, in which my performance was completely harmless for both sides, and I won my varsity letter.

My favorite sport was ice hockey. I played at the club level for two years, becoming captain of the all-club team, and (dare I use the word?) starred on the junior varsity team. I scored three goals in beating Andover in the season finale against our big-time rival. It was the crowning achievement of my Exeter sports career and won me a new title – "Hat Trick," my favorite nickname by far.

My moment of fame melted away as quickly as the hockey rink ice in the spring thaw, as I readied myself for the next big step – entering the freshman class at Harvard. The same line-up of Lamonts that had attended Exeter had gone on to Harvard, and my course was set. During that era, and especially during the war years, college admissions were much less competitive than now, and Harvard accepted sixty-five Exeter seniors; I was one of them.

Years later, to inject a lighter moment into my sales pitch at an Exeter fund-raising dinner, I informed the attendees that the school had made "a lasting impression" on me. "I picked up a case of athlete's foot in the boys' locker room at Thompson Gymnasium which has stuck with me ever since!" All kidding aside, attending Exeter did indeed have a significant impact on my approach to life. Robed in my black cap and gown I joined my classmates at the Commencement exercises at the gymnasium where Dr. Perry handed me my graduation degree, signed by Thomas W. Lamont, President of the Board of Trustees. After three years at Exeter I was ready for Cambridge town; my stay there would be short and sweet.

Anchors Aweigh

In June 1944 I moved into Adams House, a sprawling red brick Harvard housing complex just across Massachusetts Avenue from the Yard. I shared a dingy suite of rooms with three Exeter pals – Farwell Smith, Pete Fay, and Charlie Loring, not known for their serious approach to higher education. Then and later at Harvard I sought refuge in the house library when the social activity in our rooms became too intense.

My letters home often pleaded for financial aid as this one to my mother: "For God's sake send my check but quick. The creditors are pounding at the door, and the teachers are wondering why I don't have any books. I am carrying a heavier schedule than I did at Exeter, so don't expect too high marks. Physics with three lectures, two labs, and two conferences; Navigation, which is also seven hours with night observation periods; English and Math – important courses for the service and everything else."

There were three groups of students at Harvard – the physically unfit for military duty, known as 4-Fs under the Selective Service Act; seventeen-year-olds like myself waiting to be called up when they turned eighteen; and young men in the officers' training programs. One of the most popular midshipmen in the Navy V-12 unit was Jack Lemmon, not many years away from his outstanding career as an actor. Lots of parties took place that summer and fall to wish Godspeed to guys leaving for the service, or to welcome home old friends on leave from their military duties. Jack was already a very funny fellow and a talented piano player and composer. His rendition of his song "Gladys Isn't Gratis Anymore" was always a big hit.

I made it to North Haven some weekends via the Boston and Maine to Rockland and the twelve-mile ride by boat or ferry to the island. I skippered our sailing dinghy in the weekly races and reported proudly to my father in London that in the Mill River Race I had passed Governor Leverett Saltonstall of Massachusetts ten yards from the finish line by taking his wind. The governor was a fierce competitor on the water and the most congenial fellow in the world on dry land.

Picnics have long been the favorite diversion at North Haven – family day picnics to nearby islands, and in those days evening beach parties for the younger crowd, at which the minister's daughter was often the life of the party. Now the bonfire scene changed to include beer-sipping guys and vivacious girls, who sometimes paired off and slipped away into the dark beyond the light of the flickering flames. Sometimes we played a popular lights-out game called "Murder" in someone's house; certainly the boys enjoyed groping around in the dark for a girl to "strangle." However, the clock was running out for fun and games.

I had decided to join the Navy alongside my brother Tommy, and in December I received my notice to report for a pre-induction physical examination. No problem. I returned to Harvard for a month after Christmas vacation and received credit for my freshman year. My fancy Fifth Avenue dentist with the beautiful blonde dental assistant gave me a final going over, filling a few cavities, and I was ready to go. On February 15, 1945, Mother and I went down to Grand Central Station where I boarded a special train bound for Sampson Naval Training Station on Lake Seneca near Geneva, New York, the boot camp where I would take my basic training.

As everyone knows, mail call is an important event in the customarily monotonous daily routine of life in the military. Once I went ballistic writing my mother because I had not received a single letter in three mail-calls in a row: "Mail-call can be the happiest moment of the day, or the most disappointing. . . . Life is O.K., just dull." I also asked her to send me copies of *Life* and *Time* magazines and a box of cookies that I could share with my buddies in the barracks.

Our company of 120 men, from the East Coast and New England, was run by a tough no-nonsense Chief Petty Officer from Texas. On the first day he announced that he could deal with all kinds of sad sacks except blacks, only he used the "N" word. Integration of the armed forces, let alone political correctness, would come later on. We had a good bunch of guys, except for a few goldbricks who didn't pull their weight.

We "hit the deck" at 5:30 every morning and usually ran two miles double-time around the Grinder, the base running track – before breakfast. It's mighty cold during the winter in upstate New York at that hour of the day. I did not find the physical training too demanding – calisthenics, weight lifting, endless marching drills, and swimming. Thank goodness I already knew how to swim. At the first swimming session we were ordered to jump off a forty-foot tower into the pool, with burly instructors ready to prod the reluctant off the platform. Many of the boys from rural areas had never swum before. They dog-paddled desperately, trying to stay afloat, until one of the lifeguards took pity and casually extended a long pole to fish them out.

There were two survival principles for boot camp. One was to keep your bunk, your locker, and your barracks in a state of perfect neatness and cleanliness. In preparation for the weekly inspection I scrubbed vigorously between the steam radiator pipes with a toothbrush. The inspecting lieutenant wore white gloves. The other principle was to maintain a low profile. I ran afoul of authority only once. Because I had had a year of college, I was assigned to answer telephones in the master at arms office in the drill hall (and run errands and bring coffee to the officers).

Four hours on and eight hours off for two weeks – soft duty compared to other trainee jobs, such as in the scullery or the boiler room. The office was quiet at night with plenty of time to read and write letters. Everything was cool until I blew it.

One of the married officers left the office each evening to see another woman. His wife suspected that he was fooling around and called in from time to time to check up on him. I, as the seaman on telephone watch, was supposed to cover for him, and convincingly, when his wife called. Unfortunately, the officer had not fully briefed me about the sensitive nature of my role, and when the lady called I simply replied that the lieutenant was out, whereabouts unknown. Evidently, his wife was not persuaded that her husband's absence from the office was for official business, and let him know it. He, in turn, angrily chewed me out. However, he didn't fire me, and I was now ready with a reply the next time the lady called: "The lieutenant's not here at the moment. He was just ordered to report to base headquarters."

I had only one really bad experience at boot camp – in the dentist's office, where I suffered two hours of the most excruciating pain I have ever endured. A dental examination and treatment are standard procedure for boot camp recruits, and it was now our company's turn. Unfortunately, the Navy dentist felt compelled to remove all my fillings, some just recently installed, and replace them with fillings using the Navy formula. He put it to me this way: "Your fillings might last ten years, but there are three ways to do things – the right way, the wrong way, and the Navy way." Then he added the shocker: "Regrettably, I've run through my quota of Novocaine for the day. Hang on!" pointing to the padded arms of the dental chair. I later wrote my mother, "He handled a drill like he was drilling a street"; and I was the street.

Feeling terrible and very sorry for myself, I greeted my mates back at the barracks. Many of these boys, from poor rural backgrounds, had never been to a dentist in their lives and their teeth were in awful shape. In their case the Navy dentists had found too many teeth beyond repair and simply yanked them out. I have never seen so many smiles with gaping holes in one room in my life. I felt a little better: misery loves company.

That was my worst experience in a dentist's chair. Some years later when I was working in Paris I sought out a dentist to attend to a painful wisdom tooth. My friends had recommended a certain older English dentist. I wasn't especially impressed with the state of most English teeth I had observed, but no matter, I made the appointment. My confidence was not bolstered when I noted that his office was adorned with stuffed fish and golf trophies – not a framed university dental degree in sight. But the old fellow performed a smooth extraction, and then his comely young nurse escorted me into a smartly furnished recovery room. She smoothed the soft white pillows on a chaise-longue, and I lay down to rest. A few minutes later she reappeared to offer me a glass of Merlot from a silver tray. That was my best experience in a dentist's office.

Some of the boot camp training exercises I found enjoyable and interesting. Rowing the big Navy lifeboats on Lake Seneca was fun, and, having rowed since boyhood during summers in Maine, I was ahead on the learning curve. We also spent many hours on aircraft recognition, developing our ability to quickly identify Japanese Zeros and our own planes, Navy Hellcats, Corsairs, and the rest. Picture cards and slides, flashed on the screen for a fraction of a second, were our training tools. (Military aircraft recognition technology has advanced light years since those days, yet there have been some frightful blunders. An American cruiser shot down an Iranian commercial airliner with two hundred passengers in the Persian Gulf war, a deplorable tragedy and huge black eye for the U.S. Navy, with serious consequences in American foreign relations. There have also been downings of friendly aircraft by American forces in military operations.) I never begrudged the hours spent in sharpening my ability to identify aircraft, given the Navy's battle role in the Pacific, where my brother Tommy's submarine was on war patrol. The instant spotting of enemy planes was crucial for survival.

When the smoking lamp was lit some of us would gather in a little room to smoke and exchange the latest gossip and rumors, usually about future assignments after boot camp – specialist school, Seabees, general sea duty, and so forth. Our mood was somber when we received the news that President Roosevelt had died. We viewed him as an inspiring wartime leader. Furthermore, most of the boys came from families who had struggled through the Depression and looked upon F.D.R. as a friend of the working man.

Following interviews and tests I joined a handful of recruits on the base who qualified for the Navy Reserve Officers Training program, formerly called V-12. NROTC midshipmen, after an accelerated college course, including naval studies, received ensigns' commissions with their degrees, followed by assignments to active duty. The Navy Department hadn't yet decided to go forward with a new NROTC class, however, and I would not learn my fate until I returned to Sampson after boot leave.

Now the smoking room conversation turned to how we would live it up on boot leave, only two weeks away. Maybe I had read about the new Broadway musical "On the Town," the hilarious adventures of three sailors on their first liberty in New York; maybe I was ready to live up to that "Playboy" designation by my Exeter classmates. After two and a half months of boot camp, I was ready to head home and paint the town red.

My first stop was Sherman Billingsley's celebrity-filled Stork Club. I was wearing my new tailor-made dress blues, with a black neckerchief, form-fitting jumper and bell-bottoms, and white cap at a jaunty tilt. True, I was a lowly Seaman 2/C, but I thought I looked pretty salty. The maître d' was delighted to show off the club's democratic attitude toward rank and ushered my date Joan and me to a good table. I was one of the few sailors in town who could afford the swanky club; there was plenty of gold braid around but no other enlisted man in sight.

We joined the bobbing crowd on the dance floor and found ourselves foxtrotting beside Leo Durocher, the colorful manager of the Brooklyn Dodgers, and his girl friend movie actress Laraine Day. All of a sudden Joan gasped and looked panicky. "I've got to get to the ladies' room," she whispered. "Garter belt broke!" I looked down and her long nylon stockings had tumbled down around her ankles, severely disrupting her maneuverability. She tottered off for repairs and got fixed up.

Midnight, the military curfew hour, was approaching, and all the officers started to leave, warning me to get out as they passed by our table – "Time to move it, sailor," with growing intensity. I had paid the bill and was waiting for my change, which the waiter was hoping I would forget. He finally reappeared, I tipped him, and we exited with only a moment to spare. My Scottish heritage permitted no compromise in such matters.

A few nights later I was again the only sailor on board in the Plaza Hotel's elegant Persian Room, where Hildegarde, the celebrated cabaret chanteuse, was performing in a radio broadcast. Susan and I were quietly enjoying ourselves when suddenly the spotlight focused on our table, the band struck up "Anchors Aweigh," and Hildegarde announced to her band leader, "Bob, I understand we've got a sailor in the house. Come on up here, sailor!"

Amid great applause I went up to the bandstand where after a little banter Hildegarde declared that she had a present for me – a carton of cigarettes. I had failed to note that the sponsor of her radio broadcast was Raleigh cigarettes and wondered why the band leader whispered "Raleigh" when she asked me to name my favorite brand. "Chesterfield," I replied loud and clear, naming the popular brand in short supply during the war years. Hildegarde was stunned momentarily but recovered quickly, "These satisfy too, sailor," she said, handing me a carton of Raleighs. Next, gazing at me, she sang her signature song, "Darling, Je Vous Aime Beaucoup," while I stood grinning sheepishly. Hildegarde was a lovely lady, even though up close her pancake makeup and lipstick looked about a half inch thick. She then gave me a big kiss, leaving a bright red smear on my cheek, and wished me luck.

After leaving the Plaza Susan and I took a stroll in Central Park and ended up relaxing on a park bench. In a little while one of New York's finest, a big Irish cop, came along and told us we had to leave: "Sorry, sailor, but the park closes at midnight." While stretching out on the bench my leg had gone to sleep, and when I got up I stumbled and then, grabbing Susan's arm, staggered off a few steps. "Gosh, sailor," said the officer, "I'm so sorry. You've been wounded! Where did you get it? The Pacific?"

I waved back indicating "not to worry" and limped off into the night.

On my return to Sampson I became a member of the Ship's Company working in the Motor Pool (Navy for garage) while I awaited my next assignment. My duties were simple enough – washing Navy vehicles of all kinds and fixing flats, tasks I have tried to avoid ever since. The hours were good, eight to five, with only a few night shifts and liberty every other night and weekend. Some nights I joined a friend from Harvard, Austin Lyne, in drinking Navy beer at Ship's Service. Austie was Boston-Irish with an upbeat personality and a wide, engaging smile, a very likable fellow who would become a lifelong friend. He was in the same NROTC group with me, awaiting orders. It was difficult to get the job done with two percent beer, but we did our best.

I went to Geneva, the nearby town, on liberty a couple of times – not much happening except a few bars and restaurants overrun with sailors from the base. However, a pretty hostess at the USO taught me to jitter-bug, instruction that has served me well ever since. My favorite liberty town was Rochester – a short hitchhike or bus trip away, where I stayed with my Miner grandparents and enjoyed a little R&R, civilian style. I also spent some on-base hours cheering on the Sampson baseball team, led by Mickey Owen, the fine ex-Brooklyn Dodger catcher.

One day the Chief Petty Officer in charge of the motor pool told me, "I want these vehicles squeaky-clean. They're going to pick up the Bob Hope troupe in Buffalo tomorrow." We worked into the night polishing several station wagons until they sparkled in the morning sun. Bob Hope and his sidekick Jerry Colonna entertained thousands of sailors that afternoon. For openers, a shapely and scantily clad blonde crossed the stage followed by the leering Hope, who wisecracked, "I just wanted to remind you guys what you're fighting for," invoking a chorus of wolf whistles and cheers. Bob's jokes often needled the brass, including the base commander, and the boys roared with laughter.

Bob Hope's record of entertaining our troops overseas in almost every military action since World War II is well known. He brought happiness into the lives of millions of men and women in the armed services, and laughter into the living rooms of millions of American homes. Will Rogers, Jack Benny, and Johnny Carson were very good, but in the pantheon of American humor Hope is surely the outstanding comedian of the twentieth century. For over sixty years he led the way for others who adopted his fast-paced, cocky style of delivery.

When I lived in Washington years later I attended a golf tournament and observed Hope's quick wit in action. Bob was playing in the celebrity-pro division on the first day. The sponsors had selected the aging, white-haired Clark Griffith, the owner of the Washington Senators baseball club, to hit out the first drive in the opening ceremony. He swung and topped

The crew of the U.S.S. Snook. Tommy was a crew member for three war patrols before the submarine was lost with all hands following action in the Pacific in May 1945.

Skiing and sailing were Tommy's favorite sports.

Tommy wanted to join the fight as quickly as possible.

the ball, which rolled along the ground ten yards. Hope quickly grabbed the microphone and hollered, "Run it out, Mr. Griffith, run it out!"

On March 25, 1945, my brother Tommy wrote his Grandmother Miner from Guam, "Hold the fort, and I'll be home one of these days when you least expect it." It was his last letter home.

In mid-May my parents received the dreaded telegram from the Navy Department informing them that Seaman 1/C Thomas W. Lamont II was missing, following action in the service of his country. Tommy's submarine, the U.S.S. *Snook*, on war patrol east of Hainan, had lost radio contact with the fleet on April 8. She was never seen or heard from again. The Navy never learned what caused the loss of the *Snook* and her crew of eighty-five, although it was known that a Japanese submarine, later destroyed, was operating in the area at the same time. I worshiped my older brother, and it was a heavy blow. Tommy had possessed amazing maturity, understanding, and intellectual curiosity as a teenager, and all of our family recognized that he was the rising star in our generation. Two weeks after the telegram arrived I was assigned to the NROTC unit at Princeton University and reported to my new station on July 1, 1945.

Life at Princeton had a welcome collegiate flavor, but we were still Navy trainees – in uniform and subject to orders and regulations such as evening curfews and restrictions on leaving town. The course load had a heavy Navy bias – Naval Science, Seamanship, Communications, Engineering and Damage Control, and Navigation, plus a few electives. I had a congenial bunch of roommates in the venerable '01 Hall, taken over for Navy housing, including Austie Lyne, my buddy from Harvard and Sampson.

The month of August brought days of sadness and celebration in rapid succession. I received special liberty to attend the memorial service for my brother Tommy in The Island Church in North Haven, and wrote a short piece for the occasion, extolling his moral and physical courage. As a Seaman 1/C he had turned down the Navy officers' training program and volunteered for submarine duty, "the silent service," because he wanted to get into the fight as soon as possible. And he did. On his first war patrol the U.S.S. *Snook* devastated a Japanese convoy northeast of the Philippines, sinking four vessels and winning the Navy Submarine Combat Pin and Citation for its crew. Tommy had written his father acknowledging the strain of combat: "It is no damn picnic. . . . At sea I am pretty happy. I like the roll of the ship and the bright southern stars at night. I came out of action with a deep sense of satisfaction – something that I hadn't felt before." Hearts filled with emotion at his service, we sang the Navy hymn which ends, "Oh, hear us when we cry to Thee for those in peril on the sea." Three days later Japan surrendered. The long night that followed the day of infamy had ended.

I later learned about the remarkable record of the U.S. Submarine

Force – 16,000 men on 288 boats – in World War II. Despite being less than two percent of total Navy personnel they sank 1,178 Japanese merchant ships, 214 warships, and scores of smaller navy vessels – about fifty-five percent of all Japan's maritime losses including thirty percent of Japan's entire naval losses. However, the toll in human life was high. Fifty-two boats were lost, and 3,505 submariners made the supreme sacrifice for their country.

On VJ Day, war-weary people around the world joined in joyous celebration, and I wrote home about the festivities in Princeton. "All the swabbies and marines piled out of the barracks and cheered and sang the Marine hymn and 'Anchors Aweigh.' Then we got liberty in Princeton and really went to town. I rode around on the fire engine for a while. The servicemen were wearing crazy outfits. All the girls in town were running around kissing the sailors. Everyone seemed to have a bottle of beer in one hand and a girl in the other and was making as much noise as possible. All the bells were ringing and horns were blowing. Afterwards we went over to a big victory bonfire on the campus, and then to a party at a girl's house where I played the piano and we sang songs." I didn't tell my parents that later all the boys and girls stripped down to their shorts and bras and panties and jumped into the pool. That's how we celebrated the end of the war. The Navy would claim me for another ten months; however, it eased its tight discipline over our lives.

Another football season had come around. I planned to return to Harvard when I left the Navy, but for the time being I was a rabid Princeton football fan. You had to be. Old-fashioned college spirit was in high gear at Princeton, certainly compared to the scene at Harvard. When the P-rade marched to the rally on Friday night before a big game, the cheerleaders charged into the dormitories to prod any laggards into joining the marching ranks. Back at Harvard most of the fellows stayed in their rooms sipping drinks as they watched the band and a handful of stragglers march by on their way to a halfhearted rally. That fall of 1945 I joined my fellow Princetonians at Palmer Stadium to cheer on Coach Caldwell's Tiger team. I even contributed modestly to Princeton's athletic program, playing without distinction on the soccer and junior varsity lacrosse teams.

With the relaxation of Navy restrictions, I now spent more weekends and holidays in the city. New York was a joyful town during Christmas vacation, the first peacetime holiday season since 1940. There was usually a merry gang in the evening at Larue, a nightspot in the East Fifties that for the white shoe crowd was what Rick's bar was for Casablanca. The club featured a crowded bar and a small band playing bouncy arrangements of popular standards such as "It Was Just One of Those Things." Many guys were back in town after their military service, and it was fun to catch up with old friends around the bar at Larue, or at the holiday dances.

Years later I introduced George Plimpton, the speaker of the evening, at a dinner at the Piping Rock Club on Long Island. I informed the audience that I could claim some modest credit in launching George's remarkable career and told them the following story.

One winter night in 1945 I attended a dance at the Plaza with George, who was at the time an Army private temporarily stationed at Camp Kilmer in New Jersey. His regiment was scheduled to board a troop ship the following morning bound for Italy, where it would replace veterans serving in the occupation forces. We were having a fine time. The girls were pretty and vivacious, and the champagne was flowing. However, it was getting late and George had a big day ahead of him, so a couple of us volunteered to escort him back to his base. At that hour the only possible means of transport was a taxi, and it was going to be tough to find one late on a snowy night. Luck was with us: We were able to hail a cab just outside the hotel; maybe it helped that we were all in uniform. We jumped in and told our tale, and the driver agreed to take us to Camp Kilmer. Then I noticed that the young man at the wheel was no ordinary driver. He was wearing a tuxedo, and the lovely girl beside him wore a white evening dress. They had gotten into the taxi after another party, but the driver, claiming he was off duty, refused to take them home and instead had driven to the taxi garage and simply left them. The couple then had "borrowed" the cab to drive home, and stopped to pick us up en route.

The snow was really coming down as we crossed the George Washington Bridge. We were a strange looking bunch, and I remember well the astonished look on the toll taker's face when our taxi passed by his booth. About ten miles shy of Camp Kilmer we ran out of gas and ditched the cab at the side of the road. George hitchhiked into camp and rejoined his regiment in time to ship out, and the rest of us made it back to the city. A couple of days later a *New York Times* story carried the following headline: "Taxi Stolen From Garage – Police Investigating." George became an ace reporter for *Stars and Stripes* in Europe, a promising early step in his outstanding literary career.

I received my honorable discharge from the Navy on June 22, 1946, and left Princeton, having completed my sophomore year and harboring good memories of my days at "old Nassau." Princeton's student body lacked the diversity of Harvard's, a drawback. On the other hand, the blasé attitude of Harvard students could have benefited from an injection of the enthusiasm that Princetonians felt for their college and its teams.

That summer my Navy training proved useful on a cruise that I joined with some guys from North Haven on a forty-five-foot yawl. Our destination was Digby Cove, Nova Scotia, and then on to St. John, New Brunswick. The St. John River was beautifully scenic with good water for miles running through meadows and farmlands. The social highlight of the voyage was the warm welcome given us by The Royal Kennebecasis Yacht Club, whose members honored us as the first American vessel to come by since before the war. After a sumptuous lobster and corn picnic we engaged in international trade with our hosts. They wanted American cigarettes, we wanted Scotch whiskey, in short supply back home, and we struck a deal.

Coastal Maine is renowned for its dense fogs, and in those days we did not have radar or a GPS plotter, standard equipment nowadays. Navigation was by dead reckoning, and charts, compass, parallel rulers, dividers, and speed gauge were the tools of the trade. Constant vigilance to spot buoys and landmarks or hear whistle buoys or waves breaking on the shore was essential in the pea soup fog. We avoided trouble. However, another seagoing venture that summer did not.

In the annual Pulpit Harbor dinghy race in North Haven, with a summer girl friend named Nancy as my crew, the former midshipman who had trained to become an ensign neglected a fundamental responsibility for an officer – vigilant supervision of the conduct of his crew. As skipper I normally held the mainsheet in one hand and the tiller in the other. Nancy, an engaging blonde and a novice at sea, was getting bored and pleaded for something to do. We were barely moving in a flat calm, so I gave her the sheet and did not notice when she cleated it down later to sunbathe. The North Haven dinghies are extremely tender and capsize easily. Suddenly out of nowhere a narrow gust of wind struck the boat. I was unable to free the mainsheet in time to empty the wind from the sail, and dark green water poured in. We were completely swamped. Luckily we were close to shore and I was able to beach the dinghy, bail it out, and continue the race – coming in dead last by a wide margin. It was an embarrassing performance. Nobody could figure out what had happened to us, because it was such a calm day: "What went wrong, Ted? Did you hit a rock?" It's great to date pretty blondes, but don't let them hold the mainsheet.

Fair Harvard
and Its Sons

Eliot House, one of the big Georgian red brick college houses over-looking the Charles River, would be my home for the next two years. It was known as the preppies' favorite house and for its legendary house-master John Finley, a professor of Greek civilization and a gentleman of infinite sophistication and culture.

During my junior and senior years I had a bunch of roommates in three adjoining suites, including Harvard hockey player Dave Abbot, loquacious and jovial Bobby Cobb, and my fun-loving Navy buddy Austie Lyne, all hailing from the Boston area. Our rooms were hardly a haven of tranquility conducive to serious study, but that's what libraries are for. Dr. Finley was unfailingly courteous and friendly in his relations with his boys. As a housemaster he was tolerant of the adolescent behavior of his charges; as a role model for the boys he was superb.

Each Wednesday afternoon Dr. and Mrs. Finley hosted a tea party for the Eliot boys. I attended one the day after the first Brinks armored car robbery. The robbers had made off with millions of dollars and left the police completely baffled. Mrs. Finley observed that the thieves appeared to be a very clever bunch. "My dear," replied Dr. Finley, "I trust that you do not value virtuosity over virtue."

Majoring in American history, I signed up for two courses taught by the renowned professor Samuel Eliot Morison, the official U.S. Navy his-torian of World War II and an acclaimed author of books on history including the voyages of Columbus. His brilliant lectures sparked my life-long interest in American history. His podium personality seemed arro-gant. One of his rules was that students wear jackets to his lectures. One day a fellow appeared with his jacket thrown loosely over his shoulders, and the professor demanded sternly that he put the jacket on properly. The young man struggled to obey. He was a wounded veteran missing an arm. The professor relented.

For sports I played squash and hockey on the Eliot House team. I had wanted to join the Harvard rugby team, which received a free trip to Bermuda to play games against other colleges over spring vacation. Many Harvard football players were joining the rugby team for the same reason. I tried out for the team on the first day of practice, which turned out to be my last day. In a one-on-one tackling drill I was matched up against Paul Lazaro, the varsity fullback, two hundred pounds of solid muscle and fast, too. I could never catch Paul even to attempt a tackle. On the other hand, he caught me every time and brought me down hard – end of my rugby aspirations. I did vacation in Bermuda later on and watched a rugby game between Yale and a British submarine crew that had just come into port. The Brits were a pale and scrawny lot compared to the hale and beefy Yale team, which fielded many former football players. Yale overwhelmed the submariners by sheer brute force with a huge running back, nicknamed "The Bull," shedding British tars right and left as he rumbled down the field; rugby skills had little to do with it.

I joined the Hasty Pudding Club and participated in its annual show, written and acted by the club members whose performance as hairy-legged chorines had become a comic tradition at Harvard. I played the part of a pilgrim in a musical farce entitled "Speak for Yourself, John," based on the legendary Myles Standish, John Alden, Priscilla Mullins romantic triangle. I also was ticket manager for the show, which had several performances in Cambridge before hitting the road – Vassar, Philadelphia, Buffalo, and New York. The audiences, filled with local young ladies, were enthusiastic, and the show business paper *Variety* gave the musical a fine review: "In its first full-scale postwar production Harvard's Hasty Pudding Club has hit a fast stride in straight musical comedy in contrast to its prewar rah-rah college revues. It's sock entertainment in any college league and compares favorably with all but the biggest league of pro musical shows. . . . All male cast handles the singing, acting and dancing assignments with plenty of capability, avoiding the usual shenanigans of males in petticoats. . . . Should pack them in on the road."

In New York, Jack Lemmon, ex-Hasty Pudding player and composer, invited the cast to be his guests one evening at the club where he was performing, the "Old Knick" on Second Avenue, and the first stop in Lemmon's celebrated career. Jack's cabaret ranked well down on the scale of Manhattan nightclubs, and I was reminded the next morning of the poor quality of the whiskey we were served. Jack's act was great: He wore a derby and striped jacket in keeping with the Gay Nineties décor, played the piano, sang, and chatted up the audience.

Years later when Jack won an Academy Award for his performance playing Ensign Pulver, the likable and bumbling ensign in the movie "Mr. Roberts," I wrote him a fan letter. Some months later I received a postcard from him. He was in Trinidad making "Fire Down Under" with Rita Hayworth and Robert Mitchum. He wrote that the movie was such a "turkey" that the next time I saw him it might be back at that crummy nightclub in New York.

There was a little more show business left on my agenda after the Hasty Pudding tour. Austie and I had become big fans of Al Jolson, the famous jazz singer, playing an album of his hit songs over and over until we knew them by heart. When Loews State Theatre in Boston announced that it would stage a Jolson singing contest to promote its latest attraction, "The Jolson Story," a movie about the singer's life, we decided to give it a shot.

George Plimpton beat the bass drum in the Exeter marching band, and I carried it.

Singing "You made Me Love You" in the Al Jolson contest, Loews State Theatre in Boston, 1947 . . .

. . . At our wedding reception with Lansing at the piano, San Juan, 1951.

. . . At our 50th wedding anniversary, 2001, with Austie Lyne.

. . . At parties (to a captive audience).

I thought it would be a good idea to enter the contest under the stage name of "Ted Larue." (Remember that Manhattan nightspot.) Austie flunked out at the audition, but I passed and performed from the theatre stage at the Saturday night show with a half a dozen other wannabe crooners. I was nervous, but I took comfort in knowing that a large contingent from the Hasty Pudding Club would be in the audience applauding with gusto no matter how I performed.

I sang "You Made Me Love You" in the best Jolson impersonation that I could muster – the whole gamut of facial expressions, widespread arms, and other gestures. The audience gave me a big hand even though I came in second. Not bad. The winner, a gentleman named Bert La France, was training to be a professional and put on pancake makeup before he sang, which I considered a bit much. His reward was a handsome watch, and I received a bunch of free movie tickets.

I was pleased with my performance, but concerned about my father's reaction to the *Boston Herald* article the next day. "Lamont Scion Shows Rich 'Mammy' Voice" was the headline of the story, which reported, "Harvard student Edward M. Lamont added mammy singing, Jolson style, to the famous banking clan's accomplishments last night." An astute reporter had uncovered Ted Larue's true identity. The *Harvard Crimson* laughingly reported, "As bobby-soxers shrieked, old-timers joyously acclaimed a return to the golden days of vaudeville, and theatre manager James Tibbets rubbed his hands in delight over his new minstrel discovery. 'Jolson would be proud of that boy,' he enthused. 'He's one of the best singers I've heard in years'."

The so-called "final clubs" at Harvard recruited and screened prospective members at a series of parties and outings during the "punching" season. Following this process I had joined the Delphic Club, known as the "Gashouse," which like other clubs consisted of a clubhouse with an active bar, dining room, and pool table where like-minded fellows could hang out. There was a raucous black-tie dinner each year at which many of the lads got roaring drunk, as they sang the club anthem and passed around a silver porringer filled with the traditional lethal punch. Despite their earnest efforts, the old grad members were unable to foster the mood of solemnity that they felt the ritual deserved. Girls were not part of the club scene, so I didn't spend much time at the Gashouse. Most of my crowd had girl friends, and so did I. Muriel was a quick-witted, fun-loving New York City girl, East Seventies, who was a student at Pine Manor in Wellesley, a junior college sometimes referred to as Pine Manure by the jokers.

The mothers of Boston debutantes naturally sought a well-populated stag line at their daughters' coming-out parties, and Harvard clubs provided a plentiful source of eligible young men. These frolicsome gatherings, whether on the North Shore of Boston or Long Island, offered an intoxicating mix of wine, women, and song. The champagne flowed and we danced to the lively music of Lester Lanin and the other society band-leaders. Obligations often accompany good times, however, and it behooved me to dance with the daughters of my parents' friends, some of whom were quite unexciting.

I attended almost every Harvard football game in Cambridge and drove down to Yale for the football and hockey games played in New Haven. In commenting on the makeup of the Harvard football team I wrote my dad, "There are quite a few names that are difficult to pronounce, and this is always a good sign," but I was not a fan of veteran coach Dick Harlow's ultra conservative style of play.

After the home games the parties in Eliot and other houses got quickly into full swing, and we moved from one to another. In our suite we served a potent fruit-flavored brew called "Fishhouse Punch," calculated to make merry and loosen the inhibitions of girl friends. Sometimes we went on to Jim Cronin's for hamburger plates and pitchers of beer, or attended dances at Eliot House or the Hasty Pudding Club. I have to smile when I read articles from time to time revealing with dismay that students at colleges indulge in excessive drinking, wild fraternity parties, and the like. It reminds me of actor Claude Rains, playing the French army officer in "Casablanca," feigning absolute shock in discovering that patrons were gambling at Humphrey Bogart's café. Guys have been partying on college campuses for at least one hundred years. Remember those preppies with raccoon coats and silver flasks at football games in the Roaring Twenties? In later years their grandsons disrobed to become streakers or "moon" their adversaries in the stands across the field.

On winter weekends and holidays our gang, boys and girls, often headed for the ski country, North Conway or Big Bromley and Mt. Mansfield in Vermont, staying in the inexpensive ski lodges catering to the college crowd. Any sprains or bruises suffered while skiing under frigid and icy conditions were soon dissipated in the exuberant après-ski parties.

I also went skiing down Park Avenue. In late December 1947 a record-breaking blizzard dumped twenty-six inches of snow on New York. An eerie silence enveloped the city streets as surface transportation ground to a halt, but shouts of joy resounded through Central Park as Manhattan families frolicked in the new winter resort at their doorstep and happy sledders swarmed down Pilgrim Hill overlooking the lake.

For many New England college skiers, skiing down the headwall at Tuckerman's Ravine on Mt. Washington was a time-honored spring rite. I lugged my skis up the Fire Trail and the face of the headwall to a tiny snow platform below the lip. The face was so steep that my uphill ski was level with my chin as I traversed the slope. The moment of truth comes when you make the downhill turn to change direction or schuss on down the wall. A fall meant tumbling and cartwheeling several hundred feet to the bottom, skis and poles flying every which way, and we had seen a few. My pals yelled "Chicken, Chicken!" at the skiers who delayed their turn too long, so after twenty yards I made the move and, barely in control, went into an angled schuss, hurtled downwards, and survived. For me it was one of those once-in-a-lifetime things – like the journey up the Nile to explore Egyptian antiquities – a great experience, but once was enough.

I drove an old family car at the time, a '34 Chevrolet coupe with a rumble seat that got lots of use when everyone piled in for a drive out of town, perhaps to Wellesley for touch football with the girls or to a club outing at some old grad's house in the country. On Saturday nights I drove Muriel slowly and carefully back to Pine Manor after the evening's festivities. My only run-in with police had nothing to do with my driving. One night Muriel and I were parked in Lovers' Lane discussing great books when suddenly a beam of light shone into the car. As we hastily disengaged the policeman behind the flashlight calmly told us that we were illegally parked and must move on. He certainly knew how to ruin a beautiful evening.

During the summer between our junior and senior years at Harvard Austie and I took construction jobs with Connolly Brothers, a building contractor on the North Shore of Boston. We stayed with our friends Alan and Betty Parker in Swampscott. The project we worked on was building access roads at a nearby plant, transporting and shoveling landfill – hard physical labor at $1.10 an hour. Each morning Austie made breakfast and I prepared the sandwiches for our lunch. We were dead tired by the end of a long day.

One evening we donned our tuxedos to attend a dance at a Marblehead yacht club, relaxed for a moment in the living room before going to the party, and fell fast asleep, completely missing the dance. (Since then I have always sought out white-collar jobs.) However, we did have a fine time at a Longwood Cricket Club dance in Brookline following the national doubles tournament, having met a few of the girl players while serving as volunteer ball boys during the matches. Maureen Connelly was the star women's player and tournament sweetheart. "Little Mo" was very good and later became the first woman to win the Grand Slam of tennis. Gussie Moran's lace trimmed panties were the number one fashion topic, drawing far more comment than the backless skin-tight tennis outfit of Venus Williams or sister Serena's form-hugging "cat suit" nowadays.

On my twenty-first birthday I received some special greetings. A telegram from the Corliss Lamonts, signed "The Family on the Left," read, "Now that you are twenty-one, life has really just begun. We hope that you have heaps of fun, but take care when you pick the only one. Happy Birthday." Sound advice, but marriage was farthest from my thoughts. A fine letter from Grandmother Lamont concluded, "It isn't everyone who has a grandson of high character, fine mind, but who can relax and sing Al Jolson, too." What a lovable matriarch! Grandmother was a real gem.

The story of my college years may sound like a steady diet of fun and games, but I hit the books, too, and my courses in government and American history, my college major, stimulated an interest that has grown through the years. If I missed a few lectures I could call on a studious Radcliffe friend, who had taken copious notes that I could review before exams. I put together a run-of-the-mill collection of a few B's and lots of C's. With a smile and a wink people sometimes refer to "Gentlemen's C's," implying that the recipient of this grade is somewhat easygoing in his work habits – an image that was well captured in verse by Judge Robert Grant, Harvard class of 1873:

The able-bodied C man! He sails swimmingly along.
His philosophy is rosy as a skylark's matin song.
The light of his ambition is respectably to pass,
And to hold a firm position in the middle of his class.

Mine was not a stellar academic performance, but not bad company to keep. After all, President George W. Bush was a C student at Yale. In recent years about half of the grades awarded to Harvard undergraduates have been A and A-, leaving my academic record at college in the dust. Are these sons really that much smarter than their dads, or are these high grades just another form of inflation, which, some say, started during the Vietnam war years when college deferments were a way to avoid the draft and many students and professors opposed the war?

In June 1948 I joined my cap-and-gowned classmates for the awarding of our Bachelor of Arts degrees at the pageantry-filled commencement exercises in Harvard Yard. The traditional ceremony retained most of the trappings and rites of my grandfather's 1892 graduation. My parents and I then adjourned to Eliot House, where Dr. Finley, with great panache, handed each Eliot House graduate his sheepskin.

Foreign Affairs

Three weeks after graduation my Harvard friend Todd Parsons and I embarked for France on the *Marine Tiger*, a former troop ship chartered by organizations sponsoring student trips overseas. Our ultimate destination was Chambon-Sur-Lignon, a small town near St. Etienne in central France, where we would spend a month doing construction work at a private Protestant high school, Le Collège Cévenol. The Congregational Church, the financial backer of the school, had organized the program for foreign students to donate their labor and receive lodging and meals at the school. Todd and I thought it was a great way to visit France, learn the language, and do something constructive at the same time.

I wrote my parents about our nine-day ocean voyage with some six hundred students and teachers. "The *Marine Tiger* was sensational. . . . Crowded, uncomfortable, but what fun." Todd and I fell in with a dozen college boys and girls who hung out together. During the day there were French classes, travel briefings, and meetings to discuss subjects ranging from foreign policy to religion. Many of the student groups were church-sponsored, and the prevailing political views were decidedly liberal. Henry Wallace and world federalism were popular. There were a few socialists sympathetic to Russia and communism at a time when the signs threatening a full-blown Cold War were apparent. My "fellow travelers," in both senses of the term, were well-educated, agreeable companions, and our lively debates over politics were not heated. We slept 150 to a room in the same three-tiered bunks used by thousands of soldiers before us. At night, to escape the stifling heat of the bunkroom, we brought our blankets up on deck and sang songs under the stars; "You Can Roll a Silver Dollar" was apparently popular everywhere.

We disembarked at Le Havre, took the train to Paris, and spent the first night in a Youth Hostel tent camp. We got out of there in a hurry the next day, moving to the modest Hotel Bedford on Rue de l'Arcade near the Champs Elysées. It was my first visit to Paris, and for the next week we did the town – hitting all the high spots from the Arc de Triomphe, brilliantly lit for Bastille Day celebrations, to the legendary Left Bank cafés.

Paris was loaded with American tourists, and by just hanging around American Express and Café de la Paix you were sure to run into some old pals. I wrote my parents about seeing the Folies Bergère the kind of letter a young man writes his parents about the Folies: "Classical music is played a great deal, the scenery and costumes are lavish, and naked girls are only used occasionally as a backdrop to the scenes." For the record: The "backdrops," shapely long-stemmed beauties with sequin-adorned G-strings, were sensational. I have gone back to the Folies several times since then, once joining a group of tourists selected to do the Can-Can on the big stage. The audience laughed and cheered one fellow when he announced that he was from Brooklyn. I can only surmise that the reason for this fond identification with Brooklyn was that they had seen some of the many American films with army sergeants or taxi drivers from Brooklyn in comic roles.

Our train trip from Paris to Chambon was a nightmare. Our group of four Cévenol campers, including two Harvard graduates, mistakenly boarded a train for Nîmes instead of St. Etienne. The conductor blithely punched our tickets and said not a word. We rattled and rolled along, sitting on our bags in a packed third-class car, getting deep into southern France before we realized our mistake. Clearly our understanding of French, written and spoken, needed work. More bouncing around the countryside in third class, an uncomfortable night in the waiting room of a rural train station, and finally a crowded bus ride – naturally no seats – winding through the Cévenne Mountains completed the journey.

Le Collège Cévenol consisted of a large farmhouse, a barn, used as a gymnasium, and a half dozen Quonset-type barracks and classroom buildings. However, the summer campers slept in their sleeping bags in tents. There were about eighty of us, half Americans and half Europeans, all boys and girls about my age. The Europeans were accustomed to wartime shortages and hardship, but to the Americans, mostly students who had not seen military action, the conditions seemed decidedly spartan. There were no showers, mirrors, or even hot water for washing. Once a week we paid fifty francs to take a bath in a bathhouse in the town of Chambon.

The food was terrible – mainly potatoes, bean soup, noodles, more potatoes, lettuce, and occasionally tripes and indescribably grisly bits of meat. I had fortunately dined well in Paris – it would be hard not to – because I lost ten pounds during my month at Cévenol. I wrote home, "As for comfort and food, Cévenol ranks several pegs below Sampson," but not to worry, I was having "a grand time."

We got up at 6:30 and worked in the mornings – mainly pick-and-shovel labor building roads and leveling a playing field. The afternoons were free time, and often I attended the lectures and discussions on the daily agenda. Our gang took a few weekend camping trips into the mountains, bringing along canned goods bought at the Collège canteen, loaves of French bread, cheese, and a few bottles of *vin ordinaire* from the town *épicerie*, and eggs from a local farmer. At night we lit a fire and placed our sleeping bags around its dying embers. One weekend we took the train to Nice. Swimming off the popular beach, bright lights, and cafés were a welcome respite from the austerity of Collège Cévenol.

The political beliefs of many of the townspeople of Chambon, the school staff, and European campers were an eye-opener for me, presenting viewpoints I had not encountered before face to face. The town was a unique center of Protestantism and pacifism in France. The local pastor, a town leader who had been active in the underground helping Jews escape to Switzerland during the war, was an ardent pacifist. Even in wartime he had preached the passive resistance, non-violence philosophy of Gandhi. After one of his talks I discussed pacifism with a fellow American camper who replied, "I was a conscientious objector myself during the war and served as an Army medic. I'll tell you about it."

There were English, French, Italian, and Dutch campers, and several young Germans, former prisoners of war, fulfilling work obligations in France; there were also three Czechoslovakians who were not permitted by their Communist government to discuss politics. Our divergent views became the grist for spirited debates. The Americans were mainly liberal Democrats; the Europeans were by and large socialists. They were "a good deal to the left of the Time-Life, Harvard, Lamont family views," I wrote home.

The daily agenda of topics for discussion covered the political and economic systems in different countries, communism, pacifism, U.S. foreign policy, the Marshall Plan, and so forth. I was soon arguing with socialists, communists, and even a fascist, who admired the authoritarian efficiency of Germans and relished his experience in a German youth brigade during the war. The French campers declared that Americans were too materialistic, culturally challenged, and ruled by corporate power. While the French had been sniping at Americans for years along these lines, in my first direct exposure to these views I was stunned to hear such criticisms coming from well-educated young Europeans.

I especially bristled at the charge made by some campers that the Marshall Plan was an act of economic imperialism by the U.S. Talk about biting the hand that feeds you. At the June 1947 Harvard commencement exercises I had heard Secretary of State George C. Marshall announce his historic plan for a huge U.S. program of economic aid – about $100 billion in current dollars – for war ravaged Europe. By the summer of 1948, the time of our trip, the Marshall Plan to support economic recovery was in full swing in Western Europe. (The USSR had rejected the assistance for itself and its satellite countries behind the Iron Curtain.) Grain and other foods, fuel, machinery and equipment, and various commodities urgently needed by these countries were being shipped abroad in growing volume. The recipient nations established the Organization for European Economic Cooperation to coordinate the program in Europe, the first step, as it turned out, toward the Common Market and European Union. Along with humanitarian concerns, the U.S wanted to help Europe recover her economic strength and restart the flow of international trade, which would also be good for American business. Furthermore, it was critical to deter the spreading threat of Russian-backed communism in Europe.

Many historians have declared that the Marshall Plan was the most generous deed by a nation in the history of international relations. Three years later, after graduating from Harvard Business School, I would join the Economic Cooperation Administration, which administered the Plan.

I was often the point man at Collège Cévanol in defending the Marshall Plan against the charge that the U.S. was seeking the economic domination of Europe, and in advocating the American economic system based on private enterprise as compared to the socialist and communist orders governing most European countries. But there was one criticism I could not deny – the growing witch hunt mentality in the U.S. toward persecuting communists – real and alleged.

I was ready for a few square meals and joined my parents in Paris for the last week of August. The highlights were fine dining and our side trip to view the magnificent cathedral of Chartres with its towering Romanesque and Gothic spires. Our next stop was Geneva, Switzerland, where I planned to return in October to attend the university. In 1948 thousands of Americans, many of them veterans with GI Bill benefits, headed for European universities – Oxford, Cambridge, the Sorbonne, Grenoble, and others including the University of Geneva, which Austie Lyne and I had chosen to attend. My father had spent a year after college at Cambridge, but the winter sports and good living in Switzerland compared to austerity-stricken England couldn't be denied. Switzerland, having maintained its traditional neutrality in World War II, was prospering compared to the rest of war-weary Europe. Our GI Bill benefits would pay our tuition and provide $75 a month for living expenses.

With Dad at the wheel we next drove to Grindelwald, took the cable car up the Jungfrau, and then continued on to Interlaken and Lucerne. The mountain scenery was spectacular – snow-covered alpine peaks, green mountainside meadows resplendent with wildflowers, and little brown chalets with geranium-filled window boxes. After my parents departed for home, I set off on my own tour for a couple of weeks before going on to Geneva for the start of the fall term at the university.

My first stop was The Hague, where I stayed at the home of Annemaricke De Kanter and her family. Annemaricke, a friend from Collège Cévenol, was eighteen, a pretty blonde and a happy camper, both figuratively and literally on our weekend camp outings at the Collège. For ordinary folk at that time private cars were a rarity in Holland. Annemaricke and I bicycled around town and along the Promenade, Sheveningen's famous seaside boulevard, and joined the spectators watching the Netherlands' newly enthroned Queen Juliana drive by in a gilded carriage with her military escort, to take up her official residence in the royal palace.

On to London where Lewis Douglas, the American ambassador to the United Kingdom, and his wife, good friends of my parents, had invited me to stay at the Embassy residence while visiting the city. Ambassador and Mrs. Douglas were very hospitable, and so was their attractive and vivacious daughter Sharman, who graciously included me in her busy social agenda. "Charmin' Sharman," as the London tabloids dubbed her, partied with the royal princesses and seemingly went out every lunch and evening to mingle with the cream of English society, often bearing noble titles. One night we went nightclubbing with the Marquis of Milford Haven, who told me it was okay for me to call him "David." Another night I rented a tuxedo to accompany Sharman to a movie premiere and a big reception for the party-going society crowd.

It was not my cup of tea, as I wrote home. "I've heard more boring cocktail conversations about race horses and society than you can imagine." Sharman was most considerate, and I did my best to keep pace with English upper class conversations and doings, but I was not in my comfort zone. One free evening I asked the Embassy butler if there was a first-class pub nearby, so that I could experience that side of British life, but he advised that that was not a good idea.

I spent the next weekend at the farm estate of Lord Rennell of Rodd – the senior partner at Morgan Grenfell, in which J.P. Morgan & Co. had an ownership interest, and a good friend of my parents. Two Rodd daughters had stayed with our family during the war to escape the hardships and Luftwaffe bombing in wartime England. I enjoyed horseback riding with daughter Joanna through the rolling meadows and farmlands around The Rodd, the family manor in the rural west country. Life was very peaceful there, a far cry from the London social frenzy. An old colonel who came for tea was the spitting image of C. Aubrey Smith, the actor with the sweeping military mustache who once played the part of British army officers in the movies. He talked about fertilizing crops and about pigs and horses, too, but in this case, farm horses.

I set off again and at the old city of Chester was amazed to see a bunch of English schoolgirls playing lacrosse, the game originated by American Indians, outside the ancient Roman walls surrounding the town. It was a striking example of cultural globalization (before the word was invented). Nowadays the globalization of sports has advanced so far that Russian girls, some of them lithesome beauties, are in the forefront of women's tennis, a game that for years was played mainly in elite WASP clubs and venues like Newport and Wimbledon. V. J. Singh from Fiji was the world's leading golfer in 2004; a bevy of Koreans excel in women's professional golf tournaments, and Dominican and other Caribbean baseball players star in our national pastime.

In Oxford, an elderly porter pointed out a masonry drainpipe which generations of Oxford students had clambered up to get back into their rooms after hours when the front entrance of the college was closed. One of them, he said, was William Fulbright, a Rhodes scholar at the time, who later as a U.S. senator initiated the Fulbright scholarship program for study abroad. Back in The Hague I sang my Al Jolson version of "Toot Toot Tootsie, Good-bye" to Annemaricke at a party, kissed her good-bye, and boarded the train to Paris. En route I checked out Brussels and the beautiful old town of Bruges, a medieval magic kingdom built around a maze of canals connected by arched footbridges. I met Austie in Paris, and we celebrated by café crawling in Montmartre, looking for "Gigi." No luck. Running low on money we took the night train third class to Geneva, which would be our home for the next nine months.

L'Etudiant

Austie and I shared a double room in a small pension, near the University of Geneva, run by a nice elderly white-haired lady named Madame Perez. A half dozen other boys and girls, all students, were staying there – American, Swiss, Greek, and Italian. A few more came in for meals, where we all spoke French. Proficiency in the language varied markedly among the diners, but no problem. Good humor prevailed, Madame's cuisine was first-class, and it was always a merry gathering around the long dining room table.

The top items on my initial agenda upon arrival were 1) write home for more money and my hockey skates, 2) buy a bicycle, the only way to get around town, and 3) select my courses at the university. I bought a shiny crimson and chrome three-speed bike. At the university I signed up for courses in international law, the economies of postwar Europe, international finance, the United Nations charter, and foreign trade, all taught in French. I also chose a course in the American Revolution that was taught in English – to gain the European perspective and earn an easy high mark if my grades needed bolstering. The gravitas of my academic program was impressive, but its implementation would have to wait. Two girls from New York, Eleanor and Sophie, who had a small Renault, invited Austie and me to join them on a three-week automobile trip through Germany to Denmark, the Low Countries, and France. It was too good an opportunity to turn down.

The castles on the Rhine were lovely, but my outstanding impression of Germany was the devastation caused by the wartime Allied bombing, as we progressed from Stuttgart to Frankfurt and on to Hamburg. Stuttgart and Frankfort had been leveled, and little clearing up and reconstruction had taken place aside from moving the rubble out of the streets. In Frankfort, people were living in hollowed out caves in the ruins of the empty burnt out shells of buildings. We often ate in the Army PXs, which were open to American tourists, and chatted with the soldiers manning the bases. Some had fraulein girl friends, and they all were making the best of it in desolate surroundings far from home. We watched the Berlin airlift in operation at the American air base in Frankfort. The access roads to Berlin had been blocked by the Russian army, forcing the U.S. Air Force to fly in food and other supplies to the beleaguered city. The operation appeared to be running in the routine fashion of a commercial airport.

We crossed the Kiel Canal, spent a night in Odense, the home of Hans Christian Andersen, and three days in Copenhagen, where we toured the local cathedrals and palaces. I got a special kick from visiting Elsinore Castle, with its ramparts view of Sweden just across the straits, having just seen the movie "Hamlet" starring Lawrence Olivier as the conflicted Danish prince. After those PX meals, we dined well in the home of the smorgasbord.

For European travelers in 1948 it paid to be informed about currencies and exchange rates. There were only two hard currencies, U.S. dollars and Swiss francs, that were convertible everywhere. The other soft currencies were of little value outside the country that issued them. Accordingly, it was important not to get stuck with a lot of local currency when leaving a country. In Denmark we overplayed the game and ran out of Danish crowns at the same time that our car ran out of gas while still in Denmark. No problem. We bought gas with American cigarettes, another useful medium of exchange, and headed for Paris.

Changing U.S. dollars at the black market rate to get the highest return in French francs was the common practice followed by foreign travelers; the French government for its own reasons chose to look the other way. There were plenty of money changers hanging around outside the hotels and American Express office. As a result, the good life in Paris was far less expensive for tourists than nowadays, and I often indulged my taste for *bifteck* and *pommes frites* along with a *salade de tomates*, a glass or two of *vin rouge*, *pâtisserie*, and *café* in one of the many good little restaurants.

However, the best dinner we had was at a fancy Right Bank restaurant where the Harvard Club of Paris was dining at the same time that the Harvard–Yale football game was being played in Cambridge. The club received telegraphed reports each quarter on the progress of the game. Most of the members, many of whom were former professors or graduate students at Harvard, didn't have a clue about the rules of American football, and we did our best to explain the basics. It was not all that easy in French. "Il y a quatre 'downs' pour gagner environ dix mètres. Comprenez vous?" However, the wine flowed, everybody cheered when Harvard won, and several of us serenaded the members with "Ten Thousand Men of Harvard" and other football songs.

But the party wasn't over. Across the street the Yale Club of Paris was meeting in another restaurant, and according to tradition the losing club treated the winners to a case of champagne. More singing and cheers. French passersby must certainly have wondered, "Qu'est ce que c'est qui ce passe ici?" A few weeks after the Harvard–Yale game a mysterious looking oblong package arrived in Geneva, sent by our former Harvard roommate Bobby Cobb. It was a piece of the goalpost cross bar from The Game, inscribed with the date and score.

Years later I would enjoy another Harvard–Yale game in a completely different setting – Dallas, Texas, where I was attending a conference.

Skiing at
Gstaad with
Buz and Austie.
Our academic
agenda at the
University of
Geneva was
not onerous.

Le Hockey Club de Genève with Lyne and Lamont far right.

Study group at
Harvard Business
School, 1951.
Roommates Dick
O'Keeffe and Perry
Bartsch at far left
and right. The first
year was no walk
in the park.

A friend had invited me to join him at a joint luncheon of the Harvard and Yale clubs of Dallas at a large restaurant where the game would be shown via special hookup television. Half a dozen big screens, a mariachi band, plenty of Bloody Marys, and barbecued ribs contributed to the noisy and happy gathering. About half the guys came in big hats, string ties, and cowboy boots. The other half chose the Ivy League look reflecting their college years – tweed jackets, button-down shirts, and striped ties, raising the question of how long it takes to feel like a real Texan. Football is huge in Texas, and true Texans understand and appreciate a well-played game. However, they were watching a typical Ivy League contest full of fumbles, dropped passes, penalties, and other screw-ups. At half-time a fellow at my table turned to his wife and said, "Come on, honey. Let's get out of here. We'll drive over to the stadium and see the rest of the S.M.U. game." No one ever said that Paris and Dallas had much in common. *Vive la différence.*

Back in Geneva several girls in the Smith College year-abroad program invited Austie and me to their lodgings at the Hôtel de Russie for a Thanksgiving turkey dinner; it was good to be with compatriots on that very American holiday. Two weeks later we celebrated a Swiss holiday honoring a famous event in the history of Geneva – the "Escalade," Geneva's victory over the Savoyards in 1602. My birthday fell over the same weekend. Madame Perez presented me with a birthday cake and served a grand dinner with wine and toasts celebrating the Escalade. I played the piano and my fellow lodgers danced into the night. Over the weekend the city was decked out in heraldic banners and streamers, and a pageantry-filled parade of local gentry wearing the garb of seventeenth-century Genevois marched through the torch-lit streets. In 1602 a Genevois housewife had thrown a cauldron of boiling soup down on the enemy invaders attempting to scale the walls; in 1948 we threw confetti on the heads of marchers.

Prices in Vevey, France, a two-mile bike ride from Geneva, were about half of Swiss prices for those of us with Swiss francs or dollars to exchange. I biked across the border from time to time to buy clothing and liquor. With the Christmas season approaching we needed to invigorate our holiday punch bowl, and imported liquors in Switzerland were prohibitive in price. The trick was to smuggle your purchases through the Swiss customs inspection on the ride back into Switzerland to avoid paying the high duty on imports. The customs agents often examined travelers from France. I wore my newly purchased clothes and taped pints of cognac to the back of each of my legs, and it worked. I was very careful in swinging my leg over the center bar as I mounted my bicycle after passing through the border station.

My modest hockey playing career took a new turn when Austie and I joined Le Hockey Club de Genève, sponsored by the city, which provided us with handsome crimson uniforms and equipment. We looked good until we hit the ice; at the start of the season we were a very bad team. In 1948 Genevois youth wanted to take up hockey seriously, but there was no ice rink in Geneva for practice and games. Only two other players on the team had much hockey playing experience, both Canadians attending a corporate management school in Geneva. The local boys were all novices, including the coach's son who played goalie.

We took the train to Lausanne, the nearest town with a rink, for the season's first game; it was the first time the Geneva team had been on the ice together. I started at right wing and soon ran out of gas, as did the rest of the team. There were only two lines, and our lack of conditioning and practice was evident. The Lausanne team beat us easily. Still, after a few practice sessions later at their rink we felt encouraged about the full season of games that lay ahead.

One problem facing the team was that the Americans and Canadians played an aggressive brand of hockey with body-checking that was not acceptable to Swiss referees. Accordingly, we frequently had a player in the penalty box, severely handicapping his teammates on the ice. Later in the season the Swiss coach sent a letter to the foreign players warning them that their hockey style was "trop nerveux," meaning, in this case, "too physical." As I was the least combative of the North Americans, I was often on the ice playing short a man and with my tongue hanging out. I kept urging my teammates to listen to the coach; in Switzerland do as the Swiss do.

Austie and I spent Christmas of 1948 with the family of Major Victor Conley, commanding officer of the U.S. Army School of Standards, in Zell am See, Austria; Mrs. Conley was a Lyne cousin. We skied the local mountain and Kitzbühl, a popular Austrian ski resort, where we encountered long alpine schusses in deep powder – something new for guys who had skied only New England's icy trails. There were several one-legged skiers on the slopes, young Austrian amputees wounded in the war, but very few foreign tourists. No-frills austerity governed living in postwar Austria. When we went into the hotel bar for a beer after our runs, a small band started playing Viennese waltzes. We were the only customers in the place, and it was kind of sad.

All the Army base officers and their wives came to Major Conley's house for a Christmas Eve party. One upwardly mobile lieutenant made sure that my host was within earshot when he informed me that the major was an "absolutely outstanding" commanding officer.

On Christmas morning I went downstairs early to find the Austrian butler pouring the remains of whiskey highballs from the party the night before into a bottle. The Army PX supplied liquors for the American military personnel, who lived well, but the Austrian people were still facing hard times.

Christmas day with the Conley family was a delight – presents under the tree, Santa Claus for the kids at the officers' club, and a caroling party by jeep that evening. The whole scene of the little alpine town with its church and bell tower surrounded by snow-covered hills was right out of "The Sound of Music." I left Austria with great respect for the professionalism of the American military personnel and their efforts to have friendly relations with their Austrian neighbors, like giving holiday parties for the local kids. Both Conley sons spoke fluent German. Unlike Germany Austria was regarded as a liberated country, not an occupied one, as it awaited the negotiation and signing of a peace treaty to settle its future status. As for Russia, most U.S. officers thought war was inevitable.

A few days after Christmas we boarded the Arlberg Express for Zurich and Zermatt, where the Hockey Club de Genève would play in a three-day tournament. The club provided first-class lodgings for the team at the Beau Site Hotel. I wrote my parents about the massive pyramid-shaped Matterhorn looming over Zermatt: "The Matterhorn at sunset with a small snow cloud blowing off it, like a pennant on a masthead, is one of the loveliest sights I have ever seen." Paramount Pictures certainly agrees, and has used the spectacular peak as its corporate symbol introducing movies for many years.

Geneva won the hockey tournament, beating the teams from Brigue, Lausanne, and Zermatt, which briefly made us local hockey heroes. I played right wing on the line with the two Canadian players, who were the heart of the team. The Zermatt townspeople were keen about hockey, despite the modest level of skills on display, and I received a couple of intriguing proposals. One evening, when her duties as an entertainer were finished, the vivacious red-haired piano player in the hotel bar invited me up to her chambers; and the Zermatt hockey manager offered to hire Austie and me to coach his team for a week or so. However, I decided not to compromise my amateur standing and declined.

After the hockey tournament we joined the University of Geneva Ski Club group, which had just arrived in Zermatt. We had a great time skiing the sunny open slopes and the run down into Italy, stopping for a bratwurst and glass of hot spiced red wine at the little mountainside restaurants. However, some of the foreign visitors did not fare so well.

Zermatt had long attracted English tourists, including Edward Whymper, the leader of the first climbing party to reach the peak of the mighty Matterhorn in 1865. During our stay in early 1949 some Brits were returning for the first time since before the war, but because of British foreign exchange restrictions they were on very tight budgets and forced to use their old prewar skis and boots. Most had not skied since before the war and were pretty rusty. They were a plucky bunch, but a few took nasty falls. Nevertheless, they gamely joined the après-ski merriment as they hobbled around on crutches in the hotel bar.

Maybe we just couldn't handle victory. The Geneva hockey team lost its next two games, both rough outings, first in Châteaux d'Oeux, and the next day in Gstaad. Bone-tired and black and blue from my sports-filled Christmas vacation, I was glad to return to Geneva to take it easy and renew the regular student routine.

I will be forever grateful to the University of Geneva for bringing me together with Camille Buzby, my dear wife to whom I have been married for the last fifty-plus years. American students packed the French language classes, and there were half a dozen pretty, fun-loving girls that hung out together in my class. One was Camille, whom we all called "Buz." I stood out in class because I could not pronounce the sound of the letter "R" in French to the satisfaction of the professor. Accordingly, he instructed me to stand before the class and press a pencil against my lips, which was intended to produce the correct guttural sound when I spoke words like "Français." Buz thought my attempts to get it right were very funny.

After a hockey game in Grindelwald Buz and I skied together for the first time. Buz had not skied much before. She had grown up in Puerto Rico, where Mr. and Mrs. Buzby, who came from Philadelphia and Elmira, had met, married, and decided to live and raise their family. Buz had just graduated from Middlebury, where she had been captain of the women's volleyball and tennis teams. Like me she had chosen to spend a student year abroad. She was impressively game in tackling the mountain at Grindelwald. I admired her spirit and loved her enthusiasm and good humor.

The Geneva hockey club played out its schedule in different towns around the Swiss and French Alps, with mixed results. We traveled with a happy band of camp followers, and went skiing at the local mountain resorts after the games. At Megève we lost the game, but enjoyed great skiing. At Chamonix the skiing was steep and tricky in dense fog, and we were glad that life nets were strung in places where the twisting trail ran perilously close to the edge of the precipice. France was inexpensive for us, and we lived and dined well. Later we joined the University ski club trip to Davos. The Swiss students said that Davos and Kublis, connected by a spectacular ten-mile run, provided the best skiing in Switzerland. It was sheer joy to schuss with your pals through sunny snow fields, forested slopes, and mountainside hamlets.

Mid-year exams were coming up, and the officer in charge of veterans' affairs at the U.S. Consulate had a message for me. The Veterans Administration had just decreed that all students on the GI Bill must take the upcoming exams. The good news was that the V.A. would accept minimal achievement on the exams for students to continue to qualify for benefits, because the requirement was being imposed for the first time. The bad news was that many of the guys were skiing or traveling all over Europe with no thought of returning to Geneva for the exams. "Do your best to get the word to them," the officer told me. I informed the ones I could reach by telephone and telegram, and everyone got back in time for the exams except for two fellows crossing North Africa in a Land Rover, who were in big trouble with the V.A. upon their return. My understanding of French had improved, and I passed my exams easily.

Back in Geneva Austie and I embarked on a modest change of lifestyle. We moved from our room chez Madame Perez to a small, somewhat run-down apartment on the Bourg de Four, a little square in the old city near the university. We wanted more independence, and the price was right. The apartment was across the street from La Clémence, our favorite student café featuring delicious pâtisseries, beer, and cheese fondues.

For spring vacation we joined a group of fellow students touring Italy. My letters home listed the historic sights and places we visited – Leonardo da Vinci's "Last Supper" in Milan, the Cathedral and Plaza de San Marco and Palace of Doges in Venice, and more. Everyone was highly amused when I slipped and fell into the murky waters of the Grand Canal in disembarking from a gondola. I was not rushing ashore to avoid getting stuck with the check, as some suggested.

By train and bus we made our way to Florence via Bologna, where we dined at Papagallo's restaurant. I reported home that I was becoming a big fan of spaghetti and ravioli with a glass of Chianti on the side. After our stay in Florence I said I was becoming quite "arty" as I reeled off the names of the art treasures we had visited – the Pitti Palace, the Michelangelo statues of David and Moses, Botticelli's Venus, Raphael's Madonna, and so on. We checked out the gravity-defying tower at Pisa and headed south to Naples and Capri.

I knew that organized crime flowered in Naples, junior only to Sicily in this regard, but I still had some off-the-books business to transact – exchanging American dollars at the free market rate for Italian lire. I agreed to meet a young street dealer outside our hotel (no well-lit hotel lobby for him) and we settled on the exchange rate for the transaction. I had a packet of traveler's checks and he had a large roll of lire, apparently the correct amount as he shuffled it for my inspection before the trade. Nervously we made the swap, and he took off like a rabbit. I quickly examined the roll of lire, and my fears were confirmed – big bills on the outside and small denominations on the inside, falling well short of the amount agreed on. I chased the youth down dark and narrow streets and eventually cornered him in a cul-de-sac. Now what? I expected a flashing stiletto to appear at any moment, or perhaps his gang members were already coming up behind me. Fortunately, he was more nervous than I was. We reversed the swap, and I hastily retreated to the security of our hotel.

Capri was a rendezvous point for more traveling Geneva students and the Smith girls as well. We enjoyed the beautiful scenery from the orange groves to the Grotto Azurro and took over a local café in the evenings. From Capri we bused along the lovely Amalfi Drive to Salerno and on to

Pompeii, the town buried by a volcanic eruption in 79 AD and later uncovered, fascinating historians and tourists ever since.

Italy in springtime has long been a mecca for foreign visitors, and especially Rome at Easter time. In 1925 the Easter service at St. Peter's, crowded with tourists, had reminded Grandmother Florence Lamont of a bustling railroad station. Attending the same service in 1949 I reported that I felt "more like being in Grand Central Station than in a place for meditation and prayer." However, I was moved by the beauty of the huge basilica – the mosaic images, the choral chants, and Michelangelo's "Pietà."

We spent a week in the Holy City, and, like millions of other tourists, covered Rome by foot and bus tours – from the four basilicas to the Sistine Chapel where one literally felt the presence of Michelangelo's genius. In viewing the famous central image of God reaching out a hand with extended fingers to give life to Adam, one tourist with a sense of humor broke the spell. He told me that God was saying to Adam: "Let's keep in touch!"

I wrote home that the Coliseum, seating sixty thousand, had a greater capacity than either the Polo Grounds or Harvard stadium. The Coliseum and the Baths of Caracalla were the first of many similar Roman ruins I have seen in my travels since then. The Sybaritic ancient Romans erected stadiums and bathing pools and steam baths wherever they went in their spreading empire.

The high point of our Roman sojourn was our audience with the Pope. I revered the papacy and its role in the world, although I had heard of reports criticizing the Pope for not speaking out forcefully against the Nazi atrocities and persecution of the Jews during World War II. On the other hand, his defenders said that he feared the Nazis would retaliate viciously against Catholics in Germany and other occupied countries if he censured them.

At the Vatican our group of Geneva students joined another band of tourists and proceeded through a couple of anterooms, manned by color-fully uniformed Swiss Guards, to the main reception room to await His Holiness. Everyone had brought crosses, medallions, and other religious articles to be blessed by the Pope. One lady could barely tote her heavy load of Bibles and rosaries. I had some St. Christopher and St. Bernard medals to give to my Catholic friends back home. The Pope went down the line of visitors, stopping to chat briefly with each one. His demeanor was both serene and cordial in welcoming his guests. I told His Holiness that I was a student on vacation from the University of Geneva, and he smiled and wished me a pleasant holiday.

Back at the university for the spring term I focused on my courses in international law and finance at L'Ecole des Hautes Etudes across Lac Léman from the university. I was especially interested in the proceedings of the international conferences taking place at the United Nations offices nearby, and wrote home about them.

"I have attended six of the Economic Commission for Europe conferences at the ONU. Ambassador Averill Harriman was there first, but then he left, and Paul Porter took over as head of the U.S. delegation. . . . Of course, it was a fight between the East and the West from the word 'go.' The Eastern nations' big kick was the use of export licenses by the U.S., which greatly restricted commerce, they claimed. I was favorably impressed with the competence of the U.S. and British delegations. The U.S. had facts and figures in their arguments that could not be denied. The Russians, however, went in for a lot of name calling, repetition, and completely wild statements, such as that the Marshall Plan had caused widespread unemployment in Europe." At the time, in contemplating the future, I was leaning toward a career in international business or government, and, as it turned out, my first job would be with the Marshall Plan. Almost fifty years later I met Porter at a Harvard conference for Marshall Plan alumni, and we reminisced about the early days.

In June Teddy Janeway, a friend from Long Island, showed up in Geneva with a couple of Yale friends. They were on their way to Paris and the châteaux country in the Loire River valley, and I was glad to join their tour. We spent a few days in Paris staying at the small Left Bank Hotel Idéal, whose name was a gross exaggeration, and then we checked out their great châteaux – Chinon, Amboise, Chenonceau, and the rest, while dining well in small country inns.

My last fling in Europe had been a good one. I flew back to New York with fond memories of my student year abroad. It is good to have a buddy in life's adventures, and sharing this one with my congenial pal Austie made it very enjoyable. I had learned a lot from the experience, not so much in classrooms as about the people in different countries and how they lived. I had greatly improved my skiing and my French and met my future wife, a happening that would bring a lifetime of happiness.

Love of My Life

When I got back home, I was at loose ends about my next move. I vaguely aspired to getting into international business of some kind, but had little knowledge of business and finance. Business was never discussed in the Lamont household. Good books, public issues, politics and so forth, yes, but never business. I had only a remote idea about what my father, the banker, did all day at the office. He and Grandfather Lamont felt that talking about making money at home with the family was simply not done. In truth, I did not press Dad on the subject. Too bad. I might have learned a lot about the world of business.

The obvious solution, recommended by my father, was to attend the Harvard Graduate School of Business, a two-year course leading to an M.B.A., a master's degree in business administration. I had a decent enough résumé, but July was after the prescribed period to apply for admission. Dad, who was a prominent and generous Harvard alumnus, had a word with Dean Donald David of the Business School, and after submitting the application forms and being interviewed, I was accepted into the first-year class starting in September. I roomed with two good college friends, Dick O'Keeffe and Perry Bartsch.

I have never worked so hard in my life as during my first year at Harvard Business School. I had a lot of very smart classmates. Still, my pilot light burned steadily and I hung in there, but not everyone did. One afternoon my friend Bill, a dedicated party animal, showed up in our room wearing his tuxedo. He was about to drive to Providence for a debutante party. A midterm exam in Marketing was coming up and when Bill inquired, "What's all this wholesale and retail stuff about, boys?" we suggested that he skip the dance and hit the books. But he would hear none of it, declaring his attendance a family social obligation that he must keep. He departed from Business School following the midyear examinations, and he was not the only one.

Gradually, I began to get on top of my work load. During spring term I received the equivalent of a mix of B's and C's similar to my college grades. In one sense it was like golf: You can play a number of rounds quite differently and still come up with about the same score each time.

The courses in securities analysis, with Graham and Dodd as our bible, and accounting were the most valuable. Understanding financial statements is of course essential in business. Yet as we know all too well today, if companies like Enron, in collaboration with their auditors, hide their liabilities and create phony profits, the statements become virtually worthless. The Marketing course was kind of obvious; for starters, watch television commercials. Administrative practices amounted to using common sense in human relations. "So you believe that your supervisor treated you unfairly in denying your request for time off" was the suggested response to an angry employee complaining about his boss. All you had to do was let the fellow sound off for a while until he calmed down, the same technique you use with children. Ad Prac required students to submit a paper by 8 p.m. on Saturdays, and Buz was often a godsend in typing my paper to make this deadline. A good secretary is an asset in any office.

Buz and I were "going steady." She worked in Manhattan as a secretary at the Girl Scout headquarters and rented rooms in a fine old brownstone on West 11th Street in Greenwich Village. People go to the Village to have a good time, and our favorite watering spots were Jack Delaney's, a congenial Irish bar, and Nick's, an acclaimed jazz club featuring the great clarinetist PeeWee Russell. Buz often came up to Cambridge on Friday night while I was at Business School, and after my Ad Prac paper was out of the way, sometimes not until late Saturday, the fun began and lasted until I dropped her off at South Station on Sunday afternoon for the train ride back to New York. I loved Buz with all my heart and asked her to marry me over a ravioli dinner at an Italian restaurant in Cambridge one evening. To my great joy she accepted my proposal.

During the summer of 1950 I worked at J.P. Morgan & Co. at 23 Wall Street. I was impressed by the bank staff's meticulous attention to accurate bookkeeping. One afternoon at the close of business, twenty cents of the total cash in the teller's cage was unaccounted for. Morgan bankers could not accept even this small discrepancy. The cash and books had to balance, and two of us stayed on well after hours until we could reconcile the difference. Later on I had the job of teller one Friday, a payday for many firms on the Street. At lunchtime hordes of office workers descended on me to cash their checks. By then I was thoroughly imbued with the importance of an errorless performance. So careful was I in carrying out my duties that I soon had a line of people stretching out the bank's front door onto the sidewalk waiting for the slowest teller on Wall Street. But the books balanced at the end of the day, and I was on time for my date with Buz that evening.

Buz had met my family in New York, and it was now time for me to visit the Buzby family on their home turf in Puerto Rico. Latin Americans are the greatest dancers in the world, and while Buz's heritage was English–French, she had grown up in the Latino culture of Puerto Rico. She was fluent in Spanish and a superb dancer, as scores of dancing partners have declared over the years. I, on the other hand, had not

Buz and brothers Scott and Milton Buzby.

The lovebirds before their wedding in San Juan, 1951.

The newlyweds and their parents at the reception.

Our wedding party enjoyed a week of sun and fun in Puerto Rico.

progressed beyond the foxtrot, jitterbugging, an occasional waltz if I couldn't avoid it, and the conga line. It appeared that the samba was the fashionable new Latin dance at parties, and I decided to master it before visiting Puerto Rico. So one afternoon I took a personal samba lesson at Arthur Murray's dance studio, the only dance lesson I've ever had. Now I was ready for the nightlife of San Juan. However, when we went dancing several times, to my chagrin not a single samba was played – just rumbas, not at all my strong suit. The samba, of course, is a Brazilian dance. I now do a very smooth rumba.

The Buzbys – Jesse and Helene, Buz's parents, and Milton and Scott, her brothers – were a great boating family led by Captain Jesse, who had been sailing his boats around the Caribbean for years. You get to know folks quickly on a sailboat; we cruised out of St. Thomas for several days in the Virgin Islands and hit it off well. We planned the next step over rum punches on the terrace of Bluebeard's Castle overlooking Charlotte Amalie Harbor: Our wedding bells would chime in San Juan after I graduated from Business School in June, 1951. After our honeymoon we would head for Washington, where I had a government job in the works.

I have had a longstanding love affair with The Big Apple and knew I would miss its many attractions. New York is simply the greatest city in the world, the center of global finance and the media, a cultural capital with fabulous museums and free Shakespeare in the park on summer evenings, home of the Yankees, glamorous Lincoln Center, and glittering Broadway. In the spring Central Park is a lake-studded emerald island, surrounded by the city's soaring skyscrapers, the exciting skyline familiar to people everywhere.

New York is the great American laboratory of urban living. Two hundred years ago Gouverneur Morris observed, "To be born in America seems to be a matter of indifference at New York." As a major port of entry for immigrants, it is a human mosaic of different races, cultures, and religions, packed into their neighborhoods shoulder-to-shoulder. New York is the perfect home for the United Nations. For those fanatics who believe that they alone possess the only true belief and way of life, New York, a monumental symbol of what America is all about, was the ideal enemy target to strike down on 9/11.

Bursting with energy in corporate towers and street life and full of bustle and razzmatazz, the city projects a unique dynamism. I can walk for blocks and blocks along its streets and avenues and never get bored, which is more than I can say for country lanes or forest trails. Marathon runners say that the changing urban scene and crowds invigorate them. New Yorkers are fast talkers, fast walkers, fast eaters, and fast spenders. They don a variety of attire, but the ubiquitous cellphone and a bottle of Evian or Poland Spring are common accessories. "New York, New York," the Sinatra version played at Yankee Stadium and other public events, is the perfect theme song capturing the spirit of the city. Some say that the rest of the country has a love-hate relationship with New York. Yet judging from the happy throng of tourists outside the NBC studio in Rockefeller Plaza for The Today Show each morning, and the country's response to the destruction of the World Trade Center, there is a lot of love. An out-of-state volunteer relief worker stated, "I'm here to rebuild a city that was a diamond and got a little bit of tarnish on it. We've got to get it off."

During my student years I had enjoyed living near Boston, the home-town of Democratic political candidates who are regularly scorned by Republican opponents from other parts of the country as "Massachusetts liberals." Two of the greatest universities anywhere, M.I.T. and Harvard, have added immeasurably to that city's culture and stature, and you can't beat the Boston Pops on the Fourth of July or any other evening. The city possesses a comfortable charm, from little sailboats and racing shells skimming by on the Charles River to the elegant town houses on Beacon Hill and the tastefully restored and popular Faneuil Hall Marketplace. The living is good in Boston and its suburbs, where I have many friends who are so happy with their lives that they have never contemplated moving west of Dedham. They ski and sail and wear old frayed collar button-downs instead of sport shirts.

Bostonians are more frugal than New Yorkers. Maybe that's why they have sold some of their high profile assets out of town over the years, such as the *Boston Globe*, which went to the *New York Times*; Macy's purchased Jordan Marsh, Bank of America acquired FleetBoston, Manulife of Canada bought the John Hancock, and several substantial old-line investment firms with dozens of mutual funds were sold out-of-state. While New Yorkers build new stadiums at the drop of a hat the Red Sox still play in Fenway Park, the nation's oldest baseball stadium.

In sports, New York acquired Babe Ruth from Boston, which triggered the Yankees' dynasty of success, a transaction that sportswriters brought up for years at the end of Red Sox seasons after the Babe's departure and the team's last World Series championship in 1918. Buz and I were at Shea Stadium for the World Series game in 1986 when the Red Sox came close to grabbing the brass ring, only to succumb to "The Curse of the Bambino" and New York Mets, relative new boys on the block. Nothing lasts forever, even curses, and in October 2004 the Red Sox Nation went wild over their new world championship team. New Englanders were already in love with their Super Bowl winning Patriots, who came through again in 2005. All of a sudden venerable Beantown – the home of Cabots and Lowells, Kennedys and Kerrys, and pontifical Harvard professors – had become the sports capital of the nation, and old men died with a smile on their face. Boston Brahmins can also demonstrate a bit of chutzpah. Is there any other city where the premier and most exclusive golf club is called "The Country Club" with no further identification?

The phrase "proper Bostonians" is still apt. I fondly recall from recent years the crewcut chairman of the Visiting Committee to the Harvard Library – a proper Bostonian trust officer who was challenged by the developing culture of political correctness. In his rumpled brown suit and bow tie he opened a meeting by thanking all the "girls," referring to members of the library staff and faculty wives, for organizing a fine dinner the previous evening. A young librarian politely pointed out that while the thanks were appreciated, the reference to "girls" was not. The chairman was eager to make amends: "I meant to say 'ladies,' of course, my dear." The feminist movement was still not satisfied: Calling them "women" would be more appropriate.

In 1951 Tony Bennett's record of "Because of You" and Mario Lanza's "Be My Love" were top song hits, and Ethel Merman was belting out "You're Just in Love" in her Broadway show, "Call Me Madam," as we planned the Buzby–Lamont wedding in Puerto Rico for June 23. Not all my Boston friends qualify as "proper Bostonians," and my ushers, ready and eager for tropical isle adventures, came early and stayed up late, enjoying beach parties, Planter's Punches, San Juan nightlife, and one of Captain Jesse's Virgin Island cruises.

I had chosen dark blue flannel jackets and white slacks for the ushers' wedding uniform, not a smart move for Puerto Rico in June, even with the trade winds blowing. No problem. I have never seen the weather spoil a good wedding party. At the reception I sang "You Made Me Love You" and my dad cut loose with a tap dance he had learned for the Harvard Hasty Pudding show thirty years before. Finally the guests pushed the bridal couple out the door for their limousine ride to the Condado Hotel and its honeymoon suite.

The first stop on our Caribbean honeymoon was the Ibo Lélé Hotel, Port au Prince, Haiti, in a lovely tropical hilltop setting. In Haiti women did the heavy lifting, balancing huge bundles on their heads as they walked to market. It was Third World poverty beyond the tourist resorts with a little voodoo on the side, some for the tourists and some for real. Next stop: the Tower Isle Hotel in Ochos Rios, Jamaica, featuring grèat beach life, rum drinks at the poolside bar, and steel bands playing calypso songs like "Jamaican Lullaby." Then on to Havana, Cuba, in those days truly "The Pearl of the Antilles."

Havana was a swinging town in the pre-Castro era, with hotels, nightclubs, bars, and gambling casinos packed with American tourists and the streets filled with American cars. Buz and I returned to Havana in 1999. After decades of communist dictatorship and the U.S. trade embargo the city was run-down and desperately poor. Prostitutes were openly plying their trade, and the beautiful Spanish colonial houses, now cut up into multiple apartments, were dilapidated, unpainted, and festooned with hanging laundry. Only the automobiles looked the same: The embargo had banned automobile imports since 1962 and Havana thus has the greatest collection of working 1950s automobiles in the world, including some splendid fin-tailed Cadillacs. Two positive social developments had emerged under the Castro dictatorship, as we observed on our later trip – basic health care and education. Cuban longevity and literacy were high in comparison with other Latin and Third World countries. Yet how frustrating it was for thousands of educated young men and women to end up in menial jobs, the only employment available. Castro's harsh political repression has continued without letup. It is no wonder that hundreds of thousands of Cubans have fled from an economic wasteland and dictatorship that they feared and despised. However, Cuban–American political clout, driven by hatred of Castro, has bound the U.S. Government to a trade embargo that has not changed Castro's regime and instead has enabled him to blame the U.S. falsely for Cuba's abject poverty.

On our honeymoon, Buz and I drank daiquiris in Hemingway's favorite bar and strolled along the Malecon overlooking Havana Harbor and Morro Castle, the Spanish colonial fort on the far shore and mirror image of the Morro Castle guarding the entrance of Puerto Rico's San Juan harbor. The two former Spanish colonies would undergo great changes in the coming years, especially Cuba. The young Marxist revolutionary Fidel Castro was already secretly plotting to overthrow the government and install a Communist dictatorship.

Our next port of call was Mexico City, where we took in the local sights including the Aztec pyramids, floating gardens of Xochimilco, and Sunday afternoon bullfights at the big city arena. Bullfights are a cruel, exciting, and very colorful feature of Hispanic culture, from the traditional brassy musical salute to the execution of the noble beast. The lead matador at our event did a superb job in smoothly and expeditiously courting and killing his bull without prolonging the agony. His cape and sword work was brave and graceful, and the huge crowd responded with thunderous cries of "Olé!" The judges awarded him the tail and both ears of the bull for his performance.

There were lots of American visitors in the crowd that day including U.S. Ambassador William O'Dwyer, the former mayor of New York, and his pretty young wife, ex-model Sloan Simpson, who were seated in a ringside box. The matador, slender and handsome in his tight fitting "suit of lights," started his triumphal tour around the ring, proudly holding on high his well-earned trophies. When he reached the Ambassador's box, he stopped and graciously presented the bloody appendages to the Ambassador's wife. Some American women would have fainted dead away or at least retreated at this turn of events. Not Sloan Simpson, who, clearly knowledgeable about the protocol of bullfights, cordially accepted the matador's compliment. The matador and the pretty model chatted briefly, and the crowd roared its approval of the Ambassador's wife. She was *muy simpática,* and some even said that America had scored a diplomatic triumph thanks to Sloan Simpson.

On we went to Acapulco, the deluxe Pacific resort featuring young divers plunging from towering cliffs into the foaming ocean surf, and charming Taxco, noted for its exquisite colonial church and skilled silver craftsmen. We bought a silver tea set even though we never gave tea parties. The bus ride back to Mexico City seemed endless to one who was afflicted with the Mexican tourist disease. It has sometimes been known as "The Aztec Two Step," and President Jimmy Carter once lightheartedly told the president of Mexico that he had suffered from "Montezuma's Revenge" on a previous trip to his country. El Presidente was not amused.

I know of one Mexican president who did have a grand sense of humor. In 1921, Wall Street banker Thomas W. Lamont had visited Mexico City to negotiate a settlement with the Mexican government regarding the country's foreign held bonds, which had been in default since 1913. He first arranged an appointment with President Alvaro Obregon, the black-mustachioed caudillo who was Mexico's current strongman – a revolutionary survivor, one tough hombre, and quite a joker. When Lamont was ushered into his private office, the president summoned an attendant. "Bring whiskey, wine, and liqueurs! At last, Mr. Lamont, you are in a free country," he declared with a beaming reference to Prohibition in the United States.

Cuernavaca, the lovely old colonial town beyond the smog of Mexico City, has long attracted the nation's elite, including icons from both ends of the political spectrum. Buz and I gazed at the intriguing murals of Diego Rivera on the walls of Cortez's Palace, portraying his strongly leftist viewpoint of Mexican history. Rivera had also painted a bad portrait of his left-leaning fellow traveler Corliss Lamont and given it to him as a gift.

It's a small world. In his youth my uncle Corliss had been enamored of Anne Morrow, his Englewood, New Jersey, and North Haven neighbor, but Anne fell in love with someone else. It was in Mexico City and Cuernavaca that Charles Lindbergh, who had just completed a goodwill flight to Mexico in 1927, met and charmed his future wife Anne, the daughter of Dwight Morrow, the former Morgan partner and U.S. Ambassador to Mexico at the time. Morrow had a handsome weekend retreat in Cuernavaca. In 1951 the Lamont honeymooners agreed that Cuernavaca, with its abundant gardens filled with blooming geraniums and bougainvillea, was a delightful setting for romance.

Buz and I next flew to Merida in the Yucatan to visit Chichén-Itzá and other ancient Mayan ruins, great stone pyramid temples with carved inscriptions and reliefs. The Mayan culture, we learned, could be pretty savage. We saw the stone ball court where the losing team sometimes paid with their lives, and the deep pool into which, it was said, young virgins were thrown as a sacrifice to their gods. The Spanish conquerors in the sixteenth century were even more bloodthirsty. The conquistadors did more than just slaughter and enslave the Indians. Spanish priests burned most of their literary works, written in hieroglyphs on paper made from the bark of wild fig trees. The priests were determined to convert the Indians to Christianity, and destroying the records of their pagan religion and culture served this end. Mao Zedong and Adolph Hitler were merely latecomers to the tyrants' practice of book-burning to subjugate their peoples.

Washington to Paris Shuttle

Earlier in 1951 I had taken a U.S. Government Civil Service examination and done well. My goal was to work in the Economic Cooperation Administration, which ran the Marshall Plan, providing economic aid to the war ravaged countries of Western Europe. After several interviews I was appointed to the position of junior management assistant in the Northern Europe and Sterling Area Division in the Washington office. My annual salary was $3,450 with an expected raise to $4,250 and promotion to international trade and development economist after a six-month probationary period. I thought I was underpaid, but those were the times. Even Ted Williams, with the highest salary in baseball, was paid only $125,000 a year and historically I was in pretty good company: America's first Secretary of the Treasury, Alexander Hamilton, was paid an annual salary of $3,500.

In my FBI security check the agents were especially interested in my wife's background growing up in Puerto Rico, because in 1950 two Puerto Rican nationalists had attempted to assassinate President Truman at Blair House, where he was staying while the White House was being renovated. I reported for duty on September 4, and was soon getting great on-the-job training in economics – balance of payments, national accounts, trade analyses, and the like. The vacations were short, the hours were long, and the honeymoon, in the fullest sense of the word, was over.

Later, ECA became the Mutual Security Administration, a new title linking it to the growing importance of the North Atlantic Treaty Organization. Secretary of State Dean Acheson had taken the lead in building up NATO to meet the threat of Russian aggression in Europe. Two senior economists directed my research leading to constructing pro forma gross national product and balance of payments models for the United Kingdom for 1952. Our purpose was to determine the amount of dollars the U.K. would need to purchase the essential imports – foodstuffs, fuel, machinery, and equipment – that it required to help the economy recover. Secondly, the U.K. must become strong enough to make a fair contribution to the NATO defense buildup. I was fortunate in having a good and patient teacher working in our division – Murray Havens, a former economics professor at the University of Alabama. My other supervisor was a competent woman who lost her cool regularly under the pressure of late hours and short deadlines. Based on our balance of payments forecast we recommended a grant to the U.K. of $350 million for 1952 (about $2.5 billion in current dollars), an amount that survived all the higher-level administration reviews and was later appropriated by Congress for aid to the U.K. that year.

Our division even had an economist assigned to little Iceland with whom I worked from time to time. Dick Birnbaum from New York was no Viking. He looked like Woody Allen and was just as funny. What oil is to Saudi Arabia, fish is to Iceland, and we compiled fishing revenues and attended inter-agency meetings to discuss Iceland's ongoing disputes over territorial fishing rights with its seagoing neighbors. Dick and I estimated that there were more economists covering Iceland in the U.S. government than in the entire Icelandic government.

One evening my division chief, a pipe-smoking academic, invited us to dinner. I was low on the bureaucratic learning curve and contributed little to the fast-paced "inside the Beltway" conversation among the guests about politics and national voting trends. My comment that in the 1948 presidential election many voters had been turned off by the stiff and formal style of Thomas E. Dewey, reminding some of the little top-hatted figure on wedding cakes, drew only condescending smiles.

Buz wanted to go back to work and took a job on the Hill in the office of Senator Estes Kefauver, who was starting his campaign to seek the Democratic nomination for president. In 1950 I had joined millions of Americans watching the televised hearings of the Senate Crime Investigating Committee headed by Senator Kefauver, in which Mafia boss Frank Costello, a very nervous witness, had permitted only his hands to be shown on camera. A year later I attended a high-spirited office party at which the tall Tennessean handed out coonskin caps, his campaign trademark, to all the staff members, who then broke into song. "We'll all be on the payroll when he wins" (to the tune of "She'll Be Coming 'Round the Mountain When She Comes"). But the Democratic convention rebuffed Kefauver's bid and chose Illinois Governor Adlai Stevenson to be their candidate for president.

Buz and I stayed with some Washington friends until we found a suitable apartment, a fourth floor 1 BR walkup at 2239 Q Street for $125 a month. We had our own built-in Stairmaster and a nice view of the Turkish Embassy and Buffalo Bridge in Georgetown. On weekends and holidays we explored Washington and its environs. Country club life was still in the future, and we played tennis on the Wisconsin Avenue public courts. One Saturday we went over to Byrd Stadium in College Park, Maryland, to watch a football game between Maryland and Missouri. Why the players were several sizes larger and considerably more skilled than their Ivy League counterparts was explained by the sales pitch of the teenager selling programs: "Names, numbers, and salaries of all the players!"

Washington summers are hot and humid, and at our stage in life none of us had swimming pools. Sometimes we picnicked in the nearby

Virginia woods and splashed about in the rocky bed of a brook called Difficult Run, which ran down into the Potomac upstream from Washington; it was hardly swimming. A great swimming hole, but a long way away, was a large abandoned quarry in Virginia's Shenendoah Valley, where we dived from rocks and floated about in inner tubes. However, I had my eye on the elegant pool in the gardens of Dumbarton Oaks, the lovely Georgetown estate given to Harvard that housed a rare collection of Byzantine art and long-haired scholars. I asked my father to see if he could persuade Harvard to permit its alumni in Washington to swim there, and eventually our family was given access to the pool after pledging to keep our privilege top secret. I'm sorry that the other fellows didn't make the cut.

I saw President Harry S. Truman only one time, and not on official business. Coast Guardsman Scott Buzby, Buz's brother, was in Washington on the U.S.C.G.C. *Courier*, a vessel newly equipped with an extremely powerful transmitter to relay Voice of America programs behind the Iron Curtain from its port near Greece. Buz and I attended a dedication ceremony on the *Courier* before her departure for the Mediterranean, along with other families of the crew, President Truman, Secretary of State Dean Acheson, and assorted officials and top brass. On the cold and drizzly day we took our seats, about thirty feet away from the President's, on the top deck. He appeared in fine fettle as he walked jauntily up the gangway, wearing a broad-brimmed fedora, while the Coast Guard band played "Hail to the Chief." The President made appropriate remarks, as did Secretary Acheson. The contrast in their styles of delivery – flat Midwestern twang versus urbane Grotonian articulation – was marked. Yet these men of quite dissimilar personalities and backgrounds worked well together, and with great mutual respect in developing the Truman–Acheson foreign policy initiatives – from the Marshall Plan to the Berlin airlift to the formation of NATO.

In fact, NATO was about to play an important part in our lives. In September my boss informed me that the Mutual Security Administration had to assign an international trade and development economist to Paris for several months to assist the NATO Secretariat in its Annual Review of the defense efforts of its member countries. I agreed to go.

Because my NATO assignment would last only until completion of the Review in mid-December, Buz and I chose hotel living. The street outside our hotel turned out to be a popular rendezvous point for ladies of the evening and young Frenchmen seeking female companionship. On many evenings a bittersweet little drama unfolded. Around eight o'clock one or two cars filled with exuberant guys armed with bottles of wine and champagne drove by and scooped up a half dozen or so pretty girls. However, one plain-featured girl was repeatedly turned away. It was sad to watch her smile bravely to her girl friends, pretending she didn't care, and then dejectedly slump off into the night as the cars with their merry-making occupants sped off to the party. I hoped that this real life Ugly Duckling story would have a happy ending.

After the Review NATO requested that I stay on until mid-March 1953, to help prepare the program for the next ministerial meeting. A French–American couple whom we knew, the Girauds, lent us their small apartment near Port St. Cloud while they were traveling. When they returned we rented a couple of rooms in the private home of a French lady near Napoleon's Tomb.

Shopping and cooking in Paris were a new experience for Buz. Supermarkets had not yet come to France, and she queued up in lines at half a dozen stores – the *épicerie,* the *fromagerie,* the *boucherie,* and so forth – to supply our cuisine. You brought your own bag or newspaper to carry your purchases home. Like many Parisians the Girauds had no ice-box or refrigerator, so Buz placed everything on the windowsill to keep it cool. With no refrigeration, shopping for food was a daily chore, or diversion, depending upon your outlook.

The Buzbys and son Scott joined us in Paris at different times. In 1917 Buz's father Jesse had been driving a U.S. Army ambulance not far from Paris on an exposed road, when a German artillery shell smashed the vehicle and he was wounded in the neck by shrapnel. We drove outside Paris to the area where he identified the road and spot where his ambulance had been hit, and the house in the nearby village where his wounds were dressed before he was taken to an army hospital. Scott Buzby, three wars later, the third one "Cold," was on leave from his U.S. Coast Guard cutter stationed at the Isle of Rhodes.

My office was in the NATO headquarters at the Palais de Chaillot, overlooking the Seine and the Eiffel Tower. For the first two months until the end of the Review we usually put in ten- to twelve-hour days six and sometimes seven days a week. Long lunch hours were a European custom, and the NATO cafeteria served wine in little carafes. Thus meetings often did not get going in the afternoons until after three o'clock.

I worked with a congenial group, all young economists, including a walrus-mustached Englishman, an earnest blonde Norwegian, and a humorous Portuguese duke. On December 10 we celebrated my birthday at a merry office party with these good colleagues and their ladies at a Left Bank restaurant. They were believers in the NATO mission, not time-serving civil servants, and staff morale was high. Within the Economic and Financial Division my primary assignment was to examine the economy and defense contribution of Norway to NATO's program. How well had Norway met the military targets set one year earlier?

One of my duties was to assemble all the relevant papers about Norway and see that they were distributed on time to all interested parties. Much of the material that we studied dealt with military matters and was classified as top secret. The NATO label for this highest security classification was "Cosmic." One day I went to the special room where these papers were kept under guard, to pick up a document. The officer on duty first inquired about the status of my security clearance: "Have you been cosmicized, sir?" I assumed that he was not referring to some psychiatric therapy and answered affirmatively.

The defining exercise of the Review was to question each national delegation about any shortfalls in meeting the military goals that had been set, and how they intended to improve their performance. These meetings took place in formal fashion in a large conference hall. The delegations were headed by defense ministers or top diplomats who sat at a large circular table, with their staffs sitting behind them whispering in their ear or handing up papers. The key Secretariat officials and assorted generals and admirals were also seated at the table, and there were simultaneous translation headsets at each place. These meetings clearly had an important purpose, but, as I wrote my father. "There's an awful lot of hot air expended on fairly trivial things – phraseology, order, protocol and the like."

At the meeting to examine Norway's defense effort the Norwegian delegation was headed by a very senior and distinguished ambassador. The meeting chairman from the NATO Secretariat, M. Sergent, was an equally prominent French diplomat. I sat behind Walter Salant, an American who was NATO's chief economist on Norway. Americans by now dominated international relations, and English was the working language of the Secretariat. Most of the international staff, which included a number of very able Brits, were more fluent in English than French, and Lord Ismay, the Secretary-General, was English. This use of English dismayed the French, who were desperately trying to maintain French as the language of diplomacy in a futile effort to portray France as the world power that she had not been since Napoleon.

Chairman Sergent announced that the meeting would, of course, be conducted in French, and the Norwegian delegation and others began fiddling with their headsets in order to receive the English translation. The Norwegian ambassador appeared to have some difficulty in fitting the headpiece comfortably over his bald head and adjusting the little dials to get good reception. Finally he took it off, slapped it on the table, and stated, "Mr. Chairman, we all know that you speak excellent English. Would you please consider conducting the meeting in English as a personal favor to me?" There was a long pause before M. Sergent shrugged his shoulders and replied, "Just for you, Ambassador Skaug, we will conduct the examination in English."

The final meetings of the Annual Review were attended by the highest-ranking ministers from the member countries. I was tremendously impressed with the performance and style of Secretary of State Dean Acheson, who led the American delegation. With his British military mustache and his pinstriped sartorial elegance he was the quintessential diplomat as he smoothly articulated the American position. At the final press briefing a reporter observed that the NATO countries had failed to achieve the prescribed military targets for the past year by a significant margin. Wasn't this shortfall in the common defense effort a very serious blow for NATO?

Acheson coolly replied, "Oh, no. I wouldn't characterize this result as a shortfall or failure in any way. There has simply been a moderate slowing down in the defense buildup due to unforeseen economic factors, and we fully expect recovery to occur in the coming year."

In a letter home I said, "I certainly take my hat off to Secretary Acheson after seeing him conduct himself at these meetings. His contributions were almost always pertinent and good ones. He is extremely admired and respected by all the foreigners I have talked to, and got a fine hand from everybody when he bid them farewell. [With the election of Eisenhower, a new administration would soon be in place.] Of course, his contribution to NATO in particular, from its very inception, has been enormous. It was his 'baby'."

Buz and I spent Christmas in Nice with her parents Jesse and Helene, who were driving about Europe. An out-of-season resort in the dead of winter is a lugubrious sight; the only other people in the luxurious Plaza Hotel dining room were two ancient bejeweled dowagers who had been wintering on the Riviera for decades.

Back in Paris during the early months of 1953, with the Annual Review behind us the work pace slackened at the Palais de Chaillot. Our main task now was planning the defense goals of the NATO countries in preparation for the ministerial meeting in April. The winter weather was abominable; we rarely saw the sun between November and March, just day after day of leaden gray skies, cold drizzling rain, or damp fog. In the office, in the streets, in restaurants and cafés people appeared pale and drawn, suffering from colds or worse, and I succumbed to bronchitis for a week. No wonder the arrival of spring and sunshine was welcomed so joyously. Lovers embraced on park benches, and children played in the Tuileries and the Jardin du Luxembourg. Couples sipped wine at sidewalk cafés or strolled along the banks of the Seine or up the Champs Elysées. Composers write romantic songs about April in Paris, and they're right.

One Saturday we watched the steeplechase races at Auteuil in the Bois de Boulogne, a colorful event popular with Parisian society. Some weekends we rented a small Renault and toured the surrounding countryside. We visited Fontainebleau and Versailles, and picnicked with friends from NATO at Port Royal near the old abbey ruins. We also sampled some Parisian theatre and nightlife – "Don Juan" at the Comédie Française, and the Lido nightclub with its spectacular and erotic floor show, so popular that it was later exported to Las Vegas. Most of the magnificent topless showgirls at the Lido and the Folies were English, high-quality British exports along with Rolls Royce cars and Scotch whisky.

One day, quite unexpectedly, I ran into a pompous old phony when I checked in at Morgan & Cie. on Place Vendôme to say hello to the partners who were colleagues of my father, a senior officer at the parent bank in New York. One of the gentlemen invited us to a black-tie dinner at his home, and I replied that while we'd like to come, unfortunately, we had not brought evening clothes with us for our short stay in Paris. "Oh, well," he replied. "Sorry you can't make it. Be sure to tell your father that we tried to get hold of you."

Earlier I had touched base with the World Bank, expressing my interest in working there. Apparently they were favorably impressed with my recent work experience, and I received an encouraging reply about a possible position in the Department of Europe, Africa, and Australasia. I would end my MSA/NATO job on March 15, take some accrued vacation time in Spain, and report to the Bank in Washington in May.

We spent the last week of March in Mallorca, where the warm sunshine was a welcome change from the dreary Paris winter. Bullfights can be good or ugly. At the one we attended in Palma the picadores gouged the bull unmercifully with their lances, and the matador, too timid to go over the top, kept stabbing away until the poor beast, covered with blood and gore, at last succumbed. On to Madrid where the highlight of our visit was the magnificent paintings of El Greco and Goya at the Prado. Flamenco dancing and the late dinner hour at restaurants did not appeal.

Returning to Washington I nailed down my new job at the World Bank and bought our first house – a traditional 3 BR home with a small back yard on Reservoir Road, not far from Foxhall Road and Georgetown. It is said that a man's home is his castle, and after bouncing around in small apartments, hotels, and rented rooms for so long it was a joyful new experience to be the lord and lady in residence.

I liked Ike, along with most Americans, and had voted for him in November 1952. Upon our return to Washington in 1953 President Dwight D. Eisenhower's new administration was firmly in place and ex-President Truman had gone home to Independence. Truman was a very partisan politician, no rarity in Washington, who had scorned Eisenhower since the general's election campaign in which Ike had aggressively attacked the record of the Truman administration. Furthermore, Eisenhower had not stood up to defend President Truman's Secretary of State George C. Marshall, the Army Chief of Staff and Ike's strong backer during the war, against the false and reckless charges of Senator Joseph McCarthy, who impugned Marshall's patriotism in his conduct of foreign policy.

Years later I would read *Plain Speaking – An Oral Biography of Harry S. Truman* by Merle Miller. Miller reported that Truman had told him the following story. One day in 1945 when Eisenhower was Supreme Commander of the Allied Forces in Europe, General Marshall came to the White House to brief his Commander-in-Chief. The U.S. Army Chief of Staff reported to the President that Eisenhower had sent him a private cable stating his intention to divorce Mamie to marry Kay Summersby, his attractive British driver and aide, to whom he had become very attached. General Marshall was furious at this revelation by Eisenhower and fired back a cable to him immediately stating that Ike's promising career prospects in the Army would be finished if he persisted in this disgraceful course of conduct. Miller, the author, emphasized that he was simply reporting what President Truman had told him. There was no corroboration of this exchange in the U.S. Army cable files or anywhere else.

I related this account to my friend Joe Downer, who, after serving as an artillery officer in the Italian campaign, had been assigned to a communications unit on General Marshall's staff in the Pentagon. Joe replied, "I remember the incident well. I was in the cable office and saw the outgoing cable to Eisenhower in which Marshall pointed out that Ike was in line to become the next Army Chief of Staff and very firmly urged him not to jeopardize his career by taking this step regarding his marriage." Thus President Truman's recollection was confirmed.

This nugget of historical gossip in no way diminishes my admiration for Eisenhower as a great military leader in wartime and an effective and immensely popular president in peacetime. I firmly believe that we should judge our leaders on their merits and not focus in on their private peccadillos, like extramarital liaisons, in the past. Many people of great accomplishment operate on two quite separate tracks, and a number of distinguished leaders have pursued less than exemplary conduct in their private lives. There are skeletons in lots of family closets, and since half the marriages in America end in divorce, one can assume that oftentimes someone was fooling around. However, we do expect our leaders to clean up their act when they achieve high office. Rudy Giuliani, for example, tarnished the end of his successful mayoralty in New York by his public affair with his future wife during the loud and messy divorce proceedings with his wife at the time. Yet all was soon forgiven when he demonstrated outstanding leadership in guiding a city in shock after the terrorist attack on the World Trade Center.

President Clinton's personal conduct involving a young female intern was disgraceful, marring an otherwise successful and very popular presidency of two terms. However, the House of Representatives should not have trivialized the U.S. Constitution by wrongfully interpreting its provisions for partisan gain in impeaching President Clinton – an action that threatened to upset the carefully designed system of checks and balances between the branches of government that have served our country so well. Clinton's conduct should have been severely censured by Congress, but it did not come close to the standard for impeachable offenses required by the Constitution.

It is interesting to ponder what would have happened if President Thomas Jefferson had been impeached and driven from office for lying when he publicly denied having had sexual relations with his slave mistress Sally Heming. There might have been no Louisiana Purchase, almost doubling the area of the United States, or Lewis and Clark expedition, exploring and charting the Northwest. The honorable reputation of a true founding father of this nation and author of the Declaration of Independence would have been badly stained. Of course, in those days there were no so-called "independent counsels" to investigate and expose sexual indiscretions in the private lives of presidents, like some sleazy tabloid reporter. I sincerely hope that we have seen the last of these prosecutors who pursue political objectives at the expense of fairness and the national interest in preserving people's confidence, at home and abroad, in the stability of the American government.

The World Bank

After a breaking-in period during the summer of 1953 at the World Bank, my department head informed me that the Bank wanted me to return to Paris in September to serve as an assistant to the Englishman who ran the bank's small representative office at 67 Rue de Lille. I did not welcome the proposed assignment. We had just bought a new house, Buz was expecting, and going back to live in Paris for a few years did not appeal at that time in our lives. The Paris office was basically an information-gathering outpost and base for traveling missions from Washington, out of the mainstream of the bank's business with no direct role in the lending operations. Nevertheless one rejects one's first assignment at a new job with some trepidation.

I told my boss, another Englishman named Stanley Cope, that I would go to Paris, but expected return by mid-December for the birth of our first baby. Cope, formerly of the Royal Navy, replied that while it was essential for me to participate in the laying of the keel, it was not necessary for me to be there for the launching of the vessel. However, as a Navy veteran myself, albeit of modest experience, I stuck to my guns.

Upon my arrival in Paris, a taxi driver reminded me of how proud the French were of their language and how intolerant they were of others who did not speak it perfectly. To my request, "Je voudrais aller aux Champs Elysées" he repeatedly and rather sharply replied "Je ne comprends pas." My French accent would never be confused with that of a native Parisian, but it isn't all that bad; I did not pronounce "Champs" as in "champion." Americans, on the other hand, and especially passengers in New York City taxi cabs, are quite accustomed to hearing mangled English spoken by the foreign born. If all the city cab drivers were gathered together in an auditorium, the scene would bear a distinct resemblance to a meeting of the General Assembly of the United Nations. We were all immigrants once so it doesn't bother us that a Haitian or Bangladesh cab driver can barely speak our language. Indeed we often find a foreign accent quite charming. Just look at the popularity of French actors Charles Boyer and Maurice Chevalier. And Arnold Schwarzenegger is in a league by himself.

The fall of 1953 was not a particularly happy period in my life, with Buz back home expecting our first child. It was depressing to eat dinner alone in the hotel restaurant. I did a lot of walking along the banks of the Seine and around the city during weekends and got together with some pals from my previous tour in Paris and a French colleague at the office,

Yann LeRoux. Yann's evening boat parties on the Seine were merry affairs; we were usually a multinational group, and the cuisine and wines were good and plentiful. Yann, the office manager, was a jovial bon vivant and an excellent Paris tour guide. Visiting staff members from Washington were delighted to have him escort them around town to the best restaurants, Left Bank *caves*, and glamorous nightclubs. Looking after our guests from headquarters was a pleasant duty. I gave one vice president a guided tour of the Louvre, making sure that he saw three star attractions – the Winged Victory of Samothrace, Venus de Milo, and the Mona Lisa.

The office work, as I expected, was unexciting. My boss and I attended a number of OEEC (Organization for European Economic Cooperation) meetings, and I took notes and wrote reports that were soon buried in the files. A number of Europeans seeking employment at the World Bank descended on the Paris office, and with only four months on the job myself I assumed the role of a personnel officer in screening and interviewing applicants. The office was the European center for disseminating information about the Bank, and I answered a flood of inquiries.

The office was small, so there was no opportunity to learn from and enjoy the company of other colleagues. My boss was a decent fellow but a rather dry and stuffy academic. He wanted me to return with my family after some home leave, to become his assistant, but I respectfully declined. I had had enough of Paris for the time being and was overjoyed to arrive home in time for Christmas with Buz and my family.

On January 3, 1954, Edward Miner Lamont, Jr. was born, a fine looking baby with healthy vocal chords. Over the Christmas holidays that year we took our son to Rochester to visit his great grandparents, and we have a wonderful picture of Edward G. Miner, age 91, and his great grandson, E.M.L., Jr. age 11 months. We chose "Ned" as our son's nickname, the same as that of his great grandfather. Ned was christened at Rochester's St. Paul's church, and the next time I went to St. Paul's was for Grandfather's funeral the following year. A large crowd paid their last respects to a much loved and honored citizen of that city.

While my first two years at the World Bank were unexciting, I learned how to structure project loans to underdeveloped or Third World (the more politically correct contemporary term) countries. The loans were all to governments or government-guaranteed. Following a feasibility study of the project to be financed – perhaps building a hydroelectric dam or developing a seaport – and its expected economic benefits, we prepared an economic forecast for the country including its ability to earn hard currencies to repay the loan. The World Bank loans were virtually all in dollars in the 1950s. I worked largely on the Bank loans to Turkey and Italy. Under the terms of the loan to the Industrial Development Bank of Turkey we screened individual loan applications, such as a cement plant

Introducing Ned to his great grandparents, Edward G. Miner and Helen R. Miner, in Rochester, 1954. Grandfather Miner was also called "Ned."

With Ned in our first house –
4604 Reservoir Road, Washington, D.C.

Laden with golf trophies our resident pro gives her son a lesson.

Kim and Helen join the scene at Sky Farm, 1964. (They now prefer Camille and Helena.)

or a textile mill, before approving drawdowns from the Bank loan. The Bank loan to Italy was to the regional authority promoting economic development in the depressed area of Southern Italy.

I was too lowly in rank to work directly with Eugene Black, the American president of the Bank and a former Wall Street banker. Black was courtly mannered and distinguished in his well-tailored double-breasted dark suit and black homburg as he traveled across the country promoting the sale of World Bank bonds. The staff enjoyed the story of his introduction to Marilyn Monroe at a reception in Hollywood. The famously shapely Miss Monroe inquired breathlessly if she could obtain a loan from the World Bank. Mr. Black, so the story goes, replied that he was sorry. The Bank charter clearly stipulated that the Bank could make loans only for the development of underdeveloped areas, and clearly Miss Monroe did not qualify.

My sophisticated European colleagues were very knowledgeable about the wonderful world of wines, both connoisseurs and masters of the jargon that is such an important part of the game. I have never claimed to have a sensitive palate, one good enough to tell the difference between good and great wines. Indeed, I believe that a number of my friends who drop phrases like "crisp and clean," "good acidic backbone," and "long spicy finish" would fail the blindfold test, for sure if they had a couple of drinks beforehand.

One summer evening a friend from the Bank, Jack Evans, gave a party in the patio of his Georgetown house, and a number of my colleagues from the European winemaking countries attended. Following a spirited cocktail hour we sat down to dinner, whereupon a robust red wine was served from crystal carafes to accompany the beef bourguignon. Frenchmen, Belgians, Italians, and the rest of us complimented our host on his excellent selection and speculated as to the wine's identity. The names of famous château vineyards were dropped with assurance. Jack had aimed and now he pulled the trigger, announcing that he was serving a Maryland red wine. The expressions on the faces of his European friends ranged from shock to disbelief, and even embarrassment.

When my Belgian friend Jean Blondeel gave a dinner to welcome his uncle from Belgium, only champagne cocktails were served beforehand. There would be no dulling of the taste buds to spoil our appreciation of the great wines to be served at dinner. Uncle, who had a vineyard at his château in Belgium, was also a bit of a curmudgeon and, when dinner was served, loudly disparaged the quality of the wine offered by his nephew. We all pretended not to notice the embarrassing exchange. Bourbon and sour mash whiskeys are revered around the world as the finest liquors of American origin, but at that time in Europe imported American whiskey was extremely rare and expensive. I had observed during cocktails that when the rest of us were sipping champagne, Uncle was consuming Jack

Daniel's with gusto, downing several strong drinks the color of iodine. By dinnertime he would have had great difficulty discerning the difference between Manischevitz and Château Mouton Rothschild.

My own winemaking experience would come years later when I planted sixty Chardonnay and Riesling vines in a small enclosed meadow near our house in Laurel Hollow, Long Island. My vineyard never produced any decent wine. The stifling summer heat and humidity, unrelieved by any breeze, produced a grape-withering fungus each year – powdery mildew, downy mildew, and finally the *coup de grâce*, the black rot. Fungicides and advice from experts were no help. Despite these setbacks, miraculously one September we were able to pick a modest harvest of grapes, thanks to the rare occurrence of benign weather that growing season. Buz and I had already purchased all the necessary equipment, including two small oaken casks, to produce a fine wine whose brand name, with some presumption, we had also selected – Laurel Crest.

We were ready to go. We got out the winemaking manual and faithfully followed the instructions for crushing, pressing, racking, and storing our precious brew. Finally, the eagerly anticipated moment arrived for sampling the first glass of Laurel Crest. We raised our glasses in a mutually congratulatory toast and sipped a drink as clear as crystal and as golden as sheaves of grain.

It did resemble a fine wine, but, as they say, looks can be deceiving. We had no idea what had gone amiss in the winemaking process, but we had produced a pale dry sherry, which I thought, with complete objectivity, was first-class. Unfortunately, I never had the opportunity to capitalize on my sherry making skills, because our vineyard gave up the ghost and never again produced a decent crop of grapes. However, I keep a bottle of Laurel Crest at my bar for venturesome imbibers.

Some of our friends in Washington were in the State Department or the Foreign Service. Some said that they were but were actually Central Intelligence Agency operatives. Two of these fellows were congenial Harvard party-goers that I had known before; obviously, distinguished academic performance was not a prime requirement for C.I.A. employment. Their C.I.A. identity was supposed to be hush-hush, but our friends at State knew that they were not working there, and the word spread. Saying that they worked at the Department of Agriculture or the Veteran's Administration would have been a better cover, because nobody knew anybody in those departments, although friends might have wondered what on earth they were doing in such unlikely and unglamorous jobs.

My cousin, Bill Macomber, who had a distinguished diplomatic career including ambassadorships to Turkey and Jordan, started off in the C.I.A. He chose the Fish and Wildlife Service as a cover. We also had Cliff Dweller friends, the Chevy Chase Club crowd, and the combination with our pals in government service made for party conversations ranging from golf scores to Cold War strategies to who could remember the most quotable lines from "Casablanca."

Having seen a lot of Europe, but not much of the U.S., Buz and I decided to drive across the country to San Francisco for our summer vacation in 1955 – one of those once-in-a-lifetime projects. We made it to Denver in three days, and the towering Rockies were a welcome sight after the monotony of endless plains and fields of corn and grain. We visited our friends Tom and Ginny Russell on their cattle ranch in Yampa; then the four of us headed north. Jackson Hole, Yellowstone Park, Glacier National Park, Lake Louise, Mt. Hood, and Crater Lake informed our itinerary with the most beautiful mountain and lake scenery in North America. Nikita Khruschev and Charles de Gaulle, neither one a big fan of the U.S.A., had visited San Francisco and praised its beauty. Tony Bennett loved it, and so did we. One drive across the country was enough. We sold our second-hand Oldsmobile and flew home.

Back in Washington even minimal skiing in the winter was better than none at all, so we headed to the very modest hill at the Homestead in Hot Springs, Virginia, with Charlie and Dale Cabot one New Year's weekend. The champagne flowed freely at the New Year's Eve party, and I had carefully planned to restore my vigor at the famous spa the next morning, indulging in sauna, steam, Jacuzzi jet pool – the whole works. On New Year's Day I went around to the spa and was absolutely crushed to read the sign on the door: "Closed for the Holiday." Of all the days to close a spa, New Year's Day was the worst. A friend had once taken me to the New York Athletic Club on New Year's Day to partake of the pool and steam rooms; the place was mobbed with New Year's Eve party-goers seeking therapeutic aid.

We broke Ned into skiing in Davis, West Virginia, laughingly referred to as "Davos," and skied with my father in Vermont – a great opportunity for father-son bonding.

Dad had long been active in Harvard and Exeter alumni affairs and I followed in his footsteps, albeit at a more modest level. I helped organize and sold tickets for the annual Exeter alumni dinner in Washington. I arranged a boat outing to watch the Harvard crews racing on the Potomac, and interviewed Harvard admissions applicants from local high schools.

I was appointed regional vice president of the Associated Harvard Clubs and appealed for contributions to the Harvard capital campaign. I solicited my classmate Bobby Kennedy, who, as the new Attorney General of the U.S., had advanced in his career as far and as quickly as nepotism can take a person except for George W. Bush and the royal family in Britain. Indeed, many fancied Bobby in the role of the crown prince in America's royal family. Bobby and I had no more than a nodding acquaintance from college days, and I nodded first. Noblesse did not oblige in response to my appeal to support our Alma Mater.

Visiting
Historyland

As an American history buff I am chagrined to read stories reporting how appallingly little many American school boys and girls, and indeed their parents, know about their country's history. The subject should be a required course in all schools; our nation's history and especially its eventful times are the rich endowment that shapes our ongoing progress.

Living in Washington, Buz and I visited the nearby places in Virginia where so many important developments in the birth of our nation occurred. Virginia was the most populous colony and state at the time; four of our first five presidents were Virginians, and Virginians provided much of the intellectual ferment leading to the successful struggle for independence and the formation of our constitutional government. After visiting the reconstructed fort at Jamestown, site of the first surviving English colony, we toured the battlefield at Yorktown, where the Continental Army under General George Washington had won the decisive American victory in the Revolutionary War.

Mother was on the governing board of Mount Vernon representing the state of New York and attended regular board meetings at the magnificently restored and preserved home of our nation's first president. (How many have a son who jumped up and down on George Washington's bed, until his mother and grandmother with dismay discovered his transgression?) Mother's successor as a governor was our friend Priscilla Williams, who encouraged our support and attendance at some grand soirées given by the ladies of Mt.Vernon, emulating the warm hospitality shown by Washington to his houseguests and friends. Dinner parties at Mt. Vernon and at Federal Hall on Wall Street, where Washington delivered his first inaugural address, and an evening cruise around New York Harbor on Malcolm Forbes's yacht *Highlander* were classy affairs. "The father of our country" would approve of the ladies' stewardship of his beloved home.

At Stratford Hall, another plantation on the Potomac that Buz and I visited, young Robert E. Lee had grown up in the mansion of his father Colonel Henry "Light Horse Harry" Lee, a Revolutionary War cavalry officer who served under his friend George Washington. When Lee later became a Congressman, he authored the well-known Congressional tribute to Washington when he died: "First in war, first in peace, first in the hearts of his countrymen."

Washington's courage, integrity, and inspirational leadership in persevering against overwhelming odds won the battle for America's independence, and later in serving as our nation's first president he set sound precedents and a style for the presidency that have served the country well. Benjamin Franklin once said, "Wise and good men are the strength of the state, much more so than riches and arms." Thomas Jefferson declared, "The whole art of government consists in the art of being honest." As we look around the world and observe the incompetent and corrupt leaders of so many newly independent countries, we must be thankful for that extraordinary group of men, our founding fathers, who gave America its strong start, and they chose George Washington to be their leader.

We enjoyed visiting Monticello, Thomas Jefferson's beloved and fascinating home, and the nearby University of Virginia (known by Virginians as simply "the University"), which he had proudly designed and founded. However, our favorite place to step back in time in Virginia was Williamsburg, the meticulously and handsomely restored colonial capital where Jefferson and the other Virginia country squires gathered to debate and legislate in the House of Burgesses. One could almost hear the angry voice of Patrick Henry excoriating King George III in the growing opposition to unpopular royal rulings affecting the colonies.

Thomas Jefferson, a Renaissance man and political intriguer, enjoyed the good life at whatever the cost. He loved fine French wines but failed in his winemaking efforts at Monticello. I can sympathize with him. He expressed lofty ideals eloquently: In the Declaration of Independence he spoke of man's right to "the pursuit of happiness" (from which I derived my book title) and stated the principle that "All men are created equal." This assertion of moral conviction came from the Virginia Bill of Rights written by Virginia statesman George Mason, whose plantation home Gunston Hall we also visited. Acting on principle, Mason freed his own slaves, and when Washington died, his Mount Vernon slaves became free men in accordance with his will. Jefferson, however, ardent in preserving states' rights that protected the institution of slavery, and financially dependent on slave labor at Monticello, never freed his slaves.

Jefferson's chief political rivals were John Adams and Alexander Hamilton. John Adams, the second president of the United States, was the father of John Quincy Adams, who became our sixth president twenty-four years later. The only other father-son presidential duo in American history is the Bushes – George H. W. Bush, our forty-first president, and George W. Bush, our forty-third, who won the White House only eight years after his father had left it. Before becoming president John Quincy Adams had been a senator, an outstanding diplomat, and Secretary of State. George W. Bush had been an oil and baseball club executive and governor of Texas.

Alexander Hamilton, the leader of the Federalists in backing a strong central government, grew up in the West Indies and became the quintessential New Yorker. He went to Columbia and later practiced law in New York. Hamilton was Washington's military aide during the Revolution and at age thirty-three served brilliantly as America's first Secretary of the Treasury under President Washington. He founded *The New York Post*, then a newspaper, not a tabloid, which my Grandfather Lamont owned from 1918 to 1923. After he was killed by the murderous Aaron Burr in a duel, he was buried, with great honors, in the Trinity Church cemetery at the foot of Wall Street. All New Yorkers can be proud of this outstanding founding father. Grandfather Lamont, the Morgan banker, admired Hamilton and gathered a collection of historic material about his effective and precedent-setting service as Secretary of the Treasury, including a legislative resolution signed by Hamilton, now hanging in my study.

Another framed document hangs on my wall as well – a letter from Abraham Lincoln to my great, great grandfather in 1858. As a town official in Winchester, Illinois, Edward G. Miner was a friend of Lincoln, who at the time was a prominent Illinois Republican about to run for the U.S. Senate. In this letter Lincoln recommends the appointment of a certain gentleman to be the superintendent of the local "insane asylum."

In another letter to his family Miner described an incident, from around the time of the Lincoln–Douglas debates, illustrating Lincoln's propensity for telling jokes and stories. Miner and some Republican politicians were discussing politics one time in Springfield when Lincoln came into the room.

> *After some talk he says to the company, "I will have to tell a joke on myself. When I was canvassing the state last year at Winchester, I stopped at Haggart Hotel. In the morning I walked up to the square to get shaved, and a little Irishman came walking along with me, and he says, 'Ah, Mr. Lincoln, and you made a grand speech yesterday, and so ya did.' [Lincoln went on mimicking the Irishman.] After that he says, 'And now Mr. Lincoln could you give me a quarter to buy my breakfast?' I told the fellow that I was afraid that he wanted to buy whisky with it. No, indade he dident. So I gave him the quarter. After getting shaved I went back to the hotel. There was a big crowd in the street chasing the Griggsville band, and as I got among them they cried out, 'Three cheers for Lincoln,' and it was given. Then someone yelled out, 'And now three cheers for Douglas,' and I looked around and it was the same fellow that I gave the quarter to. And so we all had a hearty laugh."*

Many of the Civil War military campaigns unfolded around Washington and Virginia in the ebb and flow of battle. Buz and I visited Harper's Ferry, upstream on the Potomac, where John Brown and a small

band of followers had attacked the Federal arsenal in a prewar act of aboli-
tionist defiance, and toured the battlefields in the area. At nearby Bull Run
at Manassas the Confederates had been victorious in two engagements,
sending hundreds of spectators from Washington society fleeing back to
town in their carriages along with Union soldiers in the first battle.

The number of soldiers on both sides who died in the Civil War, some
six hundred fifty thousand, is a little more than the total number of
American servicemen killed in all the other wars in our history. The huge
number of casualties stemmed from poor medical treatment of wounds,
deadly diseases, often due to the lack of basic sanitary conditions in the
encampments, and especially the stupidity and callousness of generals
who showed little concern for their soldiers' lives. One weekend Buz and
I drove south to Fredericksburg and viewed the hill where Union troops
were ordered to charge uphill across an open meadow against fortified
Confederate lines. The repeated assaults failed, and the Union casualties of
killed, wounded, and missing amounted to twelve thousand men. We later
visited the Gettysburg battlefield, site of the major clash between the two
armies culminating in Pickett's disastrous and futile charge up a long slope
to overcome the Union forces on Cemetery Ridge. In three days of bloody
fighting the casualties on both sides amounted to fifty thousand men.

The competence of generals didn't improve much over the next fifty
years, remembering the appalling losses suffered in the trench warfare in
World War I, with a million soldiers killed on both sides just in the Battle
of the Somme; nor will Australians forget Gallipoli. Sir Robert Borden, the
Canadian Prime Minister at the time, talked about the "incompetence and
blundering stupidity of the whiskey and soda British H. Q. staff." Indeed
one can question the wisdom of some of the beachhead assaults in World
War II. The accounts and photographs, as well as Hollywood films, like
"Saving Private Ryan," which vividly depicted the D-Day landings at
Omaha Beach, remind us once again of the horrors of war.

Later we would cruise down the Mississippi from Memphis to New
Orleans on the *Delta Queen*, a stern paddlewheel steamboat, on a tour featuring Dixieland jazz, antebellum plantation homes, and Civil War battlefields. One of our stops was at Vicksburg, the Confederate "Gibraltar of
the South," where we strolled about the battleground and high bluffs
commanding the river. Following Lee's retreat from Gettysburg, President
Lincoln soon received still more good news. It was July 4, 1863, the same
day that the Battle of Gettysburg ended, that General Ulysses S. Grant
accepted the surrender of Vicksburg, a victory that gave the Union control of the full length of the Mississippi for the first time.

It is very moving to visit the Gettysburg battlefield, with its rocky
ravines and meadows sprinkled with granite and bronze monuments and
statues – each honoring the men who fought and died there. A friend
wrote me after visiting Gettysburg: "I don't know what I really expected,

but as we walked into the cemetery just before twilight, I was overcome with emotion. The stones in the encampment – row after row of small marble squares – moved me, for those poor souls, for their long ago families and friends, for us now, for all the sadness past and present. It made me thankful for those brave men, known and unknown, in a way that I could not have been before."

Anyone who has visited our beautiful national cemeteries, or those of other countries, will have felt the same emotions, as I did when I visited the U.S. cemetery near Manila in the Philippines for the U.S. Navy and Marine men and women lost in the Pacific theatre of World War II. My brother Tommy's name and rank, along with thousands of others, is inscribed on its marble walls. On a visit to the cemetery at el-Alamein, where the British army had overwhelmed the Germans in 1942 and driven them from Egypt, I read the inscriptions on the little crosses that the families of the fallen British soldiers had chosen. One was:

> *To the world he was a soldier.*
> *To us he was the world.*

It was at the ceremony inaugurating the Gettysburg battlefield as a national cemetery in November 1863, that President Lincoln gave his Gettysburg Address. In ten sentences he summed up the meaning and the goals of the great conflict with uncommon eloquence. I have recited the Gettysburg Address a number of times at the Memorial Day service at St. John's Church of Cold Spring Harbor, the perfect message for the day we honor those Americans who fought and died for their country.

A different breed of American politician, Senator Joseph McCarthy, was making headlines during our early years in Washington. He was an evil demagogue and bully who casually destroyed the lives and careers of innocent citizens in his phony communist-hunting investigations. No politician in my lifetime has blackened the good name of the U.S. Congress more than Joe McCarthy in his self-absorbed pursuit of power. In 1953 my uncle Corliss Lamont won a battle against McCarthy, whose Senate investigating committee had cited him for contempt in refusing to answer questions. A New York Court of Appeals dismissed the indictment. I was following McCarthy's reckless charges and committee investigations with growing anger.

To invigorate dull dinner table conversations about fad diets or flexible golf club shafts try posing the question, "What invention in your lifetime has had the greatest impact on peoples' lives?" Some may cite the atom bomb, or "the pill," the jet plane, or the computer. My answer is television, and in 1954 we purchased our first set, a Zenith, just in time to watch the televised Army–McCarthy hearings. It was exciting high drama featuring an intriguing cast of characters – the menacing Senator

McCarthy; two young attorneys who hated each other, Roy Cohn, the Committee counsel, and Bobby Kennedy, the minority counsel; Robert Stevens, the wimpy Secretary of the Army; and Joseph L. Welsh, the courtly old-fashioned Boston lawyer who was counsel for the Army.

McCarthy's insulting and crude conduct and wild accusations in these hearings precipitated his downfall. In one instance he gratuitously exposed the fact that a young law associate in Welsh's firm, not under investigation, had been a member of a left wing organization years before in college. Welsh turned on McCarthy with emotion: "Little did I dream that you could be so reckless and cruel. Have you no sense of decency, Sir? At long last, have you no sense of decency?"

That dramatic exchange before a national TV audience marked the beginning of the end for Senator McCarthy. In December 1954 the Senate voted to condemn him for conduct unbecoming a senator. The vilified, hard-drinking senator died three years later.

The Changing Continent

In 1956 my career took a positive turn. I joined the staff of the International Finance Corporation, a newly formed affiliate of the World Bank whose purpose was to invest in private companies in less developed countries without any government guarantee. IFC investments took the form of loans plus a share in earnings or option to acquire shares – financing subordinate to senior debt. IFC would later sell off a number of its holdings to private investors.

After working in the large and bureaucratic Bank, I found it fun to be a part of a smaller and more flexible new enterprise, and in on the ground floor as it developed new policies and procedures. The president of IFC was Robert L. Garner, a former Wall Street banker and vice president of the World Bank. Bob Garner had charisma. He was an able white-haired executive in his sixties with a twinkle in his eye and an enthusiastic vision of IFC's mission. I was one of half a dozen investment officers. At the weekly staff meetings we reported on the status of the investment projects that we were working on, and discussed new proposals. Everyone hoped to be assigned to the promising projects that would cross the finish line; we knew many would drop by the wayside. The staff was largely European and American, and a real sense of camaraderie prevailed. Morale was high. IFC had a capital of $100 million, and in its first five years when I was there invested about $50 million in thirty-seven industrial projects (around $350 million in current dollars).

I made a number of field trips to inspect my projects in Latin America and Africa. On my trips to Brazil, I got together with my brother-in-law Scott Buzby and his wife Ann. Scott was working for Goodyear Tire in Sao Paulo, the booming center of business and industry in Brazil. I had business in Sao Paulo, an investment in a brake lining plant, and in Rio de Janeiro, where an outstanding attraction is the beach at Copacabana, populated by scores of lithesome beauties sunning themselves.

Forty years later Buz and I would return to Brazil with the Buzbys, heading up the coast from Buenos Aires to Belem on the fancy cruise ship *Seabourn Pride*. "The Girl from Ipanema" and her girlfriends were still strolling the beach at Rio in their string bikinis. From Belem, we then steamed a thousand miles west up the Amazon to Manaus – a thriving city close to the equator in the very heart of the continent and in the early 1900s the prosperous center of the rubber industry in Brazil. We explored the tropical rain forest in small motorboats and toured the elegant opera house where the great Caruso once sang.

I was also working on IFC projects in Mexico City, and Buz and I later visited Mexico several times on business or to visit our daughter Helena, who lived south of the border for a dozen years. For us the cultural highlights of the region were the Spanish colonial churches, built in the 1500s in Aztec villages around Mexico City, that were central to the Catholic church's campaign to convert the Aztecs to Christianity. The church interiors are adorned with ornate Indian woodcarvings inlaid with gold, silver, and precious stones. Built decades before the New England settlements in North America, they are absolute gems.

Mexico and Brazil are the two eight hundred pound gorillas of Latin America; their large and volatile economies have periodically generated financial crises – causing major headaches for the U.S. government, the IMF, and international businessmen and bankers. Episodes of rampant inflation, major currency devaluations, and huge government deficits, along with weak banking systems and corrupt officials, are the economic wounds keeping these countries from achieving a better life for their people. Despite a growing middle class a huge income disparity still exists between much of the population and the upper tier of society, periodically spawning social unrest and violence, such as the Zapatista movement. Mexico and Brazil are getting their acts together gradually, however, and should soon break through into the ranks of modern industrial nations. It is important for Latin countries to prosper for their own sake, and for ours, too, if we are to avoid being overwhelmed by a flood of Latino immigrants clambering to come to the land of opportunity.

Very low pay and unemployment are nevertheless still widespread and chronic south of the border. Almost half of the Mexican population of a hundred million people live in poverty. Once in Puerto Vallarta I chatted with a young Mexican who had married one of Buz's cousins. He was fluent in English, well educated, and well spoken. Yet the only job he could get in Mexico was that of a restaurant waiter. He went to California periodically to get work at decent pay, sometimes as a chef, to make enough money to build a small house back in Puerto Vallarta.

The Latino businessmen I dealt with during my IFC years were for the most part a different breed from the typical hard-driving American executive. They took an easy-going *mañana* approach to work in our joint efforts to develop their proposals. In some cases they were probably on fishing expeditions for cheap loans and didn't like our proposed financing terms, but rather than say so they stalled and delayed. Like everyone traveling on business I wanted to get the job done and get on home, but oftentimes on my trips south of the border I came to realize that there was just no rushing these fellows. I once spent ten days in Mexico City on a job that should have taken half that time.

On another occasion I was investigating a proposal to invest in a textile mill near Caracas. The company president invited me for lunch, and I intended to spend the afternoon with his people gathering the information for my report to IFC management. First we had drinks in his well-appointed office suite; el presidente preferred to tell off-color jokes and talk golf rather than business. Then we piled into limousines to ride downtown to a fancy restaurant. Another round of drinks. I turned to another American guest, the Price Waterhouse man in Caracas, and quietly asked. "What gives? I've got work to do." He replied. "Ted, you're in Latin America. You've got to just go with the flow." After a three-course lunch with wine we broke up around five o'clock. The day was shot; I did not recommend an investment in the company.

This management style was not uniquely Latin American. A few years later, after I had left IFC and was a Morgan banker, I flew to the Philippines to review several projects – among them a large steel company seeking an investment. Again I was ready to go to work. But after several telephone calls the first contact I received from the company was a call from a public relations officer, who invited me out to dinner at a nightclub. This thuggish flack, who knew little about the business, brought along a pretty girl in a slinky dress who made it clear that she would be happy to spend the night with me in my room at the Manila Hotel. I politely told her just to drop me off and keep on going. I soon decided that this enterprise was not a suitable Morgan client, and departed promptly for Hong Kong and Tokyo to join the Morgan team attending the annual meetings of the World Bank and IMF.

My first business dinner in Tokyo was a polar opposite from my sleazy evening in Manila a few nights earlier. Seated at one end of a long table in a famous geisha house was my boss, John M. Meyer, Jr., the president of J.P. Morgan, and opposite him Chairman Tajitsu of the Mitsubishi Bank. Seated down each side of the table in descending rank, and generally age, were officers from the two institutions. As an assistant vice president, I was well below the salt.

John Meyer was competent and austere, not known for easygoing small talk. The Japanese chairman, struggling in English, appeared to be a pretty formal fellow, too. Conversation plodded along heavily as John picked at his sushi and other delicacies foreign to his palate. As one progressed down the table toward my end, seating the junior officers, the sake flowed more freely, and chatter and laughter filled the air. Soon the coquettish geisha girls appeared to spur on the merriment with little games like "paper, stone, and scissors" and transferring an orange tucked under your chin to under her chin without using hands. It was a scene out of comic opera.

Unlike Latin America, in Africa south of the Sahara there is little reason for optimism about early prospects for sound development, with the possible exception of South Africa. In 1959 IFC's vice president John G.

Beevor and I visited a number of African countries to inspect potential investment projects and spread the word about the IFC. Jack, a former London solicitor, was one of the nicest gentlemen I have ever known and a congenial traveling companion. The countries we would visit were all British colonies at the time except for the Union of South Africa, where the United Kingdom had long-standing ties and commercial interests.

Jack and I spent a few days in London at each end of the trip meeting with bankers and Colonial Office officials. The bankers – Morgan Grenfell, Baring Brothers and the others – liked their pre-luncheon drinks and there was lots of old boy lighthearted banter. They knew that Jack Beevor, formerly of Slaughter and May, was a fine fellow with a worthy mission, but no one expected the IFC to have much impact in these territories. The whites constituted a tiny minority of the population in the colonies, whose native populations were pushing hard to win their independence from the U.K., the sooner the better. The big concern of the British establishment was what was in store for their business interests and the thousands of British settlers in these former colonies when native African governments assumed power.

Our first stop was Salisbury, the capital of Southern Rhodesia, part of a federation with Northern Rhodesia and Nyasaland, all of them governed by the U.K. (Following independence the names all changed: Southern Rhodesia became Zimbabwe and Salisbury is Harare.) We called on Sir Roy Welensky, the federation prime minister, and worked our way down through the ranks of officials, businessmen, and bankers. There was little of investment interest for the IFC, but the government and business community welcomed us warmly at luncheons and dinners, sometimes black tie. Jack had advised me to pack a tuxedo for the trip, as we would be moving in British establishment circles where a dinner jacket in the evening was often de rigeur, even in African colonies.

We arranged to talk to a couple of well-informed Africans – a newspaper editor and a legislator. The official British line called for developing a partnership with the native Africans, but the whites on the ground in Rhodesia anticipated running the show for years to come. The Africans were frustrated in their subordinate role in government and business, however, and impatient for the day when they would take over. The native population in 1959 was over two million in Southern Rhodesia, and there were only about 175,000 whites. The disparity in standard of living was huge between whites and natives, who lived mostly in tribal villages. Racial tensions were bubbling beneath the surface; other African colonies were gaining their independence; the handwriting was on the wall. Twenty years later after sporadic guerilla warfare and turbulent political twists and turns, the whites in Zimbabwe would surrender control of the government to an African party led by Robert Mugabe. The country has become a basket case under Mugabe's brutal dictatorship.

Violent confrontations have continued between the natives and white settlers as the Africans, backed by their government, seek to acquire, by force if necessary, the rich farmlands owned by the Europeans.

En route to Northern Rhodesia Jack and I inspected the newly built Kariba dam on the Zambezi River, partially financed by the World Bank, which would supply hydroelectric power to the Rhodesias. Construction of the 420-foot-high dam and its power stations, carved out of the dense jungle in a remote area, was an impressive international undertaking. An Italian firm had won the construction contract, British companies supplied most of the equipment, and a Frenchman had designed the dam. Twice during construction the Zambezi had gone on record-breaking rampages flooding the coffer dam and washing away bridges, roads, and buildings. But the work force persevered, and Kariba went on line in 1960.

We then flew to Lusaka, the capital of Northern Rhodesia (later named Zambia when the territory became an independent republic in 1964). The British governor gave us a welcoming black-tie dinner, inviting his top ministers and their ladies, formally attired in flowing evening gowns. After dinner the ladies left the gentlemen, who, led by the governor, lined up under a starry sky to urinate at the edge of the lawn that met the vast veldt stretching beyond. Afterwards we adjourned to the billiard room for brandy and cigars. The evening was a pleasant lily-white affair, as were the other receptions and dinners that we attended in Africa.

The British colonial officers we met took their professional duties seriously. They did seem sincerely concerned about educating and preparing the native populations for their future after independence day. However, they remained aloof from their charges and generally made little effort to cultivate personal relations with the blacks.

Copper was king in Zambia, its leading industry and export, and Jack and I visited Ndola and the Copper Belt mines of the Rhodesian Selection Trust. The forty thousand native workers in the Copper Belt were the most highly paid laborers in southern Africa. Still the European workers' unions kept them from advancing to higher and better-paid positions in the mines. Of the six operating mines Roan Antelope was not the biggest, but what an appealing name!

Well before the Kariba dam site the Zambezi River flows over the magnificent Victoria Falls, our next destination. The view from the air of the great falls – long cliffs of cascading water and rising clouds of mist with rainbows arching over the turbulence – was spectacular. En route we flew over the huge lake forming behind the dam, which would ultimately extend back upstream for one hundred seventy five miles. Over fifty thousand Batonka tribespeople had to be evacuated, along with thousands of wild animals marooned on newly formed islands, as the lake filled. Nowadays the environmentalists would be up in arms against such a project, but the Rhodesias and especially the copper industry needed that Kariba power. We chatted with the British district commissioner in Livingstone, near Victoria Falls. As a boy in England he had enjoyed sailing, but his career assignments in the Colonial Service had always been inland posts. Like a child before Christmas he was awaiting the extension of Kariba Lake so that he and his friends could go sailing in the heart of Africa. He was planning to open a small yacht club and had already selected a class of sailboats for racing on the lake waters.

Flying into Johannesburg Jack and I enjoyed a magnificent view of the great tawny sea of the veldt below us – golden brown grasslands and distant mountain ranges in the background. Following our normal routine we called on businessmen, bankers, and government officials in Johannesburg, Praetoria, Durban, and Cape Town. We toured a half dozen or so industrial enterprises and descended in a rickety wire-cage elevator into a gold mine in the Rand mining district near Johannesburg. Afterwards the native workers put on a colorful tribal show for the tourists featuring a war dance by Zulu warriors.

Johannesburg was virtually built on gold. From a small mining town in 1886 it would eventually grow into the largest and most modern city in southern Africa. In 1959 gold mining was a supremely vital force in the South African economy. South Africa produced about 60 percent of the free world's gold, which was the country's number one export. The mines employed about three hundred thirty thousand natives and forty-four thousand Europeans; thousands more worked in ancillary enterprises. The government's policy of "job reservations" for whites restricted non-whites from advancing to the better jobs in the mines and indeed throughout the economy. The Bantu workers lived in bachelor barracks at the mines and periodically took long leaves to visit their families living in the native reserves far removed from the white populated cities.

One overriding condition ordered the way people lived in South Africa during these years – apartheid – and we observed its effects throughout our travels. Of a total population of about 14.5 million, 3 million were European, 1.9 million were "coloured," or mixed ethnicity, and 9.6 million were Bantus, or African natives. The white population was the largest south of the Sahara and still is. Yet in 1959, with twenty-one percent of the total population, they ran the country as they alone saw fit. Their doctrine of racial apartheid was based on white supremacy and the physical separation of whites from other races. The Afrikaners of Dutch heritage, who outnumbered the people of English descent, believed in the biblical passage referring to the children of Ham as hewers of wood and drawers of water, or so they said. Apartheid ordered the segregation of two thirds of the Bantus in native reserves; the establishment of separate African, "coloured," or Indian townships adjoining the main urban areas for those needed to fill jobs in the cities; the displacement of most non-whites from the cities; their political disenfranchisement; and restrictions on their movements and activities.

Our government guide took us out to Soweto, a native township outside Johannesburg started ten years earlier. It was the largest black urban center in the country, housing the families of Africans who traveled by jitney bus to their jobs in the city. In 1959 the houses were tiny bare-bones huts, lacking basic amenities, but no worse than those in the tribal villages. The housing and unpaved streets were dusty, dirty, and drab without greenery. It was not a happy community or a pleasant place to live. In later years Soweto residents were in the forefront of demonstrations demanding black equality, and the town was the center of a large uprising in 1976.

Afrikaner officials whom we interviewed, such as Dr. Donges, the minister of finance, touted the Nationalist Party line: Apartheid was the best arrangement for everyone. The government's policy of apartheid was nevertheless becoming the target of strong and growing criticism both externally from other countries and internally from the opposition political party and underground African organizations. Business executives of English background, such as Harry Oppenheimer, who headed the Anglo-American and DeBeers gold and diamond mining companies in South Africa, were more pessimistic about race relations. Charles Engelhard, Jr., a leading American investor in African gold mining shares, thought that racial bitterness and confrontations would get worse substantially before public pressure brought about a relaxation of apartheid.

I left South Africa in 1959 with the impression that it was a powder keg waiting to be ignited. The wait would be long. The following decades brought sporadic outbreaks of violent confrontations with the police plus passive resistance by blacks demonstrating against the hated policy. Apartheid became increasingly abhorrent to the world at large. Countries began to impose economic embargoes on South Africa. Private institutional investors in the U.S., among them university endowment funds and pension trusts, as well as individuals, refused to buy South African securities or even those of companies doing substantial business in that country, and banks began to restrict their lending to South African borrowers.

The campaign to bring about the collapse of apartheid and institute universal suffrage would at last be successful, and Nelson Mandela became the first African president of the country in 1994. It was a triumph for the majority rule of Africans of their own country, but South Africa continues to struggle today. Incompetence and corruption in government, the inability to control criminal activity, and the rampant spread of AIDS have remained serious obstacles to progress.

In 1959 we ended our tour of South Africa in Cape Town, founded by the Dutch in 1652 and one of the loveliest cities in the world. I took the cable car to the top of Table Mountain for the breathtaking view of the city and Cape Peninsula, between two oceans and cradled by mountains.

South Africa was a beautiful country, sadly burdened by the disgrace of human discrimination against people because of the color of their skin.

In 1959 Nairobi, Kenya, was a colorful and intriguing town. The Mau Mau rebellion that had ended only four years earlier, and its implications for the future of Kenya and its white settlers, was fresh in everyone's mind. Kenya was still a British Crown Colony. Europeans, largely British, comprising only about one percent of Kenya's population of 6.5 million, occupied the rich farming region of "the white highlands," where they employed native workers to raise coffee, tea, and other crops. The largest African tribe, more than one million, were the Kikuyus. The Mau Mau were a Kikuyu secret society intent upon driving out the Europeans and gaining independence for Kenya. The Mau Mau rebellion and the trial and conviction of Jomo Kenyatta, allegedly its leader, had been headline news around the world, and at the time of our visit Kenyatta was scheduled for release from prison in a year.

The Mau Mau attacks had first been directed against their own people, the Kikuyu, to dominate and control them, and then against the white settlers on their remote farms. Thousands of Kikuyu were killed along with scores of European farmers and police and military personnel, with gruesome brutalities committed by both sides. The Mau Mau years were a very ugly chapter in African history. Many wondered if Mau Mau violence was a forerunner of uprisings to come against Europeans in other parts of Africa. Native Kenyan leaders were clamoring for independence – their attitude was "Ready or not we're coming." The urgent question in everyone's mind was how soon it would happen, and then what lay in store for the white settlers.

Jack Beevor and I made our routine calls on Nairobi's officialdom, starting off as the luncheon guests of Sir Evelyn Baring, governor of the colony. Joyce Grenfell, the bright British comedienne and movie actress, was another guest – one of the many celebrities passing through Nairobi to visit the game parks and their beautiful wild animals. Three young British colonial officers invited me to spend the weekend with them at the Amboseli game reserve, not far from snow-capped Mt. Kilimanjaro, Africa's highest mountain. From a safe distance I marveled at a herd of elephants rooting in the bush with their long curved tusks, so prized by big game hunters and poachers for quite different reasons. The lions, basking in the noonday sun, barely batted an eye as we drove by, but their growling outside our cabin at night was their reminder not to take them lightly.

On the way back to Nairobi we stopped at a Masai village of thatched roof mud huts surrounding a cattle corral. The tall, crimson blanket clad Masai, some carrying spears to protect their cattle from predators, possessed great dignity. They were proud of the pastoral way of life that they had chosen and unimpressed by the trappings of modern civilization, especially camera-toting tourists who took their picture without first asking permission and paying for the privilege.

Nairobi was also the safari capital of Africa, and the Norfolk Hotel, where assorted celebrities, adventuresome tourists, and hunters stayed before heading into the bush, was the center of action. Those were the days when rich men went to Africa to shoot big game – lions, elephants, rhinoceros, leopards, and water buffalo – a sport later banned. The bar at the Norfolk was a colorful and popular watering hole for both locals and visitors. Sunburned farmers who had survived the Mau Mau crisis were downing beers, and William Holden, the handsome movie actor, was charming an enraptured blond. One fellow told me an intriguing tale about an old-timer by the name of Colonel Grogan, who had frequented the bar for many years.

As a young British lieutenant Grogan had sought permission from his sweetheart's guardian to marry her. However, that gentleman was unimpressed by Grogan's record and turned him down. Grogan then proposed to walk from Cape Town to Cairo to demonstrate his courage and determination, and the guardian agreed that such a spectacular and bold achievement would persuade him to approve of the marriage. So Grogan did just that – finally stumbling out of the Upper Nile jungle tattered and emaciated, where he ran into a British expedition just sitting down to dinner in their mess tent. He told the leader that he had just walked up from Cape Town, and that gentleman reportedly replied, "Good show, old man!" Grogan joined them for the rest of the journey, married his girl, and they settled down happily outside Nairobi.

At breakfast one morning at the Norfolk an old North Haven friend, Harry Cabot, and his wife Colly greeted me. They were leaving in a few days on a month-long hunting safari organized by Robert Ruark, the *New York Post* columnist and author, and invited me to attend the pre-safari departure parties that Ruark had planned. Ruark was a fine writer whose lifestyle reminded one of Hemingway. He had a villa in Spain and was a bullfight afficionado; he loved big game hunting and enjoyed hard drinking evenings with his pals.

As it happened, I had just read Ruark's brutally honest novel *Something of Value*, based on the Mau Mau rebellion, and praised the book when Harry introduced me to him at his sundowner party at the Norfolk. Ruark thanked me, pulled me aside, and said, "Ted, you're a good friend of the Cabots, but I really don't know them very well. I invited them to join me on this safari on sort of a spur of the moment impulse at a party one evening. We're going to be out in the bush together for some time, and I'm especially interested in their drinking habits." We sat down at a small table and Ruark pulled out a notebook and pencil: "Does Harry like martinis before dinner, and how about Scotch highballs later on or maybe brandy?" I had seen my friend Harry in action at parties and told Ruark as much as I could about the Cabots' taste for spirits as he took detailed notes. The drinking logistics of the safari were very important to him; he had one entire lorry loaded with "x" number of cases of Scotch, gin, vodka, and so forth. He would adjust his supplies based on what I told him of the Cabots' estimated consumption of liquor. The safari set forth the next morning. I wished Ruark and the Cabots happy hunting and promised myself that the Lamonts would go on an African safari someday, but with cameras, not guns.

Jack Beevor and I next brought our IFC "dog and pony show" to Entebbe, Uganda, where we stayed at the Lake Victoria Hotel. Once again we called on the key government officials, largely British colonial officers and businessmen. Sundowner parties at the end of the day were a pleasant way to meet the local gentry. Moving on, we checked out some flimsy investment proposals that the IFC had received from businesses in Mombasa and Zanzibar, and settled in at the New Africa Hotel in Dar es Salaam, Tanganyika (which became Tanzania following independence two years later in 1961 and merger with Zanzibar in 1964). Our one and only solid investment proposal in all of Africa was in Tanganyika, making it a critical project from a public relations viewpoint. We were there to do the final "due diligence."

Before coming to Africa I had been working on a proposal for IFC to help finance the project of the Kilombero Sugar Company to grow and refine sugar for the Tanganyika market. The company would clear and irrigate seven thousand acres of fertile land in the Kilombero Valley and construct a sugar mill and refinery with an initial capacity of twenty thousand tons a year. The output would obviate the need to import sugar, a significant foreign exchange saving for a country of about nine million people with a chronic payments deficit. A Dutch company that had formerly operated sugar estates in Java would manage the enterprise. Of the total project cost of $8 million, IFC would invest $2.8 million in a mix of convertible notes, 7% debentures, and stock options. British and Dutch government-backed development corporations would be investment partners with the IFC, and we hoped that African and Asian residents of Tanganyika would subscribe to stock in the new company. The Ismailis, whose leader was the rich and powerful Aga Khan, were one of the prominent Asian groups in Tanganyika. We were told that traditionally the Khan family liked to invest in communities where their people lived.

In 1959 the Aga Khan was a young man who had recently graduated from Harvard. Before our African trip I had set up a meeting with him on his visit to Washington in hopes that IFC's president Bob Garner could sell him on the idea that the Ismailis should make a substantial investment in the Tanganyika sugar project. At the appointed hour Garner and I went around to the Aga Khan's suite at the Mayflower Hotel. Garner, white-haired and distinguished looking in his dark suit and homburg, was appropriately dressed for his part. The youthful Aga Khan, in rolled-up shirtsleeves, sat casually cross-legged on a sofa.

Garner and I described the project, emphasizing its economic and social benefits for the country at some length – foreign exchange savings, employing four thousand new workers with housing and medical care for them, developing a large new area, attracting foreign investment and so forth. We figured that our pitch would appeal to the Ismaili chief's statesmanlike and generous instincts as the leader of a large religious sect with many followers in Tanganyika. So his reaction came as a surprise. When we wound down the young man said that he had just one important question, and he went straight to the bottom line: "How soon will the company pay its first dividend?" Somewhat taken aback, Bob Garner replied that it could not be very soon, given the nature of the project. The Aga said he would think it over.

The British colonial officials in Tanganyika were all for the sugar project, but more importantly, in view of the colony's imminent independence, the local leaders that we saw were enthusiastic backers. The support of Amir Karimjee, the Ismaili assistant minister of commerce, would help in selling shares in the company to the Ismaili community. The most encouraging endorsement was that of Julius Nyerere, the head of the Tanganyika African National Union. Nyerere was the country's foremost African politician, and destined to become its first prime minister in 1961 and later the first president of Tanzania and a major power in African affairs. Beevor and I went around to see him at his small and spartan union office. Nyerere was slight in stature, soft-spoken, and unpretentious – an engaging man who smiled easily. He was modest, but at the same time confident of his ability to lead his people. He was moderate in his views, espousing peaceful change and racial harmony, as he pressed the Colonial Office vigorously for freedom from British rule. Nyerere had attended the University of Edinburgh, the first African from Tanganyika to attend a British university, where he earned master's degrees in history and economics. He was an intellectual who had translated two of Shakespeare's plays, *Julius Caesar* and *The Merchant of Venice*, into Swahili. Nyerere declared that he would encourage African investment in the Kilombero Sugar Company; the project simply must be made to succeed.

The only discordant note that we heard about the project was that a herd of elephants had just trampled down the experimental sugar cane plots, causing a minor delay. Beevor and I flew back to London and Washington and worked on the final plans and financing package. In June 1960 the agreements were executed, and the first IFC investment in Africa was announced to the public.

Safari

Ten years after my IFC ventures in Africa, Buz and I set out on our own
safari from Nairobi, now a bustling modern city of four hundred
thousand, with our friends Martha and Vic Kenyon. We eschewed the
zebra-striped vans loaded with camera-toting tourists headed for deluxe
lodges, a new development since my prior visit in 1959. We had our own
"white hunter" (even though we were only photographers) who drove us
through the bush in a Toyota Land Cruiser, pointing out the abundant
wildlife. Paul Herd was a handsome young Kenyan who could spot a
leopard in a tree at two hundred yards. We all applauded his driving
skills; our hardy vehicle easily handled the rugged off-track terrain with
only an occasional flat tire. Paul had a favorite game that he played whenever we ran across a rhinoceros. He walked toward the rhino and with
sounds and gestures incited him to charge our vehicle. Paul then raced
back to the Land Cruiser with the rhino in hot pursuit. Rhinos are big,
but Land Cruisers are bigger, so the rhino wisely always veered off a few
yards away from us. Still Martha did not enjoy the stunt. Paul ran a very
efficient camp and loved his job guiding safaris through the game-rich
rain forests and plains of Kenya and Tanzania.

While we spotted game, a truck with our tents, baggage, cooking
gear, and supplies went on ahead to prepare our campsite for the evening.
Paul's crew consisted of ten African "boys," in the days before political
correctness governed our vocabularies. My Swahili was limited, but I
greeted them with a "jambo" every morning, and they addressed me as
"bwana," which was kind of neat. There was a central mess tent, and each
couple had its own sleeping tent, with rugs, and a toilet and shower tent.
The campsites – near Amboseli, Lake Manyara, Seronara, and the Mara
River in the vast reserves south and west of Nairobi – were the bases for
our daily excursions.

Tanzania's Serengeti National Park and Kenya's contiguous Masai
Mara Game Reserve, both covering an area larger than Connecticut, were
home for the most spectacular concentration of wild game animals in the
world. The sheer number and variety of game that we saw was absolutely
awesome – at least thirty different species – not only the big five game
animals, but giraffes, impala, elands, zebra, cheetah, ostriches, several
kinds of gazelles, wildebeests, baboons, hyenas, and more. One watering
hole had so many different kinds of game (no carnivores, please) that it
looked like a casting call for Noah's Ark. We agreed with Walt Disney who
made "The Lion King"; we decided that the hyena was the meanest and

ugliest critter we ran into; nor did the warthog win many votes.

Some of the scenes we observed were brutal jungle life in the raw, survival of the fittest. The cheetah is the fastest animal in the jungle, and I filmed one stalking a bunch of grazing Thomson's gazelles. After moving closer steadily from bush to bush, he made the final explosive dash and lethal leap, sinking his jaws into the neck of the panic-stricken gazelle. We didn't hang around for dinner. On another day we spotted a leopard in the branches of a tree gnawing away at a bloody carcass that he had dragged up to his perch.

Often, however, the predators went home hungry. Near a watering hole where zebras and water buffalo were drinking, we watched a pride of seven lions move in stealthily for the kill. The zebras sensed trouble and bolted; the buffalo stood their ground, and the lions, knowing they had met their match, slunk away.

We also saw tree-climbing lions dozing in the branches of trees on the shore of Lake Manyara, resting during the heat of day before going prowling for a meal in the late afternoon. On one yellow-barked acacia tree we saw dozens of vultures, one perched on every branch, waiting to pick the bones of the lions' latest kill.

One night, when we were chatting around the campfire, we beamed our flashlights into the surrounding darkness, and a sea of little red eyes stared back at us – baboons and monkeys, according to Paul. Throughout the night our jungle neighbors kept up a steady chorus – grunts and growls from the lions and leopards, and excited chatter from the baboons. As we enjoyed a leisurely breakfast the next day in the bright morning sunlight, colorfully plumaged Superb Glossy Starlings joined our table to partake of the bread and muffin crumbs.

At Olduvai Gorge we descended through layers of earth's history to reach the level where anthropologists Louis and Mary Leakey had uncovered the earliest fossil finds of human ancestral forms. For us, the most awe-inspiring sight in the animal kingdom was the huge herds of wildebeest and zebra streaming across the vast rolling plains of Serengeti and Masai Mara, while lions lurked hidden in the rocky outcroppings and tall grass waiting to pounce on unwary weaklings or stragglers. Paul estimated that one day we viewed over five thousand wildebeest in a long winding column, several thousand zebra and gazelles, plus elephants, leaping elands, and a hundred hippopotami cavorting in the river. As in Olduvai Gorge we were looking through a crack in the wall of time at a scene from thousands of years ago.

It was time to bid farewell to Paul and the "boys" and meet our next guide and bush pilot, Malcolm Hudson, who would fly us in his twin-engine Piper Aztec to our new destinations. Malcolm was a third-generation Kenyan whose family had lost their farm to their native countrymen when Kenya gained its independence; he had stayed on despite this setback because he loved the country. We buzzed the tiny airstrip at Uganda's Murchison Falls a couple of times to scare off the animals, landed, and drove to the resort hotel on the Nile River.

At Murchison Falls the Victoria Nile takes a one-hundred-foot leap into space through a narrow rocky gorge, and then continues on its way to Lake Albert. On a launch trip to the foot of the cataract we filmed frolicking hippos and cold and beady-eyed crocodiles, exuding malevolence as they slithered off the muddy banks into the river. The next day Malcolm gave us a panoramic aerial view of it all as we flew downstream to Lake Albert and viewed the source of the White Nile, starting its sixteen-hundred-mile journey to the sea. Then we turned east, flying over completely desolate, arid, and mountainous terrain to our destination, a rustic fishing lodge on the western shore of Lake Rudolph in Northern Kenya, more than two hundred miles from the nearest civilization.

The fish were biting. Between us we caught 260 pounds of the rare Nile Perch in two afternoons. After a sporty fight I landed the biggest, at forty-five pounds. The story of my catch came in handy. When I was working on Wall Street later on, a couple of my fisherman friends used to invite me to The Anglers' Club for the annual Christmas punch and lunch, where the fellows sat around the table exchanging stories about their fishing experiences in far-flung places like Iceland and Chile. When my turn came I was ready with my tale about catching the rare Nile Perch at remote and wild Lake Rudolph. I believe the members were impressed.

Lake Rudolph was noted for its man-eating crocodiles as well as its fish, and Peter Beard, the noted game photographer, was there to take pictures of the crocs for his new book. One evening when we were having drinks, Tony Potter, the lodge's British manager, beckoned me to step down to the end of the bar. "I have really admired the U.S. and its government ever since a sad incident that happened here a few years ago," Tony began.

A young man in the U.S. Peace Corps, visiting the lodge on leave, inquired about going swimming. Tony advised him not to, warning him about the danger of swimming in a lake filled with large, aggressive crocodiles known to have attacked humans. It was difficult to see the crocodiles in the murky lake water; often they looked just like floating logs. Nevertheless, it was a hot day and the fellow slipped off to a cove on the lake for a swim. He never returned. Tony radioed the American Embassy in Nairobi. Four agents flew in and proceeded to shoot and split open thirteen crocodiles in the cove. In the stomach of the last croc they found some body parts of the Peace Corpsman. I probably looked a little skeptical, for Tony then produced several photographs from a cigar box that he kept behind the bar, commenting that they were too grisly to show the ladies. Clearly seen in one picture was the poor fellow's arm and hand wearing his watch and signet ring. The Embassy officers took his remains

Life on the
Home Front

Life in Washington was pleasant. In the winter I played squash and swam at the University Club. In the summer we played tennis and sometimes drove to Rehoboth Beach on weekends staying with a merry band of friends in a rented beach house, with everyone pitching in for meals and parties.

Then golf came into our lives. The IFC held an outing and golf tournament each year at the Bethesda Country Club near Washington. I had never learned to play golf. My father, who played regularly with his buddies, had never introduced me to the game, which in my youth I disdained anyway as a sport for older businessmen. However, many of my IFC colleagues were novices as well, and we all decided to sign up for the tournament. A few days later I was shocked to learn that Bob Garner, the president and elder statesman of the IFC, had chosen me to be his partner in the tournament, and there was no way out. I raced out to a Virginia driving range the afternoon before the outing to take a quick lesson. It didn't help much, and the next day I sprayed balls all over the course and into the woods. Our opponents beat us handily. Garner was polite, but we never played golf together again.

Buz and I decided to join the Bethesda Country Club to take up the game. The club was looking for new members, unlike the toney Chevy Chase Club where our name was at the end of a very long waiting list for admission. My letters to the family about learning to play golf could have been written last week. "Last Saturday I shot a 42 on the front nine, my lowest score yet, and then blossomed out with a 58 on the back nine. So I'm still not in two digits. I hope to break that barrier before winter closes in." To Grandmother Miner: "Camille and I usually play golf over the weekends. She is a natural athlete and has won several large silver trophies in golf tournaments. I don't believe that athletic ability has ever been present in any substantial degree in the Miner and Lamont families. I didn't inherit very much."

I have played a lot of golf since then, a few times on classy courses like Pebble Beach, Augusta National, and Shinnecock, and in Hawaii, Scotland, and Ireland. I broke a hundred, and then remained stalled in the nineties decade after decade. Different clubs work well for me on different days, but never all on the same day. Golfers will know what I am talking about. One day the long putts are dropping and drives are slicing into the woods. The next day the drives are long and straight, accompanied by three-putt greens. My most important golfing role has been that of sparring partner for my trophy-winning wife, a worthy and enjoyable mission.

In addition to her triumphs on the course, Buz has become part of golf history. Driving through Scotland one time in the 1960s, we stopped off at St. Andrews for a round of golf. Back then there was no need to reserve a tee time months in advance. After our round we walked into the Royal and Ancient clubhouse looking for a cool drink and the facilities. There was not a soul around.

We wandered about, ending up in a handsomely paneled room containing a large mahogany table and filled with golf memorabilia – ancient clubs, plaques, official scrolls, silver cups, and the like. As we looked around, an elderly Scottish retainer appeared and sharply demanded to know what we were doing there. I told him and he replied that there was a powder room for the ladies in the hotel across the street. Ladies were not permitted in the Royal and Ancient clubhouse, and he had never seen one inside the venerable structure in all of his many years of service there. Furthermore, we were in the Governors' Meeting Room, which was reserved for their exclusive use and strictly off limits to everyone else. We apologized profusely and beat a hasty retreat from the high temple of golf. Buz's pioneering invasion of the sacred premises may have been the most noteworthy breakthrough for women's golf at St. Andrews since Mary, Queen of Scots, played the new course in the sixteenth century.

The place of St. Andrews in golf history is well known. That's where the game began on the eighteen-hole links of the Old Course. My main hang-up about the game, aside from my erratic play, is that it takes too long – around four hours for a foursome playing eighteen holes. But that's the layout that the golfing fathers at St. Andrews decreed and that course designers have been slavishly following ever since. Will anyone have the courage to build a twelve- or fourteen-hole course?

We enjoyed pleasurable outings closer to home as well. Jesse and Helene Buzby had settled on Virginia's Northern Neck for their retirement years. Their house was on the Wicomico River not far from the river mouth on Chesapeake Bay. Jesse, the veteran Caribbean sailor, now kept a thirty-two-foot cabin cruiser at his dock. We enjoyed cruising about the bay and feasting on fresh oysters plucked from its waters. Tides Inn in nearby Irvington was a favorite port and resort for a good time in an atmosphere of easygoing Southern hospitality. The Buzby home was about a three-hour drive from Washington, and it was a great experience for young Ned to go boating and fishing with his Buzby grandparents.

We spent our summer vacations in North Haven with my parents, where we also did a lot of boating. Beautiful Penobscot Bay was at our doorstep, and picnicking on one of the many rockbound, spruce-covered islands in the bay was the favorite family enterprise. A couple of motorboats and usually a sailboat or two would be loaded with parents and children, uncles and aunts, baby-sitters and houseguests, picnic baskets and coolers, and off we'd go. At Hurricane Island we explored winding tunnels among the granite blocks in the old quarry, whose output in earlier times used to supply the construction of some of the great public buildings in eastern cities. Nowadays we go there and run the obstacle course of the Maine Outward Bound program based on the island.

Another favorite spot was McGlathery's in Merchants Row, which sounds like a bar but is really an enchanting isle. And sometimes we visited nearby Castine, climbing about the Revolutionary War fort built by the British army occupying the town. A U.S. naval fleet, dispatched from Boston in 1779, lacked the backbone to attack and capture the town and was later ignominiously routed by a British fleet and destroyed as it fled up the Penobscot River. It was a horrendous U.S. Navy disaster, never equaled until Pearl Harbor. The commander of the American fleet was Commodore Dudley Saltonstall. Some of his descendants, the family of Massachusetts Senator Leverett Saltonstall, are respected and popular summer residents of North Haven just down the bay from Castine; they are all excellent sailors.

The dinghy races up and down the Fox Islands Thoroughfare could be adventuresome in a good blow. On an August Saturday twenty-five or thirty boats competed fiercely, crowding and jockeying for position at the start. It was wise to have a hefty crewmember in a stiff breeze, leaning far over the windward rail when he wasn't bent over pumping, in order to stay afloat. Port and starboard tack close calls and other right-of-way confrontations added to the excitement. The final race of the year was always on Labor Day, marking the end of summer fun and return to office and school.

My five weeks of duty on a criminal jury panel at the District Court, during our Washington years, was a fascinating experience. I wrote my father, "You really find out what goes on in Washington or any big city after dark." I served on four different juries and was chosen once to be the foreman on a case involving car theft and robbing a dry cleaner. The police had arrested two teenage boys in a stolen car; on the back seat of the car they found tickets to clothes stolen from a dry cleaner earlier that evening. The government prosecutor charged the boys with committing both crimes. The boys were caught red-handed in the stolen car and admitted that they had taken it for a joyride after a party. They insisted that they knew nothing about the break-in at the dry cleaners, and there was no other evidence linking them to this crime than the tickets found in the car. In our jury deliberations I stated that while the boys were clearly guilty of car theft, there was simply not enough evidence to convict them of robbing the dry cleaner. However, some jury members disagreed. One fellow said "Look, the government goes to a lot of effort and expense to prosecute these cases. They must know what they are doing." Another said, "Let's stop talking and find them guilty as charged. I've got tickets to the night game and want to get out of here." It was a scene right out of "Twelve Angry Men." I kept them all there and talking until everyone agreed to return a guilty verdict on the single charge of car theft.

My last case presented court and jury room drama at its best. A number of persons who said they were opposed to capital punishment were excused from the jury pool for this case. It involved a charge of rape, and in the District of Columbia juries had the right to recommend the death sentence to the court for persons convicted of rape. I was not opposed to capital punishment in certain rare cases where it seemed appropriate and was selected for this jury. None of us ever considered recommending the death sentence in this case.

Four black teenagers were charged with dragging a white woman into a dark alley outside a bar and raping her. The woman, who was known to be a local prostitute, had earlier been with a man whom she had picked up in the bar. He took off like a rabbit when the boys got physical. The evidence against the boys was that the woman had positively identified them as her attackers, and they all had signed written confessions in the precinct station house after their arrest. The defense counsel claimed that the police had beaten the boys to obtain their confessions. One of their mothers who had gone to the police station testified that she had heard her son crying, "Don't hit me again!" from another room where he was being interrogated. A District-employed nurse testified that the boys showed no marks of a beating when she examined them later. After listening to testimony from both sides for a week I believed the boys were guilty.

Our jury was composed of six whites and six blacks, and for two days our votes, taken every few hours, broke evenly on color lines. The woman had not gone to a doctor after the assault, and the act itself was impossible to prove. The six whites believed the boys were guilty of assault with intent to commit rape. The six blacks believed the boys were innocent. We appeared to be hopelessly deadlocked and headed for a hung jury. Then on the morning of our third day of deliberations a crack opened up in the solid black voting block.

One white woman juror in her thirties, who was a senior nurse in the Emergency Room at D.C. General Hospital, had been gently but firmly arguing the case that the boys were guilty. It appeared that a couple of the black jurors knew of her reputation for providing compassionate care to their people who had gone to the Emergency Room for treatment. We had chosen one of them to be our foreman, an elderly civil servant who resembled ex-Mayor David Dinkins of New York City. The foreman said he had thought hard about the trial when he had gone home the previous evening, and now advised his brothers and sisters on the jury to open their minds to consider the nurse's views. One or two at a time, the black members of the jury shifted over to a finding of guilt in the course of several more ballots, and we finally announced our unanimous verdict to the court: We found the defendants guilty of assault with intent to rape. This trial with its stark racial undercurrents might have led to explosive violence in the hot summer streets of Washington – if the local media had covered and reported the story. The Washington press, wisely and responsibly, did not.

My friend Bobby Cobb, who had come to Puerto Rico for our wedding, later established Cobb's de Puerto Rico – a small enterprise to raise and sell baby chicks, his family business in the U.S. I made a modest investment in the company and along with my old friend Austie Lyne became a director. The main dividend would be the annual board meetings in Puerto Rico, first held in March 1960, where our gang enjoyed a week of golf, beach action, and rum drinks in San Juan, St. Thomas, and St. Croix. As for business, I produced the annual budget on a paper napkin over breakfast in a restaurant one morning. The foreman's first name was Jesus, but that didn't help; profitable operations remained elusive. However, we had a lot of fun losing money, and even found another way – visiting the new gambling casinos in San Juan hotels.

Gambling had been a big tourist attraction in Havana before Castro's takeover, the government confiscation of private property, and the U.S. embargo on trade and tourism with Cuba. Puerto Rican hoteliers had then seized the moment to get into the business big time. The following year we repeated our wintertime safari to Puerto Rico for the annual Cobb's Chicks meeting. The Puerto Rican landscape and economy were visibly changing as old sugar plantations gave way to real estate developments and new golf courses. In a few years the whole San Juan–Santurce beachfront would be recast with new hotels, casinos, and condo towers attracting tourists who might otherwise have headed for Cuba, had it not been transformed into a poverty stricken communist state.

In our visits over the years to the island that was Buz's childhood home, we have witnessed the fluctuations in sentiment concerning Puerto Rico's political future. There appears to be little support for the independence movement despite the acts of violence of a few fanatic nationalists. Many believe that the present commonwealth status offers the best economic and social deal for Puerto Rico, and others seek full statehood for the island. We have been adding states and stars to Old Glory since 1776, and I won't argue that fifty is a nice round number so let's draw the line there. However, the stars in our current flag are very attractively aligned. If Puerto Rico did become a state, it's interesting to ponder how the fifty-first star would be injected into the field of blue to join its brothers. Well, I won't worry about it.

For our summer vacation in 1960 we started off with a bus tour from

Madrid through the Andalucia region of Spain – Seville, Gibraltar, Grenada, and Cordoba – marveling at the Alhambra, the magnificent Moorish palace and gardens in Grenada, and the splendid mosque in Cordoba. Then on to Rome, where we rented a Fiat and drove through the hill towns to Florence to revisit the city's art treasures. Moving right along via Verona and Lake Garda, we settled down in Venice for a few days at the Monaco and Grand Canal Hotel. We sipped coffee among the tourists and pigeons beneath the great Campanile in the Piazza de San Marco and watched a moonlit performance of "Othello" in the courtyard of the Doges' Palace, a truly dramatic setting. This time I went swimming at Lido Beach instead of in the Grand Canal. We checked out the magnificent mosaics in Ravenna on our return to Rome before starting the final leg of our journey.

Our trip followed a typical American tourist itinerary – fast paced and crammed with sights that must not be missed. The Parthenon and other Acropolis temples lit up at night were unforgettable. A four-day bus tour took us to famous places of ancient Greece, such as Olympia and Delphi, that schoolboys read about. A small cruise ship, the *Stella Maris*, took us to Crete, Rhodes, Ephesus, and through the Dardanelles to Istanbul. High points were the Palace of Knossos, seat of the Minoan civilization in Crete, and the Roman ruins of the town of Ephesus on the Turkish coast. (I went back to Ephesus on a cruise more than thirty years later, and the local guide was still proudly pointing out the remains of the city brothel that served the sailors from ships in port and the local dudes out for a night on the town.) Buz and I then cruised back to Athens via the charming sun-washed Greek isles of Delos and Mikonos.

I stayed on for another week to work on an IFC investment in a refrigerator factory in Athens, staying at the Grande Bretagne Hotel. The Grande Bretagne was the hostel long favored by celebrities in Athens, like Claridges in London or the Norfolk in Nairobi. I was in the lobby one morning when the elevator doors opened and out marched a squadron of bellhops carrying a mountain of matching Louis Vuitton luggage. Then came the queen herself, Elizabeth Taylor, the model of sumptuous movie star elegance. Following her was her husband of the moment, Eddie Fisher, another scrawny crooner with good pipes, but lacking Sinatra's charisma and commanding presence. Liz had more than enough for both of them as she directed her woebegone mate to take their yapping white poodle outside for a walk. Many years and several husbands later, Liz is still the queen.

23 Wall Street

After ten years in U.S. and international government agencies I decided that it was time to move on. J.P. Morgan had acquired the Guaranty Trust in New York, making the Morgan Guaranty Trust Company the fifth largest American bank. In 1961 Morgan, notoriously stingy with titles, offered me a job as a junior officer in the international division, and I accepted. I did not want to confine my career to investing in Third World countries and working in government institutions.

It was clear to me that it would take decades, indeed generations, for many less developed countries to become modern industrial nations with a strong middle class. International development banks and government foreign aid programs could give no more than a helping hand in raising these countries from poverty. The heavy lifting would have to be done by the citizens of these nations, where there was often a dearth of competent and honest leaders. Their task was to take the necessary steps to create a healthy investment climate to attract the huge amounts of private capital, domestic and foreign, needed to develop their economies.

Capital flight was a real problem. On a plane to Europe once I struck up a conversation with a Brazilian business executive. He told me he was flying to Zurich to visit his Swiss bankers. Each year he transferred most of his company's annual profits to his Swiss bank, which directed their investment in U.S. and European securities and properties on the Riviera. He left in Brazil only whatever sum was absolutely necessary to run the business. I naively observed that at least the taxes that he paid the government stayed in Brazil. His only reply was a knowing smile.

A Harvard classmate had invited me to speak at a luncheon meeting of the Harvard Club of Philadelphia about my work at the World Bank and IFC. My first talk to a large audience was a strikingly rookie performance. I recently reread my speech – too long and verbose; more of a lecture than a talk. Furthermore, there was no podium. I had a thick sheaf of papers in my hand, and when I finished reading each page, I placed it on the slowly mounting pile on the table before me. I covered the mission and modus operandi of the two international institutions, government foreign aid programs, the future economic implications of the world population explosion, and so on. I sensed that the audience was carefully measuring the diminishing supply of papers in my hand, and peeking at their watches from time to time.

In describing my grandfather's experience in dealing with Mexican loans and defaults in the twenties and thirties, I would write in *The*

Ambassador From Wall Street: "A major obstacle to economic growth in backward countries was the lack of competent leaders dedicated to improving the welfare of their burgeoning populations mired in peasant-class poverty. The ruling classes paid little heed to the concept of creating a society of economic opportunity for all citizens. The governments were often tantamount to army-backed dictatorships, with rampant corruption at all levels, and the small elite upper class that dominated agriculture and business was devoted to amassing and enjoying family wealth. Lamont was the forerunner of a parade of twentieth-century bankers who would tackle the frustrating problem of lending to Third World countries."

In my Philadelphia talk I should have emphasized that the greatest hindrance to economic progress was the widespread corruption throughout government from top officials and generals down to the cop on the beat in so many Third World countries. Developing countries must produce leaders who don't wink at the rule of law and who enter public service to improve the welfare of their people, and not simply to line their own pockets. With billions of people living in dire poverty this lack of good leadership continues to hold back progress in developing countries some fifty years after my World Bank days. The wide gulf between the have and have not nations of the world continues to spawn jealousy, hate, illegal immigration, and violence.

I looked forward to our new life – working on Wall Street and living in Laurel Hollow on the North Shore of Long Island, near Oyster Bay, Cold Spring Harbor, and the Sound. We knew the area well from visiting my parents in their country house there over many years. I had grown up living on the eleventh floor of an apartment building in the city. The elevator men were friendly fellows, but it was not the life I envisioned for my family. But first we would enjoy the summer break between jobs.

Bostonian Charlie Cabot was a good friend, a champion of worthy causes, and a fine skipper. After a foggy cruise Downeast aboard Charlie's beloved yawl *Echo*, Buz, Ted, and seven-year-old Ned departed the rock-bound coast of Maine for the Rocky Mountain scenery of Colorado. We started our grand tour of the national parks in Denver, with Disneyland as the carrot at the end of the stick to boost Ned's esprit during long days of desert driving.

After commiserating at Yampa with our ranching friends, Ginny and Tom Russell, over the low prices they received for their premium beef, we headed for the parks: Mesa Verde, home of the Pueblo cliff dwellers; Monument Valley, which has provided spectacular background scenery for so many Western movies that one could almost picture John Wayne driving a stagecoach coming around the bend; Grand Canyon, Bryce, and Zion – each unique in its natural grandeur. We are all-American tourists and had a great time watching the Hopi dances, climbing around Indian caves and canyon paths, and attending evening campfire sessions put on by the Park Rangers.

The night after viewing the serene desert beauty of Zion, we checked out the fleshpots of Las Vegas. The statuesque showgirls were lovely; the overweight women in tight shorts with blue-tinted hair playing the slot machines were not. Then on to Disneyland, the forerunner of its popular siblings in Orlando, Paris, and Tokyo and, like them, a joy for all ages.

The first order of business in Long Island was finding a new home. We bought a colonial style house on two acres in Laurel Hollow not far from my parents' weekend house. I commuted to work by taking the 7:40 train from Syosset, three miles away, to either Brooklyn or Penn Station, where I caught a subway to Wall Street. My commute took one and a half hours, one way, when everything was working right, which was often not the case. Delays were endemic for various reasons on the Long Island Rail Road. You could count on the track switches freezing in the winter and the air-conditioning malfunctioning in the summer. Governor Nelson Rockefeller declared that the L.I.R.R. would soon become the best commuter railroad in the world. That was laughable, although electrifying the line to provide direct service to New York without changing in Jamaica was a big step forward. At least on the train you could read the *New York Times* in comfort before reaching the office, assuming you weren't left standing in the aisle; it did sometimes take a bit of hustling to nail down a seat during rush hour. At the end of a long day commuters were understandably fatigued on the train ride home. The practice of meditation that involved mentally repeating your mantra was all the vogue for a while as an exercise to relieve the stress and strain of daily life and calm the inner self. I put myself into such a deep trance on the train one evening that I missed my Syosset stop and ended up in Huntington.

I was lucky. If I needed to work late, I could stay in town at my parents' apartment. Often I headed to the Harvard Club for a Vodka Gibson on the rocks followed by a steak sandwich before retiring uptown to 101 East 72nd Street. The fine old bar with its brass foot railing, Harvard sports posters, and crimson-jacketed bartenders was a convivial male bastion before the club opened it up to women. I was there one evening shortly after this politically correct breakthrough when a demure young lady came in for a drink. The male bantering ceased for a moment, as everyone eyed the latest arrival. Then my storytelling classmate Sumner chose to tell the raunchiest tale from his vast repertoire in his loudest voice. The girl proudly stood her ground, admirably upholding this significant feminist advance at The Harvard Club of New York City.

Given the commuting timetable starting with a 6:30 wake-up call, weekday social life was curtailed. The weekend was for fun and games. As a youngster I had observed that the parties given and attended by my parents, aunts and uncles, and their friends were merry affairs where the cocktails flowed freely among the social set that came of age during the Roaring Twenties. A generation later the guys still liked to unwind with a few drinks on the weekends after a week of business travel or just plain commuting three hours a day.

It all depends on your viewpoint. Once my mother observed to Paul Sheeline, an able, martini-loving young lawyer and family friend, that men who drank too much just didn't "measure up." (She must have forgotten Winston Churchill and General Ulysses S. Grant.) Our friend went on to become CEO of Intercontinental Hotels.

On another occasion after a round of golf at Pebble Beach with a Canadian golf pro and his wife, we adjourned to the bar for a couple of beers. Our golf talk turned to John Daly, and I observed that while he had great talent, he also had a drinking problem. "Ah, Ted, who hasn't?" said my companion, signaling the waitress for another round. He surely would have agreed with E. B. White that the most beautiful sound was "the tinkling of ice at twilight." I now follow the professional advice of the Harvard Medical School Health Letter that one or two glasses of wine a day may be beneficial to one's health. Surely, those Harvard doctors must have it right.

In the exuberant atmosphere of summertime cocktail parties I sometimes got carried away with my own wit: Joining a shy and demure lady friend approaching the bar, I declared, "Bartender, just make Mrs. Smith her regular – a double!" This questionable witticism backfired once when the lady in question, who appeared to be the sort to order a Perrier or glass of white wine, replied, "You've got that right. Make it a double Scotch on the rocks, with just a splash of water."

My favorite annual wingding was the Fourth of July dance at the Cold Spring Harbor Beach Club. The girls wore strapless or off-the-shoulder summer dresses displaying wide expanses of well-tanned backs and shoulders. Madras jackets and lime-green trousers decorated with little whales were popular among the men, perhaps inspired by the fact that Cold Spring Harbor was once a minor whaling port.

Everyone let their hair down at this annual summer rite. Under the big tent dancing to the fast-paced music of our local band leader, Ben Ludlow, became increasingly uninhibited – jitterbug, Latin, rock and roll, Watusi, and more. As the evening wore on, the wine flowed and decorum was discarded. Buttoned-down suburbanites started acting like Mardi Gras revelers on Bourbon Street. At first sheepishly, later with growing abandon, distinguished bankers and lawyers shed their jackets, loosened their ties, and joined the perspiring throng waving their arms and stomping and spinning around the dance floor. An alien from outer space would indeed have wondered about the strange customs of earthlings. What a degenerate, uncivilized society – an easy conquest, if worth the effort.

Laurel Hollow is a few miles away from the town of Oyster Bay, noteworthy as the hometown of President Theodore Roosevelt. His home, Sagamore Hill, now a national park, is just a few miles away – a popular tourist attraction where we often steer our guests. I have postulated that Teddy Roosevelt was the first famous person to grin enthusiastically for photographers, and everyone has been doing it happily ever since. One will not observe smiling faces on the gentlemen posing for photographs and portraits before Teddy. Leading businessmen, government officials, and other notables chose to present a solemn countenance. Only a famous celebrity could change this habit, and President Teddy Roosevelt with his ebullient, outgoing personality was the man. Of course, some folks grin more broadly than others: President Jimmy Carter clearly out-smiled President Calvin Coolidge. However, I have not seen any sign of a reversal back to those grim expressions of the nineteenth century.

Two big happenings now occurred in our family in short order. We adopted a beautiful baby girl, Helen, or Helena, as she now prefers, who joined our family in December 1961. The good Lord moves in mysterious ways. Buz gave birth to our daughter Camille, whom we nicknamed Kim, about a year later. So two little sisters joined older brother Ned in making a full and happy family life for the Lamonts of Laurel Hollow. Ned caught the school bus to East Woods School each morning as Dad raced off to catch the train to work.

J.P. Morgan was a commercial bank whose core business in the sixties was with corporations, governments, and other banks and institutions. Morgan had little consumer business. Developing good relations with top corporate officers was thus important in the bank's efforts to sign up substantial deposit accounts from corporations and other firms. It was not just good business. To be the number one bank for many of the world's top companies was a mark of prestige in business circles. It was my job, along with my colleagues, to market the bank's wares – offering all kinds of loans, credit lines, and a host of financial services to earn those deposit balances.

Some of our account-building practices now seem a bit overdone. We sent a letter to CEOs on the anniversary date of the opening of their company's account, telling them how much we valued our relationship with them. When an executive was promoted we always sent him a letter congratulating him on this well-deserved recognition of his outstanding ability. At cocktail parties and dinners for our clients (Morgan never used the word "customer") the Morgan men wore red carnations in the lapels of their Brooks Brothers suits to designate them as hosts. One friend left the bank because the task of "hustling deposits," as he put it, was distasteful.

By the same token, if you think Christmas has become too commer-cial you had better not be in the retail business. Maybe rocket scientists and brain surgeons don't have to sell their wares, but most folks – bankers, businessmen, politicians, and even professionals – do. With our salaries, benefits, and the prestigious Morgan imprimatur, we were much better off than Arthur Miller's Willy Loman, but we were still salesmen – energetically promoting Morgan's financial services as superior to those of our arch rivals, First National City and Chase.

My early years at Morgan were unexciting. I was first assigned to the U.S. Territory in the International Division, a group whose task was to advise American corporations about various aspects of their foreign operations – trade financing, Export-Import Bank loans, investment conditions and laws in foreign countries, overseas partners in joint ventures, and so forth. Sometimes I accompanied national district officers in calling on companies to discuss these subjects, mainly in the Chicago area. We still took an occasional passenger train to get around in the sixties. A stateroom and dining car dinner on The Twentieth Century Limited from Chicago was a classy way to return home from a business trip.

The uniform of the day for white-shoe Morgan bankers on the move was a gray Brooks Brothers suit, button-down shirt, and tie – sometimes one with regimental stripes replicating the design and colors of some military unit that had been co-opted by tie manufacturers. These "regimental" ties could get one in trouble. Once a fellow in a Montreal hotel lobby inquired about my service in the Royal Canadian Air Force. Perplexed at his question, I replied, "Why, none at all." He then informed me in a sharp tone of voice that I had no business wearing the official necktie of the RCAF. He was not mollified when I told him that my mother had bought the tie for me as a birthday present at Bloomingdale's just because she liked it.

Later I joined Morgan's two international subsidiaries, known as Edge Act companies. One invested in foreign banks, and the other invested in projects in developing countries and underwrote securities issues in Europe, a pioneering activity for American commercial banks at the time. A few trips – to Europe, Mexico City, Manila, Hong Kong, and Tokyo – added some spice to my regular duties at 23 Wall Street. Two memorable features of my visit to Tokyo were (1) room service massage, administered by pretty young masseuses who came to one's room, and (2) seeing the Imperial Palace where in 1927 Grandfather Thomas Lamont had received an imperial decoration from Emperor Hirohito, The Second Class Order of the Rising Sun With Double Rays. The militarists had not yet taken over, and the good guys were still running Japan then. Grandfather Lamont was given the award in recognition of his work in organizing a large international loan for Japan to finance reconstruction following the devastating earthquake of 1923.

Our office on the thirty-third floor of the Morgan building on Broad Street made for a long walk down the emergency stairs when the power blackout struck New York in 1965. In those days there were still plenty of smokers, and our group had just enough matches to light our way down the dark stairwell to the ground floor. The subways were out, but luckily a friend gave me a ride uptown in his car to my parents' building – where I climbed up eleven flights to their apartment. The city had been plunged into darkness, and all the traffic signals were out as we drove uptown, a definitely hazardous condition. But, in times of emergency New Yorkers are quick and resourceful in responding to the needs of the situation, and during the blackout ordinary citizens stepped into the streets at key intersections to direct the flow of traffic with hand signals, sometimes waving a rolled up newspaper. Furthermore, the drivers paid attention to their commands. Blackouts can also be very romantic. The Manhattan birth rate soared nine months later.

From time to time my bosses handed me speaking assignments that they didn't want. I addressed two hundred business delegates to the International Trade Conference at Millikin University in Decatur, Illinois. President William Blackie of Caterpillar Tractor and economics professor Charles Kindleberger of MIT headed the speakers' panel. It was pretty fast company for a bank assistant vice president, but I was ready to discuss my exciting topic, "Financial Considerations for Exporters to Europe and Manufacturers in Europe." Another time I spoke at a large dinner of The Bank Credit Associates of New York on "The Role of Edge Act Companies in the Expansion of U.S. Banks Overseas," and again had my audience on the edge of their seats.

Later when I was in charge of Morgan's Canadian business, I would be pressed into my most challenging speaking role. Every few years Morgan hosted a black-tie dinner at the Toronto Club for fifty or so Canadian executives – CEOs, bank presidents, corporate treasurers, and others. At the 1968 dinner John M. Meyer, Jr., Morgan's president, was to be the speaker of the evening, outlining the bank's views on international finance, the markets, the economic outlook, and so forth. International bankers were expected to be well informed and wise about these matters – part of the Wall Street mystique – and we were often questioned by clients, especially outside the U.S., seeking the latest Wall Street "take" on these issues. Often we brought our clients up to the Chart Room at 23 Wall Street, where a staff economist, using statistical exhibits and graphs projected on screens around the room, dazzled them with a high-tech briefing on the state of the global economy.

My colleague Tom Williams and I arrived the evening before the 1968 dinner to oversee the final arrangements the next day. The place cards at the dining room table were set out according to the seating plan, which carefully took into account each guest's rank, stature, and the importance of his company's account. We would be serving a great cabernet sauvignon with the Beef Wellington. There would be an oyster bar. Monte Cristo cigars from Cuba, brandy, and assorted liqueurs would be served after dinner. Later back at the hotel I relaxed in a tub; I had done my job and now could take it easy and enjoy the evening.

Around six o'clock the telephone in my room rang suddenly. I picked it up to receive some shocking news. John Meyer and Pat Patterson, Morgan's vice-chairman, were not coming to the dinner. Because of bad weather their flight to Toronto had been canceled, and I would have to pinch hit for John.

John had not prepared a written manuscript of his talk. He sketched out his ideas over the telephone as, wrapped in a towel, I scribbled notes furiously. Fortunately I kept up with current events in the U.S. and Canadian press and regularly read a variety of economic and financial publications, so I was not at a total loss. At the dinner I told the audience that I felt a little bit like George Plimpton being thrust suddenly into the role of an NFL quarterback, in *The Paper Lion*. At the end of my remarks Corporate Canada, recognizing my predicament, was very polite and gave me a nice hand.

Each December John Meyer wrote all of the bank officers to inform them of their new salaries and year-end bonuses. In my letter he added, "I wish you could do all my speeches." Assuming that was a compliment, why wasn't my bonus bigger? My reaction was not uncommon. I have yet to meet the person who believes that he is overpaid.

Time Out

L ife fell into a pleasant routine for our growing family. In the fall we sometimes took in a couple of Harvard football games, starting with the
Columbia game at Baker Field, where one sat down very carefully on the
splintery wooden benches in the old grandstands. Harvard usually beat
Columbia, which, as a big city college, found it tough to recruit good talent.

One Saturday we drove up to West Point with some friends to watch
Harvard play Army. Our seats in the stadium were in a lower row,
enabling us to observe up close a fascinating little drama. The Army mas-
cot, a big gray mule sporting a dress blanket emblazoned with a golden
A, had determined to go his own way on the track around the field and
was forcefully backing up toward the lower seats and players' bench. Two
cadet cheerleaders, a boy and a girl, tugged on his halter in vain to get him
to change direction. The girl then tried petting and sweet talk on the mule
– all to no avail. Mules are famous for their stubbornness. What to do?

Spectators in the lower rows and players on the bench were by now
stirring nervously as the mule continued on course toward their seats, its
polished hoofs flashing in the sun. The common analogy about something as powerful as "the kick of a mule" occurred to me and perhaps others. Fortunately a grizzled staff sergeant was nearby. He quickly appraised
the situation and gave the mule a mighty whack on its forehead with his
fist. The mule immediately reversed direction and docilely followed its
master out of the stadium. The two cheerleaders and future Army officers
grinned sheepishly, having learned the age-old lesson that to control a
mule one must first get its attention.

Until the 1990s when attendance at Harvard football games dropped
off, an ordinary alumnus who wanted tickets to the Yale game was seated
according to his class, which meant thirty years or so of viewing the action
from the end zone or close to it. During the early years I joined my father,
who was a member of the Harvard Corporation, the senior governing body,
in his seats on the fifty-yard line – very good duty. However, after he died I
had to scramble to avoid the end zone. I had assembled some modest
Harvard credentials over the years: I served on four Visiting Committees to
the University at different times; I was a steady, but not spectacular, con-
tributor to Harvard's never-ending campaigns to raise money; I participated
in the unwelcome task of raising money from my classmates. Most important, I had some good friends on the Harvard staff who came to my aid, and
we enjoyed good seats on the fifty for many years.

Then came the time, after my friends had retired, that I was forced to make a cold call on the Development Office to get decent seats for the Harvard–Yale game. After introducing myself, I reminded the staffer of past courtesies extended to me by his office and asked if he would be so kind as to get me two midfield seats for The Game. "Well, sir," the young man replied. "I'll be happy to arrange for an application form to be sent to you." Frustrated with this response, I started to argue the point, but then thought better of it. "You don't understand. . . . Oh, forget it." It was time to knock on another door.

The Harvard team's record against its traditional Ivy League rivals was a mixed bag. On some Saturday afternoons the Crimson team's frustrating performance left its loyal alumni in the stands little to cheer about. Still, there were some great moments. Both Harvard and Yale were undefeated going into The Game before a sold out Harvard Stadium in 1968. But the Yale team, starring quarterback Brian Dowling, who had never lost a game, and Calvin Hill, NFL Rookie of the Year one year later, was definitely favored to win.

As the game wound down to the final minute the Yalies, with a sixteen-point lead, were waving white handkerchiefs in their derisive gesture to an all but vanquished foe. Yet when the final gun sounded, the Harvard stands burst into delirious joy. In the closing forty-two seconds of play Harvard had miraculously scored sixteen points to tie the score at 29-29. Frank Champi, the back-up Crimson quarterback from Everett, a blue-collar suburb of Boston, had engineered the Harvard comeback. Following his second touchdown pass in that forty-two-second span of time, with the clock showing 00:00, Champi hit end Pete Varney in the two-point conversion pass that tied the game.

Our seats for this game were in the midfield section along with the families of the football players, including Champi's father, a modest middle-aged gentleman wearing a windbreaker. As the Harvard crowd went wild, Harvard big shots like President Nathan Pusey, University Overseers, professors, elderly alumni, and Boston Brahmins began pounding Mr. Champi on the back and congratulating him for having produced such a fine young man and son of Harvard. It was a memorable scene. "Harvard Beats Yale 29-29," trumpeted the *Harvard Crimson* later in headlining its story of Harvard's glorious comeback against its longtime foe.

Win or lose, the rousing performance of the Harvard marching band at halftime, especially in its rendition of "Wintergreen for President," was always stirring, and the social activity surrounding the games was a major attraction. Yale also had a grand musical tradition, the Whiffenpoofs, a student singing group and their alumni spinoffs, who often sang at parties. I have sometimes kidded aging Whiffenpoof songsters for singing about little lost lambs that go "Ba! Ba! Ba!," but they've never seemed amused. On Friday nights before the Yale game in New Haven we partied with our Connecticut pals – Holts, Browns, and Jewetts. Then on to the Yale Bowl where years later on a sunny November afternoon in 2001 three generations of Edward Lamonts watched Harvard sink Yale 35-23 to win the Ivy League championship and cap its first undefeated, un-tied season since 1913. In Cambridge we tailgated with friends outside Harvard Stadium before The Game, and afterwards joined the big party in the spacious indoor track cage, a great occasion to greet old pals. For graying alumni there is no finer tonic from the fountain of youth than watching your college team play in the stadium on a crisp autumn afternoon.

A promotion at the bank brought with it an increase in my annual vacation to five weeks, making a winter holiday feasible. Sometimes we sought sunshine and golf. In St. Croix Buz and I went snorkeling with our pals Linc and Truda Jewett off Buck Island. In Puerto Rico we showed young Ned his mother's old house on the Santurce beachfront, soon to give way to a condo high-rise. We enjoyed Nassau beaches and limbo dancing and beautiful Bermuda golf courses and Coral Beach Club tennis, but riding to and fro on motor bikes did not appeal. We made the first of several visits to Boca Grande, which had been Grandfather Lamont's favorite winter resort and where he had died in 1948. Boca Grande is a venerable Florida Gulf Coast resort with a large old-fashioned hotel, the Gasparilla Inn, whose interior décor features mounted sailfish of record-breaking size taken from the local waters. It was literally the last resort for aged Morgan bankers. By strange coincidence, Lamont's senior partner, J.P. Morgan, Jr. had passed away there in 1943.

Sometimes we went to sea. Our family's most perilous incident occurred when Ted, Buz, and Ned were sailing merrily along in a diminutive Sailfish way off the beach in the passage between St. Thomas and St. John's. Suddenly the rudder fell off and disappeared. In my mind's eye voracious Caribbean sharks and barracuda were circling our disabled craft, aiming to feast on my little family. I called on my Downeast seamanship skills, frantic paddling, and benign winds to save us, and they did. However, Caribbean winds are not always so friendly.

Another time we joined some friends on a cruise from Grenada to Martinique. Our vessel, the *Xebec*, was an ancient, mahogany-clad motor yacht ably manned by an English couple and two Island boys. Unfortunately, the fun of sightseeing, snorkeling, and sailfishing – plus smooth rum drinks and gourmet shipboard cuisine – was marred by waves big and rough enough to produce considerable discomfort and render shipmates Dale Cabot and Tommy Holt *hors de combat*. The rhythm of the vessel was steady rock and roll as we bucked the heavy seas on our northerly course. We were glad that the ocean on our next winter holiday cruise was far more placid. With Jesse and Helene Buzby we headed south on their cabin cruiser, from Nassau down through the Exuma cays. The many sandy isles, sometimes surrounding lovely blue lagoons, were largely uninhabited. Although the government charts lacked detail, the changing colors of the crystal clear water, depending on its depth, helped guide our navigation successfully through sandbars and coral outcroppings.

The water is dark and impenetrable off the coast of Maine, where we embarked on a cruise the following summer with son Ned, our friends Angus and Bobby McIntyre, and their son. We succeeded in navigating *The Frenchman*, an ancient gaff-rigged cutter that we had chartered out of Camden, clear of the rocky perils lurking throughout the islands of Penobscot Bay. However, our life at sea was not serene. Our only head collapsed completely – a serious blow to shipboard comfort and morale. We retreated to the boatyard nearby in Stonington for the necessary repairs.

The job would take a few hours, until after lunch, so Buz and I engaged a room and bath at a nearby motel to make use of the facilities and refresh ourselves. When we checked in the room clerk assumed that we would be spending the night. "Oh no," I replied. "We only need the room for a couple of hours." His eyebrows arched as he exchanged a knowing smile with the maid before handing us the room key.

Nor have all of our other sailing experiences been without mishap. I have run aground hard a couple of times. On the last day of a cruise in Bras d'Or Lake on Cape Breton Island we were headed for Baddeck with two other couples, the McIntyres and John and Ellie Perkins. I was below shaving when our forty-five-foot sloop ran up on a submerged reef. Our helmsman had cut inside the channel mark by a good twenty yards. In his defense, the navigational aids in the lake were short stakes, red and green, and not easy to spot.

We tried and failed to back off under power. Somewhat discouraged, we were pondering our next move when a large yawl motored up flying the burgee of the Cruising Club of America. Angus identified himself as a fellow member of the CCA and explained our predicament. We could row a line over to them so that using the engines of both boats we could disengage from the reef. We were completely shocked when the skipper of the yawl shook his head, waved good-bye, and went on his way. We were irate, especially Angus, normally a mild-mannered fellow. The other captain had ignored the time-honored tradition of aiding another vessel in distress. Furthermore, he had ignored a plea for assistance from a fellow CCA member.

Eventually by putting all our crew out on the main boom jutting out to starboard, we were able to rock our keel loose from the reef and back away safely. Back at the marina in Baddeck I ran into a fellow from the other boat whom I knew from Exeter.

"Ted," he said, "I was embarrassed when our skipper abandoned you guys. But he's the captain, and I'm only a guest."

"What was his big hurry, anyway?" I asked. "Oh," he replied, "He wanted to get to the bank before it closed." I reported this to Angus and he exploded all over again.

The mark of a good captain is how well he keeps his cool in the midst of an emergency; it is easy enough to be charming when things are going smoothly. I have cruised several times with my neighbor Bill Rothschild, who was a fine sailor and skipper. I was with him on one occasion when he and Bim Chandler brought Bill's yawl *Moonbeam* through a violent squall one night when we were crossing the Gulf of Maine, en route from Long Island to North Haven. Bill's calm amid this chaos was admirable. But you can't win them all.

One fall Buz and I joined the Rothschilds and friends in bringing *Moonbeam* part way down the Inland Waterway en route to Florida. The channel on the waterway, marked by buoys, easily silts up with shifting mud and sand despite regular dredging. Large sailboats with deep keels like *Moonbeam's* must proceed with caution, and we did. I was at the helm as we made our way south, under power, when I reported to Bill, about forty miles north of Charleston, that the fathometer showed that our mid-channel course was becoming shallower. The captain took the helm, muttering about getting "the feel of the channel" and altered our course toward the left-hand side of the waterway. Shortly afterwards we ran firmly aground, kicking up clouds of mud. Despite repeated attempts with our engine at full power, we could not dislodge ourselves.

Kedging is standard procedure to try to haul boats that have run aground back into safe water. Bill rowed out to mid-channel and dropped an anchor, with a balloon attached to mark its location. The plan was to winch in the anchor line from *Moonbeam* slow and steady to extricate the boat from the mud bank. Unfortunately, the balloon soon disappeared underwater so that we now had a submerged, unmarked anchor line stretching across much of the channel with a dozen or so big yachts, motor and sail, bearing down on us. Bill yelled out to the oncoming captains, warning them to stay clear of the line. It was a wild scene for a while. One boat, in avoiding the center of the narrow channel, went aground on the far side.

The kedging operation hadn't worked, so we pulled up the anchor and decided to relax as we awaited the incoming tide to lift us off in a few hours. But our troubles were not over. We had worked the engine very hard in attempting to dislodge *Moonbeam* – too hard. It had collapsed. So now we were floating around the narrow Inland Waterway without power – not a good situation. I hailed a teenager in a Boston Whaler, who towed us into a boatyard in McClellanville. *Moonbeam's* engine would require major surgery; she would not be going anywhere soon. Things can go wrong in many different ways on the water, even in calm seas and broad daylight.

Our family's winter sport was skiing, first with Ned, who was later joined by the girls. We usually headed up to Vermont – Big Bromley and Stratton in the Manchester area and Mt. Mansfield at Stowe. We stayed with Ted and Maru Brown and other hospitable friends or at congenial ski lodges like Johnny SeeSaws and Ten Acres. We started Helena skiing at Butternut Basin in the Berkshires, Kim a year later, and the kids quickly mastered the sport. Each time down those skis got closer together, and voilà: they were doing linked christies down the slope. You can learn a great deal about skiing by observing the form of skiers coming down the mountain as you take the chair lift ride to the top. If your goal is simply to ski for fun, skiing is not a difficult sport to master, ranking about the same as swimming or horseback riding.

Winters in Vermont can be very cold. Once I skied down Mt. Mansfield when the temperature was twenty-four degrees below zero. Not only were my hands and feet frozen, but even my eyelids froze together. I could barely see at the bottom as I raced into the base lodge to thaw out.

The two coldest resorts I have ever skied are Mont Tremblant, Quebec, and Mt. Whiteface at Lake Placid in the Adirondacks, noted for their absolutely frigid chair lift rides to the summit. On one winter weekend at the Tahawus Club in the Adirondacks I spent the whole day trying to start my car, which had frozen solid overnight in the fifty-below temperature. At the 1980 Winter Olympics in Lake Placid we could barely sit through the colorful opening ceremony because of the bitter cold. When the weather bureau announces the lowest temperatures around the country, Lake Placid and nearby Saranac Lake are often right up there with Bismarck, North Dakota.

During the sixties, before the advent of snowmaking, New England ski slopes were not only cold, but also not infrequently short of snow. So some years we headed west for a winter break – to Aspen, Sun Valley, and Vail – to enjoy the big mountain scenery, long runs, plenty of snow, sunny days, and benign temperatures. In Sun Valley we enjoyed an extra bonus – Jean Claude Killy and all the top racers competing in an international meet. We took our picnic lunches to a niche on Mt. Baldy and watched the world's greatest skiers race by down the mountain, often no more than a few yards away from us. A great racer must have super balance. Jean Claude won the competition, and Ned collected his autograph back at the Lodge.

Swimming, or more likely standing, in the well-heated big outdoor pool with the exuberant après-ski crowd was another feature of the Sun Valley scene. Before joining the pool gathering I took a sauna bath with a few other guys. After I had been baking a while, an older European fellow, clearly quite experienced in sauna protocol, pulled out a bundle of birch branches and offered to flagellate someone. I had heard that this was a traditional part of the exercise in Scandinavia, but it didn't appeal to me. The old guy went to work on the back of another young fellow, who asked to be hit "harder." I found the scene kind of weird and left them whipping away. Different strokes for different folks.

Our favorite ski resort was Vail – the ersatz alpine town at its base, the variety of trails, and especially the glorious snow bowls on the backside of the mountain. Vail was relatively easy to get to from Denver, although before the Eisenhower Tunnel was built we had some hairy drives up and over the Continental Divide in snowstorms, sometimes at night.

One time after skiing I joined the gang in the hotel hot tub. It was crowded and I could not avoid touching toes underwater with a shapely blonde in a bikini across from me. I smiled at her, shrugging my shoulders to indicate that I couldn't avoid the contact, and she smiled back. So I settled back and enjoyed life. After a while she got up and left the tub, and to my surprise, I was still making the same underwater contact. I had been playing footsie with an overweight middle-aged gentleman. I felt quite let down.

Sometimes we switched from the Rockies to the Alps. We skied Lech, Zurs, and St. Anton with Ted and Maru Brown and the kids one year, and Courcheval in the French Alps with Lansing and Ada Lamont another time. Originally we had planned to go to Val d'Isère but upon arriving in Geneva learned that the resort had been badly hit by avalanches. A score or so of students had been killed in a hotel that had been wiped out, the access roads were blocked by snow, and the French army was dropping food and medical supplies into the town by helicopter. I telephoned the hotel where we had reserved rooms and told Madame that because of the bad conditions we must cancel our reservations. "Mais non, Monsieur," she replied. "Ce n'est pas possible. I have zee deposit, and you must come. Conditions are excellent for skiing. La poudre est formidable." Madame was running true to form for tight-fisted French innkeepers. I told her that I had already heard that the snow was plentiful; deal with my travel agent; we weren't coming.

Courchevel was sunless. The light was flat, and it never stopped snowing. The upper lifts were closed, snowed under, and the skiing was tough. Just too much snow. The other guests at the hotel were French, and one night we all dined at the same long table. It was 1970, and the U.S. was hotly engaged in Vietnam, the former French colony where the French army had been defeated and driven out. A French fellow made a toast that included the phrase, "Merde aux Américains," grinning in our direction as he said it, and assuming that we didn't understand him. I was angry at the insult but let it pass, knowing that the U.S. military involvement in Vietnam was extremely unpopular in France. Still the vaunted French *politesse* was conspicuously absent that night.

We skied one day at nearby Mirabel, where slalom and downhill races were being held. The slalom course seemed straightforward; I decided to give it a shot. I got a good jump out of the starting gate and maneuvered the course without mishap. There were good strong skiers from all over

Europe on the mountain, so I didn't expect my run to rank very high. When I checked in after the race I was delighted and shocked to learn that I had come in second. A middle-aged banker on vacation beating all these hotshots? Incredible! "We will hand out the awards during cocktails at the hotel tonight," said the official." What hotel is that? "I asked. "Your hotel, sir. As you know, the races were held for the members of your group, The Ski Club of Atlanta, Georgia." I didn't show up.

Each weekend back home I looked forward to my regular men's doubles Saturday morning tennis match on the indoor courts at the Cove Neck Tennis Club, which I have enjoyed during the winter months, with changing personnel, ever since 1966. My desk at work then was in an inner room on the second floor of 23 Wall, a handsome desk that was located too close to its neighbor belonging to Sidney Butler, the vice president in charge of the Sterling Area. On Friday afternoons Sid telephoned around to confirm his tennis foursome for Saturday morning, conversations I could not help but overhear.

One Friday he was clearly having difficulty in rounding up his fourth: "Oh, you can't make it tomorrow, Bill. . . . I'm sorry you can't join us, John," and so forth. It was getting late when, after a half dozen or so calls failed to produce a player, Sid turned to me and said, "Ted, I was wondering if you might like to join our tennis game tomorrow at Cove Neck." I accepted, not revealing to my good friend that I knew that I was not his prime choice. I must have performed adequately because Sid invited me to become a member of his regular group.

Buz and I won the mixed doubles championship in paddle tennis one year at the Huntington Winter Club while our girls were figure skating and Ned was playing hockey on the Winter Club team. Come summer, the Cold Spring Harbor Beach Club was a great family gathering spot for tennis and swimming. I dabbled in golf at Piping Rock while Buz accumulated more trophies, following our strategy of labor specialization: Buz is the golfer, and I am the piano player.

More than any other sport golf can bring about sudden mood changes. Players are cheerful and chatty when they are striking the ball well, sinking long putts, and racking up pars and the occasional birdie. On the other hand look for grim demeanors and deep silence, except for under-the-breath muttering, from players who have sliced a few balls into the woods or tall grass with the ensuing double or triple bogies. I plead guilty.

Golf has its own collection of well-meaning compliments for those playing poorly. To someone who has just blasted his drive into the rough, "Wow, you really hit that one solid!" To a player whose hard putt slips past the hole for ten feet, "You almost had the perfect line!" To another who has suffered through a very bad round: "You really hit some very good shots today." I've heard them all. Too often at the end of a round when someone inquires about how I played, I've resorted to the conventional retort, "Oh, we really had a lot of fun out there today." And we did. For what an ecstatic moment it is when an impossibly long putt over an undulating green drops into the hole, or a well-hit drive soars and arches against the blue sky before dropping two hundred yards or so out in the middle of the fairway. Those are the fleeting moments that bring you back to play another day.

The game surely has a unique attraction off the links as well, inspiring far more stories, jokes, and books of all kinds than any other sport. I recall talking to George Plimpton at a party about choosing a title for his forthcoming book about his adventures in a couple of PGA tournaments. *The Bogey Man* was a very funny story. On the other hand, has anyone heard any good tennis jokes lately?

I never went hunting or fishing with my father; we were simply not a field and stream family. But I did go duck shooting one time with John Cowles, Jr., a fellow trustee of Exeter, who invited me to join him at the *Minneapolis Star and Tribune* shooting lodge, in the Minnesota lake country on the flyway from Canada. John Cowles, Sr., the midwestern newspaper owner, and his brother Mike, who published *Look* magazine, hosted the party which included a handful of corporate executives. My host supplied me with a shotgun and instructions and installed me early one frigid morning with another fellow in a duck blind bordering the lake. A flock of ducks finally flew over at great altitude, and I banged away. Amazingly one fell to the ground. My good-natured companion, noting my ineptitude at the sport, grinned broadly and observed that in fact I did not kill the duck: "It died from laughing."

On the final day, to ensure that everyone went home happy, the guides released a covey or so right at the edge of the field, flying toward the waiting hunters and eternity. It hardly seemed fair. When the guests departed on the corporate jet, they were given boxes containing dressed ducks packed in dry ice to bring home – appetizing hunting trophies for their loved ones.

When Ned was thirteen, in 1967, we departed from our North Haven summer vacation routine and took him to England and then on to Scotland to visit the land of his ancestors. In London we watched the "Trooping the Colours," the colorful military ceremony featuring Queen Elizabeth in a scarlet uniform riding sidesaddle on a compliant mare down the line of her guardsmen standing stiffly at attention. We visited Cambridge, where my father had spent a student year, and Sissinghurst, the lovely country house and gardens in Sussex of Sir Harold Nicolson, a former M.P., author, diarist, and husband of novelist V. Sackville West. As a ranking insider in London government and social circles, he had been well positioned to chronicle the life and culture of English upper classes in the final days of the British Empire. His published diaries contained an account of his weekend visit with my grandparents at Palisades – not altogether flattering to Grandmother, who was a poor "listener" in his opinion.

In Scotland Buz and I sprayed golf balls into the heather along the fairways at St. Andrews, Glen Eagles, and Turnberry. We searched in vain for the Loch Ness Monster. The Scottish biology professor who manned the observation station on the loch and scorned the appellation "monster" thought he had seen Nessie, a giant invertebrate sea worm, break the surface of the lake for a moment just a week before. He believed that the creatures had been breeding and lurking in the deepest part of the lake, which had once been connected to the North Sea, for many hundreds of years. They were trapped in the loch when an earthquake created a land barrier that blocked their exit to the ocean. The lake waters were very dark and the beasts rarely ventured to the surface. Scotland is also a leading source of UFO sightings. The legend of a monster inhabiting the lake has been so successful in attracting tourists to the region that a couple of American lakes now claim to harbor a mysterious underwater beast.

We three toured the places that I had visited thirty years before with my family – the little village of Luss on Loch Lomond and Ben Lomond, the mountain on the far shore. We climbed to the summit and looked down upon a magnificent view of the Highlands – sparkling lochs, shady glens, and purple-hued hills fading into the distant haze. Once again I explored the ruins of ill-fated Toward Castle near Dunoon, this time with Ned. The Lamonts were still a vibrant, though minor, clan after the Dunoon Massacre, and we attended their annual gathering for lunch in a country hotel in Ayrshire. The Lamonts from New York were warmly welcomed by our fellow clansmen and women attired in tartan kilts and skirts. Messages of greetings were read from Lamonts from all over, including the clan chieftain in Australia. We were well impressed by the clan's organization and esprit.

North of the Border

At age forty, I got a career shot in the arm: I was promoted to vice president and placed in charge of the bank's business in Canada, which included the Canadian banks and companies operating in the U.S. The assistant vice president for our unit was Tom Williams, an able, congenial, and very patient fellow in breaking me in. In 1966 we booked about $60 million in commitments and loans, roughly $350 million in current dollars, and a slightly smaller amount of deposits. Most of the leading Canadian corporations had accounts with Morgan, as they did with First National City and Chase. Our group was located in a spacious windowless room along with several other International Division units. Our dreary location had one distinct advantage – a door right behind my desk giving direct access to the 23 Wall Street offices of Morgan's top brass, led by President John M. Meyer, Jr. and Vice-Chairman Ellmore C. Patterson, who later became chairman and CEO.

Pat Patterson, as he was known to everyone, was not only very able. He was affable and friendly, certainly the most personable and popular Morgan chief for many years both before and after his leadership of the bank. Morgan's top ranks were often filled with Eastern establishment Ivy Leaguers. Pat, however, was a former All American football player from the University of Chicago who, while playing center, had gone head-to-head against President Jerry Ford when Ford was a center for Michigan. Pat and the President had a friendly reunion when Pat led a group of Wall Street bankers to the White House in 1975 to seek federal assistance for New York City, which was in the throes of one of its periodic financial crises. (Nevertheless, bailing out New York was not on the Administration's agenda. The *New York Post* characterized President Ford's response to New York's request as "Drop Dead!")

Pat had covered Canada earlier in his Morgan career. A board member of International Nickel and Canada Life, and several blue chip American companies, he was well known and well liked in Canadian business circles. It was tremendously helpful for the officer in charge of Morgan's Canadian business to have a senior officer so well connected in Canada and willing to assist in nurturing client relations. The door behind my desk led into a handsome reception area where the secretaries and junior officers spoke in hushed tones in deference to their high-ranking bosses occupying the adjoining offices. I often slipped through the door to Pat's office to arrange for him to host a lunch or dinner for Canadian clients, or join me in calling on them in Toronto or Montreal.

There were some great advantages to traveling with Pat: We flew first class, and we called on CEOs of Canada's leading companies and banks, who often fed us very well at lunches and dinners to welcome their popular visitor.

At the bank my promotion entitled me to eat lunch in the executive dining room, where everyone sat around a long oval table filling whatever seat was empty when they came into the room. It was a gregarious group (almost entirely men in the 1960s) as diners enthusiastically told their tales of financial transactions and amusing anecdotes. One new recruit with a real estate background said he knew he would enjoy banking, because he had "a well-developed sense of greed," an observation that evoked hearty laughter from his colleagues, although I suspect that some felt he may have crossed the line for a new Morgan officer. Other fellows would say things in ways that might lead you to believe they had important inside sources – "The word is that the Fed is going to lower the discount rate on Tuesday" – without disclosing that everything they said had come from an article they had read in *The Wall Street Journal* that morning.

The luncheon crowd was congenial. Nevertheless, every now and then I felt a powerful urge to get out of the building and stretch my legs, often heading for Battery Park or South Street Seaport to enjoy the splendid harbor and river views over a hamburger and Coke purchased from a street vendor.

In my visits to Montreal and Toronto every month or so, with occasional trips to Winnipeg, Calgary, and Vancouver, I called on our clients to make sure that they were satisfied with Morgan's handling of their accounts. Sometimes I had the unwelcome task of informing a company that their account was in overdraft or that they had to increase their deposit to compensate the bank fairly for the cost of various services. Canadian companies particularly objected to the bank's requirement that fifteen to twenty percent of loans remain on deposit, the so-called compensating balance practice of American banks at the time. Alcan, the giant aluminum company, complained bitterly that the Morgan Investment Department had sold a block of Alcan shares from the pension funds that it managed, and Canadian investment firm clients were clamoring for the Investment Department to direct more brokerage business to them. In these cases I explained that, following U.S. banking law, a Chinese Wall existed between the investment and commercial banking operations of the bank. Nowadays, after the disclosures of phony recommendations by brokers touting the stocks of their firm's underwriting clients, the need for the Chinese Wall between the underwriting and brokerage arms of investment banks is crystal clear.

I also called on non-client companies to sell them on the idea of opening an account with Morgan. For many businesses cold calls are hard going, but the Morgan name almost always opened the door for an appointment at the corporate treasurer level. While the bank provided a variety of services – merger and acquisition advice, pension fund management, foreign exchange, and so forth – my main focus was identifying good lending opportunities with our clients, employing a variety of credit lines and loans.

I covered a wide range of companies – banks, industrial and mining companies, utilities, finance and insurance companies, and more. In preparation for making six or seven calls a day including a business lunch when I was traveling, I reviewed each company's activities and its relations with Morgan – deposit balances, loan status, previous Morgan calls, gripes, key officers, and so forth. It was a real memory challenge, and often I resorted to a quick study of the company's annual report in the office building's lobby before boarding the elevator for my appointment.

While Toronto was a handsome city, bicultural Montreal, the capital of French-speaking Quebec, possessed a unique cosmopolitan charm. Château Champlain and the Ritz-Carlton were deluxe lodgings; Place Ville Marie, with its office towers and underground shopping complex and Metro links, was an I. M. Pei urban *tour de force* designed to cope with the harsh winter climate. Expo '67, with Buckminster Fuller's huge geodetic sphere serving as the American pavilion, was colorful and good fun. During the sixties the big Anglo-owned-business exodus to Toronto had not yet gathered a head of steam, a move that came later as Quebec separatists increasingly imposed their cultural and political agenda in Quebec. The separatist movement, based on Francophile emotion and intolerance of other cultures, has ebbed and flowed over the years, but never evaporated, even when Canada has been governed by French Canadian prime ministers. General Charles de Gaulle fanned the flames on a visit to Quebec when he shouted *"Viva Québec Libre!"* in a speech to a huge throng of cheering Quebecois. An independent Quebec completely defies political and economic logic. I doubt it will ever come to pass.

In my calls at the somewhat drab headquarters of two small French Canadian banks, I always indulged in a bit of small talk in French before changing over to English to talk business. The ambience was quite different at Montreal's Royal Bank of Canada and Bank of Montreal, led by well-tailored Anglo establishment types. Morgan callers received a warm welcome and often an excellent lunch in the executive dining room at these banks. We were their kind of people.

We reciprocated in New York, courting our clients with luncheons and dinners. We always took a table at the annual Canadian Society dinner, the big event of the year for Canadians in New York, and invited our clients for drinks in our hotel suite before dinner. It was a coup to have the Minister of Finance or some other high official drop by. Visiting the hospitality suites of the Canadian companies and banks and a round of table hopping at dinner was all part of the game. Bankers, like other professionals, like to gather at conventions to schmooze, play golf, and party – and even listen to a few speeches. They are usually better golfers than tennis players. At the Bankers Foreign Trade convention in Boca Raton I won a silver cup in a doubles tennis tournament and lost a modest bundle playing golf. My partner, a headstrong Morgan foreign exchange trader, kept pressing our opponents even though they clearly outclassed us.

The senior agent at one Canadian bank agency in New York, which had substantial balances at Morgan, was addicted to golf. We aimed to please our clients, but he expected too much. He wanted me to arrange for him to join the Piping Rock Club, my golf club on Long Island. His bank would pay for his initiation fee and dues. He would be leaving New York in another couple of years on a new assignment and would resign from the club. All in all, a pretty good deal for the club, he argued. John was a business acquaintance, no more, and I attempted to explain that Piping Rock was a family club, generally for nearby residents who had a number of friends among the membership. John was simply not a good fit, and I came to dread his telephone calls. Finally he was transferred out of town, and I could relax.

There were some welcome breaks from routine business travel. After our ski vacation in Europe one year I toured Morgan's European offices and called on subsidiaries of Canadian companies in Milan, Zurich, Frankfurt, and Paris. I flew to Berlin and joined a bus tour into East Berlin, passing through Checkpoint Charlie in the infamous wall. The contrast between drab and sullen East Berlin and prosperous and upbeat West Berlin was striking.

Field trips to the Canadian hinterland with groups of bankers and institutional investors to inspect projects exploiting Canada's rich natural resources were fun and fascinating. I flew to Labrador to view the site of the giant hydroelectric dam at Churchill Falls, from which Quebec Hydro would deliver power throughout the province. I visited Thompson, Manitoba, to check out the mining operations of International Nickel, for whom we were the lead banker, and the Athabasca tar sands near Fort William, where oil was extracted from huge deposits of petroleum-soaked sands.

Later I made two trips to the Northwest Territories with a side excursion to Alaska, staying in little mining towns – Kitimat, Flin Flom, White Horse, and Yellowknife – surrounded by the barren northern muskeg. These were really sight-seeing junkets, arranged for our edification and pleasure by Wood Gundy, the investment bank, and Trans Canada Pipelines; our group of financial types enjoyed themselves.

One night in Yellowknife on Great Slave Lake, we were drinking beer and singing in the hotel when two young Mounties knocked on the door and asked us to pipe down. They turned out to be fun-loving guys and stayed around for a drink. Soon one, a fine Irish tenor, was leading the group in "When Irish Eyes Are Smiling." Other diversions were golf at 1 a.m. in the "land of the midnight sun" and fishing for lake trout and river salmon.

From Anchorage we flew close to towering Mt. McKinley and the Brooks Range en route to Prudhoe Bay on the Arctic Ocean, the base of American oil drilling on the North Slope. The oil would be pumped south to the Alaskan port of Valdez through a new pipeline under construction. The construction crews successfully accomplished the Herculean task of building the pipeline over almost eight hundred miles of rugged Alaskan terrain. All reports indicate that the caribou herds are quite comfortable with the new line, which is designed with ramps to accommodate their seasonal migration.

From Prudhoe Bay we flew east into Canada and followed the McKenzie River south to the small town of Inuit, built entirely on the permafrost, which was the government's regional headquarters for research and exploration. The Eskimo inhabitants, who had abandoned their traditional lifestyle of hunting and fishing, did not take well to urban living. Many ended up on welfare, drowning their frustrations in alcohol. If it were decided to exploit the reserves of oil and gas off the Canadian Arctic shore, Trans Canada might want to build another pipeline south which would require large-scale financing.

The vastness and complete emptiness of the northern regions of Canada and Alaska that we flew over were striking. Permitting oil drilling on a small section of the huge Arctic National Wildlife Refuge seems an acceptable compromise with Mother Nature. However, creating a decidedly modest increase in domestic oil supplies ignores the main issue of curbing global warming with its increasing impact on our environment. America should take the necessary steps to reduce our burning of fossil fuels that release the harmful greenhouse gases. Many other industrial nations are ready to bite the bullet, and we should join them.

Morgan recruited and trained first-class secretaries. Mary Anne McEnerny, who stuck it out with me for about five years, as assistant officers came and went, was one of the best. Mary Anne was pert and pretty and blessed with good humor and an unflappable disposition. One Saturday afternoon we happily attended her wedding and reception at Bruno's-off-the-Boulevard, a wedding catering hall in Flushing. Bruno's produced three or four receptions that day, operating like an assembly line producing wedding parties. The final group probably did not enjoy the freshest chopped liver canapés. When we were seated at a couple of dozen round tables, there was a trumpet fanfare, and the band struck up some special "champagne" music. The red-coated waiters marched in, each carrying a magnum of champagne, and stationed themselves at the tables. At the musical climax they popped the corks in unison and with dramatic flourish poured the champagne. It was a great act reminding me of the antics of the restaurant waiter corps at Harmonia Gardens as Barbra Streisand belted out "Hello Dolly." It was a very good party.

I failed miserably at matchmaking on the domestic front. Apparently the job of nanny in the Lamont household during the sixties was a romantic assignment. First Inga, a pretty blond Swedish girl, became pregnant in our employ. We discussed the situation with her, and she agreed to stay on through our summer holiday in North Haven before leaving. There was some risk to this plan. If my mother found out Inga was expecting she would hit the roof, shocked that we would keep such a wanton girl looking after her adorable grandchildren. That summer Inga wore oversized loose sweaters even on the warmest days, and it worked. Her pending motherhood remained a secret among the three of us.

Our next nanny was Yvonne, a cheerful and responsible English girl who introduced us to the Beatles, and we became big fans of the most popular rock group of our times. When she decided to move on we were happy to hire her younger sister Maureen. Maureen was a fun-loving girl who began dating Joey, a young man who pumped gas at a local service station. Their romance blossomed, and one day she announced to us that she was expecting. She loved Joey very much, but he, unfortunately, didn't want to get married. Maybe I could call Joey and try to persuade him to marry her and give their baby a proper father? I agreed to help Maureen, although I did not relish the assignment. A few days later we telephoned Joey, and I presented the case for marrying the girl that he loved, Maureen.

I told Joey that Mrs. Lamont and I knew first hand what a marvelous girl Maureen was. She had looked after our kids with loving care and would be a wonderful mother of their children. She had a happy and cheerful personality and, by the way, she was a great cook.

"Joey, when I was your age I used to have a good time with girls and parties and all that stuff," I told him. "But after a while there comes a time, when you've found the right girl, to marry her, settle down, and raise a family of your own. Maureen would make a wonderful wife for you. She loves you very much, and I think you love her too."

"Gee, Mr. Lamont," replied Joey. "I think Maureen is a super girl. I couldn't bring myself to tell her, but I've been married before, and I'm not about to get married again soon." End of conversation. Maureen went home to England to give birth to her baby, whom she named Joseph, and the last that we heard from her she and little Joey were doing fine. Incidentally, in later life Buz and I did become successful matchmakers for two marriages of four good friends who have lived blissfully ever after.

Pro Bono
Publico

Long Island and New York City were now my home and workplace, and I was ready to engage in good works for my community and beyond. I had become a trustee of Phillips Exeter Academy in 1962, an appointment certainly influenced by legacy; both grandfather and father Lamont had served as president of the board of trustees. The Academy held three two-day meetings each year, as well as committee meetings in New York and Boston, often in the hotel at Logan Airport. The trustees, by and large, were a congenial group. Boston banker Warren Olmstead and former Amherst president Dr. Calvin Plimpton were both very able and merrymaking stalwarts during martini time at the Exeter Inn after a long day of meetings.

At first I contributed little more than backing the initiatives of my more experienced colleagues. Some of the board's moves were truly landmarks in the Academy's history. From its establishment in 1781 Exeter had required students to attend a church of their choice on Sundays. The board dropped this requirement. Since its founding Exeter had been a boys' school. Now the board decided that the time had come for Exeter to educate girls as well as boys. Both social and academic reasons led to this revolutionary change. Exeter would be a happier place to live; the importation of girls by train and bus for social events like concerts and dances had become tedious for everyone. Moreover, Exeter had to remain competitive with the many schools that had become coeducational in recent years, including Andover. Exeter today has a thousand students, about evenly divided between boys and girls, and coeducation has been a big success.

Soliciting gifts is a key task for school trustees, so I was soon raising funds for Exeter's latest capital campaign to pay for a menu of projects such as new buildings and scholarship aid. At fund-raising meetings we scrutinized lists of alumni "fat cats" and related data such as stockholdings disclosed in corporate proxy material, which would indicate their capacity for generous giving. Even the length of the Exonian's yacht and size of his house might be factored into the equation.

One of us then approached the target, armed with a glossy brochure, pledge card, and a well-prepared pitch ending with a request for a specific sum. Along with local assignments I joined Bob Kesler, Exeter's forthright vice principal, to bring the word to alumni in Texas, Arizona, and the West Coast. Bob, formerly a popular teacher and lacrosse coach, was fondly remembered by alumni and a very effective spokesman for Exeter on the creamed chicken lunch circuit. Morgan encouraged the participation of its employees in good works, and, furthermore, managed the Academy's endowment fund, an account that Grandfather Lamont had steered to the bank in the thirties. I also arranged a $3 million Morgan construction loan for the Academy to build the new buildings.

The campaign would fund the construction of two major buildings – a magnificent library designed by Louis Kahn and a multi-sport state-of-the-art gymnasium. When the gym architects presented their model for the first time to the trustees, we were startled. The design was a radical departure from conventional gymnasium buildings, including exterior steel girders supporting the structure. Cal Plimpton, clearly surprised, remarked that the building looked more like an airline terminal than a gym.

" Oh, Dr. Plimpton!" replied the architect smoothly. "That is a very discerning observation. Clearly the dynamics of young people engaged actively in different sports is indeed similar to the bustling activity at an airport on the ground and in the air." I thought that Cal suddenly looked quite pleased with himself, and, with the board's approval, the new gym was built according to the model.

Cal Plimpton was a wise and good-humored friend. One day he intervened to back our son Ned in a rather ticklish exchange over lunch with Exeter's principal, Dick Day. Dick was a dynamic leader who got things done. He did not flinch from breaking eggs to make an omelet. Sometimes Dick also appeared overly sensitive to criticism, real or perceived. Ned, then an Exeter student and president-elect of the school newspaper, *The Exonian*, had written an article highlighting a large cost overrun in the renovation of the principal's house. Ned's facts, gleaned from talks with the contractor and workers on the building site, were accurate, as I and the other trustees knew, although I had never discussed the subject with him.

The Exonian was the first to go public in reporting the significant unbudgeted expenses incurred in making over Principal Day's home, a plan that included several new amenities, fresh furnishings, and special purpose rooms, all quite appropriate for the house of the principal. Apparently Dick Day was concerned that readers of the article might infer that he had ordered up a new and fancy home costing far in excess of what was needed to house his family comfortably. Joining our table for lunch at the Inn he somewhat testily upbraided Ned for reporting the story and questioned its accuracy. I was startled and for the moment tongue-tied, but not Cal Plimpton: "Why Dick, I'm surprised at you! You should be proud of Ned for producing such a fine piece of investigative journalism."

Ned's nine-year-old sister Kim joined us at Exeter for his graduation a year later, and we all attended a reception at Principal Day's sparkling new home.

"Wow!" exclaimed Kim. "It's beautiful. How much did it cost?"

"Ask your brother," growled the principal. "He knows all about it."

In 1967 the trustees decided to permit Paramount Pictures to film "A Separate Peace" at Exeter, based on Exonian John Knowles's fine book. Student life was soon enlivened by the presence of the film crew shooting scenes about the campus. Many boys leapt at the chance to be in the movies by appearing as extras in the film. Ned declined, refusing to sacrifice his long locks to match the short teenage hair style of the forties when the story took place.

However, morning chapel, right after breakfast, was usually *not* an invigorating experience for students, and I didn't make it more exciting. Exeter trustees were invited at some point during their tenure to speak to the student body at morning chapel, and my turn came around. I believed that the time had come for Exeter to offer a basic economics course to the students, who were mature enough to understand the stories about the country's economic growth, cost of living, and so forth appearing regularly in the media. In my talk I discussed the conflict between international economic developments and a nation's ability to shape its own destiny, or the impact of, in current parlance, globalization. I suspect that my remarks glazed over many eyes, but the boys gave me a polite round of applause. Serving as a trustee of Exeter was a gratifying experience for me and good training for later board memberships in other organizations.

I went on the board of East Woods School in Oyster Bay Cove, the elementary school attended by our three children, and was also elected a trustee on the governing board of my home town, the Village of Laurel Hollow, population two thousand. In two separate tours of duty I served for seventeen years, winning my seat in eight elections, largely uncontested. We met one evening each month at the Village Town Hall near the town beach. My initial assignment was commissioner of beach and parks.

Everything was running smoothly until one summer day the police chief telephoned me to report a topless bathing suit incident at Laurel Hollow Beach. I was tempted to instruct the chief not to take any action until I could personally investigate the situation, but a few of the local mothers had already persuaded the sun-bathing young lady to cover up. Laurel Hollow would not compete with St. Tropez.

I later became Laurel Hollow's police commissioner, and for many years was the budget officer, working closely with Eleanor Foxen, the Village clerk. It was a constant battle to avoid raising taxes in the face of the ever-mounting personnel costs of the Village police force. Finally, we disbanded the force and turned law enforcement over to the Nassau County police, with significant savings for our taxpayers.

A range of issues came up for discussion at our Village meetings. Everyone was proud that the world-class biological research center, the Cold Spring Harbor Laboratory, headed by the Nobel Prize winning

Dr. James Watson, was located in our Village of Laurel Hollow. Jim Watson, who only looked like an absent-minded professor, was an ambitious empire builder who defended his projects vigorously at town meetings. Not surprisingly, there were ongoing town-gown tensions between the Village and the Lab. Was the ever-expanding Laboratory, which paid no taxes, compensating the Village fairly for police and other services? Was the Lab simply getting too big within the surroundings of our small residential community?

Usually our board decisions were unanimous, but not always. I was soundly defeated in my efforts to persuade my fellow trustees that installing Belgian paving blocks for curbing on the Village's public roads was inappropriate in our country setting.

It was interesting to observe participatory democracy evolve in the Village. In my early years as a trustee other residents rarely attended our board meetings, and only a handful of people showed up to vote for the mayor's handpicked slate of nominees at the annual elections. The residents were quite content to entrust the running of the Village to the mayor and the board.

This atmosphere changed with the passage of time as more and more families moved into new homes in Laurel Hollow, coming out from the city or built-up suburbs. Many of these new residents relished the opportunity to attend board meetings and voice their views and complaints to the mayor and trustees. Some were ambitious for political office, not content to docilely accept the establishment slate.

Certain proposals for new ordinances evoked heated debates. A very large crowd turned up when the board deliberated and passed a dog leash law. Older residents, used to their dogs running free, queried testily why the newcomers had moved to the country if they wanted to encumber their new community with all the urban constraints of their former life. The new ban on leaf and brush burning, mandated by the state for health as well as safety reasons, especially annoyed me. With a hose at the ready on a calm day, I had always enjoyed burning piles of autumn leaves and watching and smelling the smoke as it curled skyward. And, I got rid of the dead leaves and brush. Now we must pile them in huge combustible mounds in the woods. Our residents have continued to back our fundamental zoning laws, however, maintaining a residential community based on a two-acre minimum lot size, which preserve our country setting. Laurel Hollow is a delightful place to live.

In 1967 I became a member of the Visiting Committee to the Harvard University Library, a pleasant association that I would enjoy for twenty years. Harvard Visiting Committees examine the individual schools and departments of the university each year and then report their findings and recommendations to the Board of Overseers. There was a significant family connection: Grandfather Lamont had been the benefactor of the

Lamont Library, which had been serving Harvard undergraduates since 1948. The committee members came from a mix of backgrounds, including librarians from other institutions, widows of rich alumni, businessmen with a literary bent, book collectors, publishers, and authors. Barbara Tuchman, a committee member, generously advised me when I began writing *The Ambassador From Wall Street*.

The social high point of each Visiting Committee meeting was the elegant Friday night dinner, at which some erudite personage, often a distinguished professor or author, would speak on a literary or academic subject. It was always a sophisticated and classy evening. Harvard is clever at offering a range of events to attract the support of its diverse alumni. The cultural gap between a library dinner and a beer and lobster bash with my classmates at our twentieth class reunion at Chatham on the Cape was wide and deep. They were both great parties.

Fund-raising and donations are always high on the agenda of alumni participation in Harvard's affairs, and I contributed to the library's normal needs such as book acquisitions and preservation. However, I got a special kick out of meeting a library need that everyone else had ignored. Each year our committee interviewed a group of students to obtain their views about how well the library was serving their needs. Was it run in a user-friendly fashion? Each year the students complained that Lamont Library was far too noisy, a condition caused by the squeaking footsteps of people traversing the cork material covering the floors. The popularity of jogging shoes compounded the problem. New carpeting, however, had never made the cut in the library budget over the last twenty years. Nor had funding such an unglamorous project ever appealed to anyone else. I was happy to make the necessary contribution for new carpeting. Now the library is far more conducive to study and sleeping.

The most gratifying institutional relationship in my life has been serving as a member of the board of trustees of The Children's Aid Society, whose mission is to address the needs of poor children and families in New York, the first home for millions of immigrants. In 2003 the 150-year-old Society, the premier child and family welfare agency in the city, had an operating budget of $75 million and served about one hundred fifty thousand poor kids. When I was invited to join the board in 1964, the budget was about $4 million with a staff of around three hundred manning our neighborhood centers and summer camps. C.A.S. operated a group of core programs still going strong, such as foster care, adoption, homemaker services, medical screening, and after-school activities at our neighborhood centers. New programs have been designed periodically to meet special problems that emerge, such as drug abuse and the high incidence of teenage pregnancies. Children's Aid does a lot of specific things for kids. But as our social workers, camp counselors, coaches, teachers, and volunteers all know, our most important job is motivating the youngsters themselves to stay on the right track to enjoy the life that lies ahead for them.

I attended regular board and committee meetings over lunch at the Society's building on East Forty-fifth Street at which management, staff, and trustee committee chairpersons reported on the agency's operations and plans. Children's Aid had an excellent management team, led first by Victor Remer and later on by Phillip Coltoff. There are several areas where trustee expertise and input are absolutely essential – reviewing and approving budgets; the selection and compensation of the chief executive; the investment management of the charity's endowment; and fund-raising.

At the C.A.S. investment committee meetings I often pressed for a larger equity share in the endowment portfolio's asset mix. Over the long run the average annual total return on equities has surpassed the return on fixed income securities – by at least 5% during my lifetime. This is not surprising, because the economy has continued to grow, even with periodic cyclical recessions; a prolonged period of deep decline like the Great Depression seems unlikely to recur. However, our committee head in earlier years, an able and dedicated trustee, was very conservative – constantly alluding to the "uncertain times" that lay ahead. Any suggestion that we permit our investment managers to invest more than fifty percent of the portfolio in common stocks made him exceedingly nervous. He was far more comfortable in sacrificing the higher returns of stocks for the safety of government and corporate bonds. I sometimes mentioned that I had never viewed any future time as "certain" and without risk.

Trustees overseeing the investment of endowment funds of moderate size should maintain a well-diversified stock portfolio, and be wary of "The Field of Dreams" inhabited by dot-com companies and other high risk ventures. Generally fifty to seventy percent of the fund should be invested in equity securities, including moderate allocations of small company and international stocks and a hedge fund, with the remainder invested in fixed income securities. Big institutions with endowments in the billions like Harvard can afford to take on greater risks, but organizations with far more modest endowments should not. I have served on the investment committees of a half dozen non-profit organizations that have followed these investment guidelines. The committees' main job has been to set asset allocations, which we change according to the investment climate, and select and monitor the investment performance of outside investment managers. This balanced strategy has served the organizations well over the years.

Then there's the ubiquitous, never-ending job of fund-raising. Virtually every board member at one time or another has said, "I detest fund-raising." But it has to be done. Seeing the happy faces on poor kids as they played in our gyms or swam in our pools at summer camps was ample reward.

My candidate for the next president's image to be carved on the face of Mount Rushmore is that of Franklin D. Roosevelt. His leadership led the U.S., along with its allies, to victory in World War II. In domestic affairs he was the first president to introduce the notion that the government had a responsibility for the nation's economic well-being, and to provide a financial safety net for America's poor and elderly citizens during the Great Depression. He established programs that became part of our social fabric and have been added to by later administrations. The Children's Aid Society, even with its energetic and successful efforts to raise money from private donors, must rely on government funds for about half of its budget to provide services to poor children and families in New York, where about one out of three children lives in poverty. Today's minimum wage is not a living wage for a family, and nationwide the U.S. still has more children living below the official poverty level, proportionally, than many industrialized countries. This is a shameful condition for a great and powerful nation.

A Turn
in the Road

I continued to work with my father on various family matters. We converted a fund left by Grandfather Lamont for the Town of North Haven into a charitable foundation to provide college scholarships to North Haven high school graduates and fund other community projects. (My cousin, Charlie Cunningham, now heads the board of the foundation.) We negotiated an exchange of assets in a family investment holding company for shares in a Boston mutual fund, The State Street Investment Corporation, and I became a member of the board of directors.

State Street was founded and headed by Paul Cabot, my father's Harvard classmate and a colorful and delightful gentleman. Paul certainly did not fit the stereotype of a stuffy and proper Boston Brahmin, which by heritage he most certainly was. One magazine described him as a "Bohemian Brahmin." He was irrepressibly outgoing and made friends with everyone; his language was often salty, and he enjoyed the cocktail hour. He was also very shrewd, a pioneer in the mutual fund business when he started State Street in 1924, and treasurer of Harvard for many years when State Street managed the university's endowment. In a different setting I was a member of the crew on his yawl in several offshore races out of North Haven and part of the merry company when he broke open the bourbon on the run back to Pulpit Harbor, our home port, after the race.

There are many amusing tales about Paul Cabot. One time when he was attending a family wedding in Paris, he and his brother, wanting to play tennis, were introduced to an exclusive tennis club where they then encountered a major hurdle. The club pro informed them that the dress code for playing called for all-white attire, clothing that they had not brought with them and had no intention of buying. Then Paul had a stroke of genius. The Cabot brothers stripped down to their white boxer shorts and T-shirts and proceeded to play tennis without further ado.

Sons learn from the example of their fathers. I certainly did as I observed my dad in action over many years. Thomas S. Lamont was a kind and generous man with a gentle and subtle sense of humor, often marked by self-deprecating wit. He was devoted to his own family and all the members of the larger family circle. The summer gathering of the clan in North Haven was the perfect place to cement these bonds. He enjoyed dinner parties with friends and was good company. He once gave a solo performance before the Queen Mother of England, singing "We're Having a Heat Wave" with comic gestures at a New York dinner party given in her honor by his friend Ambassador Lewis Douglas. The Q.M. was heard to exclaim, "Ooh, isn't he splendid!"

Dad liked to compose poems and toasts to give at birthday parties, weddings, and other events. Here are a few lines from a toast that he gave at Mother's birthday party one year.

> *She's full of fight and dynamite, her spirits never sink.*
> *It's nice to marry vinegar and honey.*
> *Yes, my domestic weather's very sunny,*
> *The perfect mother, wife, and pal – to her I raise my drink.*

I also enjoyed celebrating such occasions with feeble poetry. "Why My Poetic License Was Revoked" is a verse from a little booklet of my poems.

> *I am the bard of Laurel Hollow.*
> *Sometimes my verse is tough to follow.*
> *Sometimes I find it very hard*
> *To be a clever rhyming bard.*
> *I generally scorn verse that's blank*
> *Though the gauge reads "low" on my think tank.*
> *And I'm not too proud to plagiarize*
> *If the line amuses and is of right size.*
> *We commemorate events that are key.*
> *Our aim is sincere. Our talent? You'll see.*

When our children were youngsters we all visited the grandparents every Christmas, as my parents had done when we were kids. Our family Christmas gathering with a tree and all the trimmings was a traditional American scene that has been rhapsodized for years in popular songs like "Home For the Holidays," "I'll Be Home For Christmas," and Irving Berlin's all-time favorite "White Christmas." At our Christmas dinners around the big dining room table adorned with holiday decorations Dad recited Eugene Field's "Just 'Fore Christmas" with dramatic flourish. I have continued the tradition.

TSL's political stance was moderate Republican, an increasingly rare breed. He voted for the candidate of his choice, rather than for the party, and his voting record included five Democratic presidential candidates. He was a ticket splitter. So am I, and by 2004 I had also voted for the Democratic candidate in five elections. A friend wrote about my father, "He was an unremitting foe of stuffiness in banking and everywhere." Another said, "He preferred for friends those whose shirts were not stuffed, who had a sense of humor, and ideas in their heads." So do I.

My father was conscientious and hardworking at his job and for his causes, especially Exeter and Harvard. He was prudent and not one to initiate bold new ventures. Yet he enlisted in the Army Air Force at age forty-three in 1942, received a Major's commission, and served as a procurement officer for the Eighth Air Force in London for two years. During his tour London was frequently bombed by the Luftwaffe, and suffered great casualties and much destruction. TSL had some close calls.

After D-Day he was stationed in Normandy for a few months until his discharge in October. I admired Dad's patriotism and courage. TSL retired as a vice chairman of J.P. Morgan & Co. when he reached retirement age in 1964. His friends and business associates respected his character and integrity. There was no more honest man on Wall Street, they all agreed, which is why what happened next was so unfair.

In April 1965, the Securities and Exchange Commission charged Thomas S. Lamont, a director of Texas Gulf Sulfur, and the Morgan Investment Department with profiting from insider trading in the shares of Texas Gulf, along with twelve other TGS officers and employees. TSL was shocked. He knew he had done nothing wrong and was embarrassed by the accusation. TSL and his Morgan colleagues cherished their well-deserved reputation for honest dealing. The *New York Times* story the next day gave him further reason to be angry and chagrined. His favorite newspaper had headlined his name in reporting the story of the SEC charges.

A year earlier, following the Texas Gulf Sulfur annual meeting, the company had announced at a press conference the discovery of a huge and rich deposit of copper and zinc at Timmons, Ontario. After the press conference reporters rushed to telephone in the news. The Merrill Lynch representative reported it over the firm's inter-office network. The *Wall Street Journal* report went out over the Dow Jones tape twenty minutes later. TSL telephoned Longstreet Hinton, head of Morgan's Investment Department, to watch for good news about Texas Gulf Sulfur on the tape, and Hinton, who had noticed earlier speculation in the stock based on rumors circulating in Canada about a major find, placed some orders to purchase TGS stock for several accounts managed by Morgan.

Before this incident the restrictions on insider trading had ended as soon as a company made a public disclosure of new information. Now, however, the SEC was attempting retroactively to establish a new rule lengthening the time for some undefined period after a public announcement before insiders could trade the stock. I attended my father's day in court when he took the witness stand and recounted his actions on that fateful day. At the conclusion of the trial Judge Dudley J. Bonsal exonerated TSL, ruling that after the news had been disclosed to the press, Lamont and the Morgan bank had been free to act. However, that was not the end of it. The SEC decided to appeal the verdict.

The whole affair had been a strain on my father. He already had a weakened heart, and now suffered increasingly from heart fibrillation. The doctors decided that he should undergo open heart surgery at

Manhattan's Columbia Presbyterian Hospital. The last words I said to him before his surgery were, "We love you. You're a tough guy and will pull through fine. I'll see you tomorrow." Dad never regained consciousness and died at the age of sixty-eight, much too soon. His death was a shock. The operation was supposed to cure him, and I had never dreamed that instead it might kill him. Open heart surgery was much less practiced and sophisticated in 1967 than nowadays.

My father was buried in the family plot in Brookside Cemetery in Englewood, New Jersey, alongside his parents. The premature death of Dad was a heavy blow that marked the beginning of a new passage in my life. I put together a book for family and friends to honor my father's memory and entitled the introductory chapter "T.S.L.: A Happy Man, A Useful Life."

Following TSL's death the SEC dropped their completely unjustified appeal. There have in fact always been plenty of legitimate targets for the SEC to go after without launching fishing expeditions. Unrestrained greed has been around forever. Consider the massive insider trading carried out by corporate executives and board members in recent years. While the insider gang at Enron presented a phony picture of their company's crumbling financial status to the outside world, they were bailing out big-time, all right under the nose of the SEC. The hitherto respected firm of Arthur Anderson, Enron's auditors, joined in spinning the web of deceit. The abusive use of stock options and exorbitant executive compensation were also a blow to the interests of public stockholders. The Enron story is a textbook of how the insiders can screw their employees, their stockholders, and the public at large.

Public confidence in the integrity of Olympic figure skating judges is desirable. But public confidence in the integrity of American business and financial markets is crucial – at home and abroad. The U.S.'s enormous current account deficit with foreign countries, stemming from the huge volume of goods that we import, is financed largely by capital flows provided by foreign investors and central banks. A sharp decrease in these investments in American securities and government debt would be a devastating blow to our financial markets and our entire economy. The recent widespread corporate deception and insider trading have been reminiscent of Wall Street during the Roaring Twenties before the Crash of 1929, with this big difference: In the twenties there were no SEC requirements for full disclosure, bans on insider trading, and other measures to protect investors that are in place today. I had always assumed that one learned the difference between right and wrong long before becoming a graduate student, but nowadays business schools find it necessary to offer courses in ethics.

The SEC's mission in all this is absolutely critical. So is the strict enforcement of corporate laws and fair and uniform accounting standards to protect investors. Accurate accounting means that debts are liabilities that must not be disguised and surreptitiously removed from the balance sheet à la Enron. Current expenses should be entered on income statements and not capitalized à la WorldCom. Cooking the books to jack up stock prices artificially is a crime, and heavy punishment should be imposed on those who try to deceive the public. When the accounting scandals were exposed, some CEOs claimed, as a defense, that they had concentrated on the "big picture" – planning future strategies – and paid little attention to financial reports, a stance, I will note, in marked contrast to the maritime tradition that a captain accepts responsibility for whatever misfortune his ship encounters.

Perhaps the most troublesome revelation of all in these debacles was that many corporate directors were asleep at the switch as company officers carried out these deceptive practices. Instead of serving as watchdog protecting the interests of stockholders, boards of directors went along docilely with management's explanations of questionable transactions without probing further. Furthermore, a number of directors on corporate boards have business relations with the company itself – a clear conflict of interest. Directors' compensation committees have also lavished inordinate remuneration on CEOs and top officers in the form of salaries, bonuses, stock options, perks, and severance pay – even when the companies were doing poorly. Professional athletes and rock stars, on the other hand, must perform well to command those big paydays.

According to an expert study in 2000, the compensation to CEOs in big American companies was on average more than five hundred times that of their hourly employees. In the United Kingdom the multiple was only twenty-five, and in other European countries, Canada, and Japan, it was even less. The U.S. gap in pay is way out of line. Clearly, too many directors have been in management's hip pocket.

Wall Street investment bankers also joined in granting special favors to CEOs with whom they did business – by giving them generous allocations of shares in initial public offerings, hot stocks in a bull market. In the Senate Finance Committee's 1933 investigation of stock market abuses the sharpest criticism of J.P. Morgan & Co.'s conduct in the booming market before the Crash was its practice of allocating hot IPO stocks from issues that it was underwriting to a "preferred list" of corporate executives, politicians, and other influential figures. The public viewed the practice with distaste then and still did seventy years later.

In 1971 I took a leave of absence from J.P. Morgan in order to take a government job in Washington that I found intriguing. My dad had volunteered for overseas duty in the Air Force at about the same age in World War II. Beyond patriotic motivation, I sensed that he had welcomed the opportunity for a break from his routine life as a banker to join a great adventure. I also felt a mid-career itch to do something new and different, having spent twenty years in international finance, and was ready for a new challenge. Buz and I had enjoyed our first tour in Washington where we still had some old friends. Public policy issues and being involved in them, if only on the fringes, had always attracted my attention, and government service, starting with my first job out of business school, appealed to me more than a banking career. The appointment that I was offered, deputy director of the Office of New Communities Development (ONCD) in the Department of Housing and Urban Development, captured my imagination.

HUD during the Nixon administration had launched a new program to help finance the building of whole new towns, to curb urban sprawl and create new growth centers away from congested areas. The program promoted high-quality, large-scale land-use planning, environmental sensitivity with ample open spaces, housing for families of different income levels, and commercial enterprises, schools, churches, and other public facilities all in one community. The secretary of HUD, George Romney, strongly backed the program.

Romney, a former president of American Motors and governor of Michigan, was greatly respected for his ability and unquestioned integrity. Under his leadership HUD made substantial advances in providing affordable housing nationwide without any hint of the political slush fund payoffs that plagued the Department later on. Romney was square-jawed handsome, friendly and easygoing with members of his staff – the kind of person who bought an extra candy bar for his assistant at the airport newsstand when we were traveling together. He was also straightforward in expressing himself – perhaps a little too much for his own good, some said. Pundits opined that he had fatally wounded his campaign to win the G.O.P. presidential nomination in 1968 when he declared that he had been "brainwashed" by the generals during his visit to Vietnam to appraise the progress of the American military campaign. It is exceedingly rare for politicians to admit publicly that they were wrong. Romney's stature and leadership were a big plus in my decision to sign up with HUD.

My credentials for a political appointment at the time were in satisfactory order. I was a registered Republican and, while not a megabucks donor, had modestly supported the Nixon–Agnew ticket in the 1968 election. I met with New York Senator Javits in the Capitol, and he backed my appointment. I believed that the Nixon Administration domestic programs were on the right track and indeed far more liberal than the right wing rhetoric emanating from conservative Republican politicians. I also trusted that President Nixon would find a way to end the U.S. military intervention in Vietnam, which increasingly appeared to be a strategic blunder of monumental and tragic proportions. In 1971, Watergate and its disgraceful aftermath involving the President still lay ahead.

Building New Towns

B ill Nicoson, a competent lawyer and key player in formulating the
New Communities legislation and regulations, was the director of the
Office of New Communities Development, and I was his ONCD Deputy.
We reported to assistant secretary Samuel Jackson, a savvy African-
American attorney with well-honed political instincts.

Sam was always aware of which developers were large donors to the
Republican party, while quickly declaring that applications would, of
course, be judged on their merits. Sam, who could be charming or crude,
depending on his game plan, spoke out especially forcefully on minority
rights issues. After all, HUD housing programs directly affected millions
of poor blacks in inner cities and rural areas around the country. Laura, a
young woman who was a junior staff attorney, once bravely reminded
him that the civil rights laws were designed to promote women's rights as
well as those of blacks. Sam sincerely aimed to lift up his people and all
poor folks in need of a helping hand. When I told him that I had once
worked for the World Bank, he responded, "That shows you care," with
an approving smile.

Sam was not subtle in revealing his ambition for his own advance-
ment. He once suggested to me that J.P. Morgan should appoint an able
black like himself to its board of directors, which was lily white at the
time, hinting that I could be the person to set this plan in motion.
(Clearly he had an exaggerated idea of my importance at the bank.) Sam
also had a good sense of humor and especially liked to kid the pretty
black secretaries at HUD: "If that boy friend of yours isn't taking good
care of you, you just let me know," he'd say with a wink. He was a firm
and able administrator at a time when it was not easy for a Republican
administration to recruit first-class African-American executives.

The best American new town model was nearby Columbia, located
between Washington and Baltimore, with a population of about sixty-five
thousand on some fourteen thousand acres. The founder/developer of
Columbia was James Rouse, who later masterminded Faneuil Hall
Marketplace in Boston, South Street Seaport in New York, and
Harborplace in Baltimore – popular and appealing developments in their
respective cities.

Jim Rouse was the dean of the new town movement in this country
and I was glad to get together with him to discuss HUD's New
Communities program. His vision of the role of cities as the vibrant centers of modern civilization and his ideas for invigorating urban life, were

154

inspiring. Residents of Rouse's Columbia enjoyed the lifestyle afforded by their new town, and Columbia was definitely a success as a well-designed place to live and work. For reasons and conditions largely beyond the control of management, however, the financial state of the development company had steadily deteriorated and now required large injections of new capital from the financial partner, Connecticut General.

Investment banks and long-term lending institutions would not assume the huge risk inherent in financing large-scale community developments with a fifteen to twenty year build-out. And yet the benefits of such well-planned development – economic as well as physical, social, and environmental – were significant compared to the small-scale, piecemeal subdivision sprawl spreading across the nation. Large-scale land acquisition, planning, and clustered development were far less costly than the conventional uncoordinated low-density growth accompanied by rapidly escalating land costs.

Hence the 1970 legislation was enacted enabling the government to guaranty loans to developers to help finance the development of new towns built in accord with conditions in the public interest imposed by HUD. Key provisions provided for sound land-use planning and a significant portion of affordable housing in the housing mix, usually in the twenty to twenty-five percent range, roughly matching the income profile of the region. The suburban new towns met a real need, as many poor families were locked in inner city slums, unable to follow the steady outflow of jobs and families to the suburbs across the country.

The amount of low and moderate income housing that HUD required, including rentals and apartments, was sometimes resisted by developers who preferred to build the more profitable upscale single-family residences. Nevertheless we held fast to this condition, which achieved an essential goal of HUD's mission.

I would later become a member of the board of the Regional Plan Association in New York; its planning is based on viewing the total metropolitan region as one social and economic unit. In a large sense the whole region is the real city, and more planning should be done on this regional scale. City and suburbs are inextricably bound at the hip.

The HUD-guaranteed loan funds, up to $50 million per project, were used by developers to acquire and develop land – installing water and sewer lines, access roads and so forth – to prepare it for sale for residential, commercial, and industrial use. During my tour of duty at HUD we approved loan guaranties for thirteen new towns whose estimated populations at completion ranged from twenty thousand to one hundred fifty thousand. Hundreds of applications flowed in from developers all over the country, and I visited many of them to inspect their new community sites and meet their development teams. I also explained our program in talks to civic groups and at real estate conferences in different cities around the country.

Visiting Morgan investment projects in the Philippines and a Morgan financed housing complex in Mishawaka, Indiana.

New Communities staff at HUD reviewing applications to help finance the construction of new towns.

Signing agreement to assist new town project of developer Floyd McKissick, 1973.

Jonathan, located in Chaska twenty-five miles southwest of Minneapolis, was the first new community approved by HUD. It was headed by Henry T. McKnight, a state senator and pillar of the Minneapolis community, and Jonathan was a first-class project to kick off HUD's New Communities program. Most of the HUD new towns were, like Jonathan, satellite communities to larger towns and cities. An exception was Soul City, developed by Floyd B. McKissick, the civil rights leader and former national director of the Congress of Racial Equality. Floyd was an easygoing person to work with and well liked at HUD. Soul City, fifty miles south of Raleigh-Durham, was a free-standing new community in North Carolina's "Black Belt," a poor rural area that blacks had been fleeing for years due to the lack of jobs. HUD approved Soul City despite recognizing that it was a high-risk experiment: To become a growth center it would need to attract industrial development and create new jobs, no easy task.

My personal favorite new town was Harbison, eight miles southwest of Columbia, South Carolina, noteworthy for its innovations, imaginative and fresh ideas more than thirty years ago. Each house had a cable television hookup; each had an advanced intra-community communications and emergency alarm system; there were pathways for walkers and joggers winding through the village with stations and equipment for simple outdoor fitness exercises. Developer Lester Gross became a good friend of mine, and later we attended conferences together in Budapest and Tehran of the International New Towns Congress, which he headed.

The developer of Roosevelt Island in the East River off Manhattan was the New York State Urban Development Corporation, headed by the prickly and colorful Ed Logue. Roosevelt Island is a popular pedestrians-only community connected to Manhattan by an aerial tramway. We had a lively debate at HUD about how to distribute the government-assisted low and moderate income housing. Housing facing the city and the setting sun behind the glorious Manhattan skyline would obviously command higher rents at market rates. From a strictly financial viewpoint, this was clearly the way to go. But should the town be segregated with all the poor folks living on the wrong side of the tracks staring at drab Long Island City and Queens? Was this enlightened public policy? Finally a compromise mix was agreed upon with some of the lower income tenants enjoying the magnificent views to the west.

There were a few lighter moments in this particular project. When the New Communities staff presented the Roosevelt Island proposal to our board of directors for approval, presenter Leonard Gordon, in explaining its location, hung a map of the area upside down. As Leonard, not quickly recognizing his goof, fumbled about looking for Roosevelt Island in the Hudson River, everyone present, led by Secretary Romney, enjoyed a good laugh.

Government officials enjoy foreign junkets from time to time, and my turn came in April 1972 when Buz and I spent a week in Paris, where I attended meetings as a member of the U.S. delegation to the Urban Environment Conference of the Organization for Economic Cooperation and Development. It is a lovely time of year to be in Paris with your girl friend. Stockholm and Helsinki were my next stops to inspect new towns near these cities.

The Swedish new town sites, linked by rapid transit to Stockholm, had been earmarked by the government many years earlier to accommodate the inevitable growth of the country's major city – a fine example of farsighted urban planning. Tapiola, on the Baltic coastline in Finland, blended attractively into its woodland setting. At the end of a long day my hosts, three Finnish officials, took me to dinner at a Helsinki restaurant. As was the custom in that part of the world, we exchanged toasts, washed down by belts of vodka – bottoms up. The Finns clearly enjoyed the ritual, and with no imminent closure apparent I was soon searching for a way to withdraw gracefully. Several ways of expressing American-Finnish friendship had already been covered, and I was racking my brain to come up with a fresh idea for a final toast to wrap things up. Then I remembered a bit of international banking history that might do the trick.

After World War I the U.S. made a few loans to assist the newly independent and struggling countries created at the Paris Peace Conference, including Finland. When the other European powers, mired in the Great Depression, canceled all their war and reconstruction debts owed to the U.S. in 1933, little Finland kept right on repaying her loan from the U.S. until it was completely retired. So my final toast in Helsinki that night was a salute to the Finnish people on behalf of the American government and all of our citizens, for repaying its loan at no small sacrifice when all the other European nations had renounced their debts to Uncle Sam. Americans admired Finland for honoring its commitment. We trusted Finland, and American bankers and investors had long memories when judging the creditworthiness of other countries as they considered new investment commitments. After a few approving nods and words from my hosts, I thanked them for their warm hospitality and suggested we call it a night; I had an early flight out in the morning.

There is a good deal of turnover in the political appointee echelons of any administration. Bill Nicoson resigned in April 1972, and I replaced him as director of ONCD. One day Sam Jackson invited me to lunch and told me that I was one of the persons that he was considering to replace his departing deputy assistant secretary for metropolitan development. I decided not to take the bait and react with enthusiasm. I got a kick out of heading my own office with its staff of sixty-five and the exciting mission of building new towns. The proposed new position involved overseeing a potpourri of housing and community grant programs. It was a horizontal move with no increase in salary. I had also watched the current deputy sitting around on too many evenings, waiting for Jackson to leave so he could feel free to go home. I liked Sam, but the job was not for me.

At the start of President Nixon's second term in 1973, Secretary Romney left and was replaced by James Lynn, who made a number of new appointments and organizational changes. In October our ONCD was reconstituted as the New Communities Administration within HUD, where there was a standard reaction to such moves: "HUD has never been organized, so how can it possibly be reorganized?" A new administrator, a real estate consultant of Hispanic background, replaced Sam Jackson as my boss, and I became the deputy administrator. A personnel officer told me that I was not offered the top post because they wanted a Hispanic to hold a senior position in the Department, although he may have said that simply to make me feel good.

Al, the new administrator, and I never hit it off well. I may have unwittingly contributed to our awkward relations by my remarks in a welcoming reception for him when I declared that the staff was proud of its accomplishments and aimed to show the new management how good we were in carrying out the program. I believe that I was well liked and respected by our staff of career Civil Service employees, who, when Mother died in 1972, had all chipped in to make an office contribution to The Children's Aid Society in her memory. Perhaps Al thought that their regard for me would undermine his personal direction of the office. He was wrong. I don't play games, and career government employees are quite accustomed to adjusting to the management style of their politically appointed bosses who come and go with some frequency.

The dour Al had another reason to hold a grudge against our office and me personally. Months before his appointment he had written offering his firm's services as a financial consultant, one of many such proposals that we regularly received from consultants. I saw no need to hire his firm and passed the letter on to our director of finance for his review. He agreed with me, but somehow the letter got lost in the system and we never replied to it. To Al this was a sign of sloppy administration, as he later told me. More importantly, we had rejected a profitable assignment that he wanted for his firm.

The growing strains in our relationship were soon apparent. Months before Al's arrival I had organized a briefing and tour for a Soviet delegation of urban specialists and given them a reception at my house; they in turn had invited me to attend an urban development conference in Moscow. When Al arrived, he cancelled my participation in the conference and attended it himself. Al then brought in two consultants whom he put in charge of the administration of the office; they were old cronies of his who added little to improving operations. However, as is often the case with a newly installed executive, Al wanted his own people around him and not the deputy administrator whom he had inherited, namely me. I invited him to join me for lunch a few times, and he declined without suggesting that we get together at another time.

Finally, he wrote me a memo, instructing me to support him energetically and visibly (which I thought I was already doing) and run the financial section, turning over all my administrative responsibilities to the consultants. I was already focusing heavily on the financial aspects of the projects that we were considering and the negotiation of our agreements with developers – the heart of the business. However, I was uncomfortable about my future relationship with Al and resigned a month later in March 1974. I had planned to return to Morgan before long, and this tawdry little episode of office politics spurred my planning to make the move. It was ironic that Al himself departed HUD just six months after me, when HUD decided to bring in a different executive and approach to managing the New Communities program.

As a going-away present the department presented me with a pleasant consulting assignment – writing a report on the British new towns movement which included a field trip to the U.K. Buz and I happily combined business with pleasure on our two-week visit in England. I toured three of Britain's new towns and interviewed a score or so of government officials. Upon my return I wrote HUD's definitive report on British new towns, which probably was read by fewer than half a dozen people before gathering dust on a shelf with all the other consultants' reports commissioned by HUD. There were in fact a few useful lessons for the U.S. government based on the British experience.

There was another reason for my sense that it was time to move on. Originally, I had welcomed the chance to join the Nixon administration because I believed that Richard Nixon was a fine President doing a good job in leading the nation in the right direction. Not high in the pecking order, I had met President Nixon only once at a social occasion at the White House. In the Clinton administration White House, hospitality to political donors in the form of coffees and sleepovers in the Lincoln bedroom attracted much media attention. Nixon employed another device – the Sunday morning prayer breakfast – which Buz and I were invited to attend one time during the 1972 presidential election campaign. Courteous, crew-cut Marines with razor-edge-crease trousers and black shoes polished to a high gloss ushered us into a large reception room where we joined a line of fifty or so guests waiting to greet the President. President Nixon was wearing his normal dark blue suit, white shirt, and conservative tie. His handshake was a bit limp as he commented on the beautiful weather and propelled me onward. While he was trying hard to appear relaxed and friendly, I got the distinct impression that he really wished he were somewhere else and doing something quite different from meeting a bunch of largely no-name supporters. However, he warmly greeted Debbie Reynolds, whose show was playing at the National Theatre; Norman Vincent Peale gave a fine upbeat sermon; a schoolboy choir sang hymns; and the fresh orange juice, coffee, and croissants were excellent.

Several years later Buz and I would attend a White House reception for Nixon's successor, President Gerald Ford. The contrast between the personalities of the two presidents was striking. After Ford welcomed everyone, he stepped down from the podium to mingle with guests and chatted amiably with Buz for a few minutes about Puerto Rico and his trips to the island.

Attendance at Sunday religious services is not always a reliable sign of virtue. By June 1974 they weren't holding prayer breakfasts at the White House, although some praying may have gone on. The White House cover-up of the Watergate break-in was steadily unraveling. In March seven former high administration officials, including Bob Haldeman, John Erlichman, and John Mitchell, had been indicted for conspiring to obstruct the Watergate investigation. President Nixon refused repeatedly to hand over the five hundred or so White House tapes to special prosecutor Leon Jaworski and the House Judiciary Committee, as they investigated the grounds for his impeachment.

They were circling the wagons at the White House, and morale in the executive branch, except for the most ardent political loyalists, was plummeting. Many felt that President Nixon's days were numbered. For me the bloom was off the rose, and, after I completed my British new towns study in June, it was time to go. In July the Supreme Court ordered Nixon to surrender the tapes, and the House Judiciary Committee approved three articles of impeachment. The tapes revealed that six days after the Watergate break-in President Nixon ordered the FBI to halt their investigation of the affair. They also disclosed the dark side of Richard Nixon – the devious plotting and crude language – and the public was shocked. Nixon resigned on August 9, 1974, and Gerald Ford was immediately sworn in as president.

While I was at HUD the New Communities board of directors met monthly to review the status of projects and act on the recommendations of the staff. Secretary Romney and his board took their duties seriously. Most of the members were top government officials with prior experience as private sector executives. One of them, John G. Heiman, was a senior vice president at E. M. Warburg Pincus & Co., the Wall Street investment bank, and I worked with him on a number of HUD projects. Yet despite a hard-working staff and board, by 1978, four years after my departure, all the HUD New Communities projects but one had defaulted on their loans – failing to make interest payments as they fell due. In some cases HUD provided refinancing and implemented work-out schemes. In others, HUD foreclosed on its mortgage and sold the property to a new developer. The good news is that thousands of families are living happily today in some of these same communities, despite the earlier financial setbacks. When the initial development company fails and is forced to give up the property, it is not unusual for the second or even the third developer to succeed in large community projects when the heavy front-end costs have already been paid and lots are ready for sale. However, HUD had to make the lenders whole on the defaulted loans and interest payments which, net of foreclosed property sales, ended up costing Uncle Sam some $200 million. What had gone wrong with this worthy government program to stimulate sensible new town development?

The federal role in assisting community developments was limited by statute to responding to the initiatives of private developers who chose the sites for their own projects. So HUD itself did not investigate and identify promising growth areas for new towns, relying instead on the judgement of developers to follow the three golden rules of real estate development – "Location, location, location!" After all, they were the experienced experts, often backed by leading citizens in their cities and states, and had spent substantial sums to put together their projects. Typically in their project presentation the development teams of architects, landscape planners, environmentalists, and others put on an impressive "dog and pony" show. If their proposal made the first cut, they worked with the HUD staff to prepare it for submission to our board for approval. As it turned out, however, many of the independent market surveys HUD required from developers missed the mark by a wide margin in their optimistic forecasts of regional growth and the timing and capture rate of new community projects.

For example, I had been intent on pushing ahead to grant a loan guaranty for Gananda, a new community project in farming country twelve miles east of Rochester, a town quite familiar to me. Several of Rochester's civic leaders were backers, and the Chase bank was providing some subordinate financing. The market consultant forecast a twenty-five percent increase in the demand for housing in the Rochester metro area in the seventies, and the project's cash flow projections were guided by this rosy forecast. The development team appeared serious and able, and I agreed with our staff that the project seemed promising. With my recommendation the New Communities board approved a $22 million loan guaranty for Gananda.

With hindsight we later realized that the market forecast was crazy. Rochester's two leading companies, Xerox and Kodak, both announced that they would not be expanding in Rochester, and the regional economy in that part of upstate New York was expected to be no better than flat in the foreseeable future. There was little demand for housing in the new Gananda development, which collapsed in a few years.

Looking back, it is clear that the cash equity investment that HUD required from approved developers was too low, given the cyclical nature of the real estate market. It takes deep pockets to ride out the bad times, and HUD developers, with one exception, didn't have them. The onset of the national economic slump starting in 1973 brought double digit inflation, soaring interest rates, and a collapse in demand for housing – the worst real estate recession since the Great Depression of the 1930s. Michael Spear, Columbia's general manager, stated, "Launching a new towns program in the early 1970s was like asking the Wright brothers to test their airplane in a hurricane and then concluding, when it crashed, that the invention did not work." The HUD New Community developers, just starting up and shouldering their heavy interest payments, property taxes, and other carrying charges, were especially vulnerable. One real estate expert estimated that a developer who borrowed $50 million at 8% would have to sell a thousand lots a year just to pay interest on his loan. That simply was not happening. High mortgage rates severely cut back building lot sales and home construction, price inflation sharply increased development costs, and increasing unemployment greatly reduced the number of potential homebuyers. The HUD new town start-ups, with no incoming revenue, were hit hard.

In the "misery loves company" department, HUD new towns were not alone in their financial floundering. Reston, Columbia, and other large-scale developments also suffered substantial financial losses during their early years, and needed large injections of fresh capital to survive. During the late sixties and early seventies unrealistic optimism had triggered massive investment in real estate development, as banks and other financial institutions rushed to finance apartment and office buildings, hotels, resorts, gated communities, and so forth.

Then the bubble burst. The over-building left empty buildings and other foundering construction projects strewn about the country and the banks loaded with bad loans. When I returned to J.P. Morgan in 1974, one of my assignments was arranging the disposal of properties acquired by Morgan after foreclosing on hundreds of millions of dollars of bad loans. And Morgan's losses were peanuts compared to those suffered by Citibank, Chase, and other large real estate lenders. Undoubtedly, many of the HUD New Community developers had been caught up in that same euphoric atmosphere about launching new projects, and we on the HUD staff, to our regret, had too readily accepted their glowing forecasts.

In 1975, the year after I left, HUD imposed a moratorium on accepting new applications and in 1983 officially terminated the program. The U.S. government's role in financing the building of new towns with enlightened social, environmental, and economic objectives was over. My final HUD assignment, the study of the British government's new towns program, highlighted the marked contrast between the approaches of the two governments. The U.S. government role was passive – designed to react to the initiatives of private developers in selecting sites and planning the projects that would have to conform to HUD's public policy objectives. The HUD loan guaranty produced the required large up-front financing, intended to jump-start the project and fuel its development until the community became self-sustaining. HUD was also supposed to steer other grants and housing subsidies to its new towns as they progressed, but overall budget constraints limited this form of assistance.

In Britain, on the other hand, the government selected the sites and planned the new towns in accord with its national growth planning strategy. Many were designed specifically to create new commercial and industrial centers to curb the draining of people and jobs to London and southeastern England. The new towns were basically run and totally financed by the government until they became self-sustaining, with the Treasury providing low interest loans of up to sixty years to plug the annual deficits. The British government felt a strong sense of commitment to the twenty-nine new towns it had started, and no new town had been abandoned since the start of the program in 1946; each was fully backed by the government in furtherance of its national growth plan. Clearly, the U.S. and U.K. governments had entirely differing philosophies regarding the central government's role in influencing the direction and quality of urban development.

There was, however, one bright star among the HUD new towns – The Woodlands, located on twenty-two thousand acres thirty miles north of Houston. The development company was owned by George P. Mitchell, a successful independent oil and gas producer. It was the largest of the HUD New Communities and generated many new jobs in the area. The Woodlands offered a good mix of housing for families of different incomes, attractive amenities like swimming pools and tennis courts, and a first-class golf course – later the site of an annual PGA golf tournament. In 1972, HUD guaranteed a $50 million loan for The Woodlands, which made all of its debt service payments promptly until the loan was retired. These days around sixty-five thousand people live in The Woodlands as did my friend Bradley Richardson, Jr. and his family for a few years. When he told me that The Woodlands was a great place to raise a family, I recalled with pride my role in financing the development of this popular and successful new town.

HUD's main mission – to increase the supply of affordable housing in communities across the nation – engaged me too, and I wrote a letter to the *New York Times* on one aspect of the subject.

"Federal subsidies for low income housing are indeed needed, but given the magnitude of this nationwide problem they can only be drops in the bucket. There has long been a wide and chronic gap between the money poor families can afford to pay and the money required to build decent minimal housing. New York City is a case in point: Planned new housing won't reach poor working or welfare families without expensive subsidies. The high and ever rising costs of housing construction must be brought down.

"Factory-built housing – modular units – offers a long range cure. Other capital consumer goods, such as automobiles, are produced at moderate prices for the lower end of the market, but the use of inexpensive manufactured housing in programs for the poor remains nominal. Expensive construction on site, which is favored by unions, prevails. Government has made half hearted attempts to promote the use of prefabricated housing, but there has been much foot dragging by all the players. Decent factory-built housing can be provided more cheaply and quickly to make a real impact on the tragic problem of the growing number of homeless."

Costly on-site, stick-built housing for those who can't afford it is a wasteful anachronism.

When I left HUD in 1974 the New Communities Administration group threw a farewell cocktail party for me at which I was the target of a poetic Roast. Here are a few lines by a staff member who had apparently felt somewhat neglected by his boss. His wit was far sharper than his poetry.

An era is ending at NCA:
Ted Lamont is departing; he's going his way.
Ted's tenure at HUD was at times rather rough.
He did the job with his tendency to be gruff.
His humor was dry and at times rather cutting.
All recipients knew into his business they were butting.
To say he was frugal would be the understatement of the year.
When asked to spend money he would quietly shed a tear.
For persons who phoned him he demanded their complete history.
There was really no reason; it will always be a mystery.
He loved talking to people connected with banks,
But to speak to researchers and others he muttered, "No thanks."
His memory was excellent, but extremely short.
He could never find his glasses, as his poor secretary was taught.
When passing him in the hall, he might mumble a greeting.
Usually his thoughts were on a just concluded meeting.
We all wish him the best in whatever he'll do.
Just don't forget NCA. We will certainly remember you.
If you need any help, just give us a call,
And wherever you go, relax, have a ball!

Fun and Games

During the three years of our second stay in Washington when I worked at HUD, we lived in a handsome house, on Tilden Street in Spring Valley, which I had purchased from brother Lansing in 1971. It had a spacious back yard, where our two girls and three collies could romp about, and a swimming pool. Eureka! No more scrounging around for a cool dip on sweltering Washington summer days.

It is a special blessing to have neighbors who become best friends. Frank and Lee Hawley and Charlie and Shirley Ames gave us a bang-up going away party when we left Long Island, and on Tilden Street we soon became good buddies with our new neighbors Dave and Stratton McKillop and John and Nancy Barnum. Dave was a former foreign service officer and ambassador; John was an attorney and under secretary of the Department of Transportation. Kim and Helena, both attending Potomac School (Ned was away at Exeter), enjoyed the next-door-neighbor lifestyle on Tilden Street, where they had playmates up and down the block. So did we, with whom we picnicked and partied – once too exuberantly.

One evening after dinner at the Barnums' house, John, who enthused over the French way of life, insisted that we cap the evening's wine consumption with a shot of "Marc," a fiery raw applejack that Brittany peasants downed to ignite their engines in the morning. It was horrible stuff, more suitable for starting an outboard motor. The night was hot and humid, and everyone soon agreed that a cool plunge in my back yard pool was a capital idea. Racing to pick up wet towels and clean up around the pool before the gang arrived, I slipped and fell heavily on some concrete curbing. The next day, as I stretched for an overhead in my morning tennis game, sharp pain shot through my rib cage. My fall had fractured a rib. Thereafter, I skipped the after-dinner liqueurs.

Mother died suddenly of a stroke in November, 1972 – much too soon – at the age of seventy-one. For years she had been surrounded by her children and grandchildren on their North Haven vacations at Sky Farm. She lived in the Big House, as everyone called it, the center of a cluster of extended wings and cottages where the next generation and their families lived. Mother was the matriarch of the clan and sometimes frustrated at her waning control over the lifestyles of her children. Yet cultural differences between the old and young are part of life; not all oldsters have rushed to become computer experts. In Mother's era wailing children had been whisked out of sight and hearing by Nanny. Now, "the young" and their teenage baby-sitters seemed to treat such eruptions so casually. Also, whoever heard of bringing dogs on a picnic? "Nini" was adored by her grandchildren and her death left a big void in our lives.

One winter holiday, instead of taking the gang skiing in Vermont or Colorado, I chartered a boat and captain for a family cruise in the Virgin Islands. The *Norseman* was a big green yawl manned by Captain Jerry and two girl friends. The weather was great, the beaches were lovely, and the New Year's Eve party at Virgin Gorda was joyful. The downside was that Captain Jerry, an ex-Navy Chief Petty Officer and control freak, insisted on doing everything himself, which did not include hoisting the mainsail. The big jib was good enough for the tourists. His daytime sour mood was enlivened by a couple of drinks at anchor in the evenings, prompting him to tell some of his crudest jokes. I'm told that there are some very congenial professional captains in the Caribbean, but I decided then and there to charter bare boat in the future and be my own skipper, or share the job with a friend.

Sailors can generally count on benign weather and good winds in these waters. There are plenty of good anchorages with clear aquamarine water and palm trees waving in the breeze over sparkling white beaches. Some years later Buz and I took Ned and his wife Annie, and Kim and her boy friend (and husband-to-be) Nick Burlingham, on another Virgin Islands cruise, sailing in tandem with the Buzby clan whose boat was skippered by brother-in-law Scott, a veteran Caribbean sailor. The highlight was a race between our two vessels up Sir Francis Drake Passage, and, with some satisfaction, I am pleased to report that we won.

We have cruised in the Caribbean with our friends Dave and Betsy Clark twice, the last time sailing from St. Vincent's south via Mustique and Union Island in the Grenadines under a blazing Caribbean sun. We observed a fascinating social phenomenon on this cruise. On many of the other cruising boats in the area, which often carried European flags, the girls went topless. Dave and I kept our binoculars at the ready. This was definitely our kind of bird watching. We then joined the many cruising vessels gathered at Horseshoe Cay in the Grenadines for the superb snorkeling and skin diving. Gazing down through my face mask at the multi-colored tropical fish, I popped my head over a coral reef to behold a magnificent sight – a topless, fully endowed, dynamite blonde just a few yards away swimming toward me. Wow! Could it be Dagmar from the Swedish sloop anchored nearby? I smiled and waved and she smiled back, I think. Just one of life's chance encounters, brief and pleasant to recall.

During one summer holiday we embarked on a new venture – dude ranching in the Grand Tetons. Buz and I had spent most of our summer vacations with our kids in North Haven, as had my parents and grand-parents before me. The preferred family choice in the summertime was seacoast and islands, not mountains and lakes. However, we felt it would be a good new experience for our girls to sample western ranch life (Ned had a summer job) and chose Trail Creek, a guest ranch in Jackson Hole.

Trail Creek was a first-class operation headed by Betty Woolsley, a former U.S. Olympic team skier. The mountain trail rides, rodeos, and pack trips were great fun, but there was one drawback. For me horseback riding was plain vanilla – unexciting, mildly enjoyable, and easy to swallow. Buz, however, suffered acute physical discomfort and stiffness after hours in the saddle, a recurring malady on each ride. A generation later we took our children and grandchildren to the Tanque Verde ranch in the dry cactus and desert country outside of Tucson and discovered that son Ned, an active athlete and marathon runner in his forties, had inherited his mother's curious anatomical flaw causing pain and suffering from horseback riding. Apparently the Buzby horseback riding affliction has not carried over into the next generation. Our grandchildren took to riding like ducks to water.

The twenty-fifth class reunion has long been a momentous celebration for Harvard alumni. My twenty-fifth in 1973 offered a smorgasbord of fun and games – golf and tennis tournaments, cocktail parties, a dinner dance, an evening at the Boston Pops, and the climactic parade of reunion classes to the pageantry-filled commencement exercises, where the class gift to the college was announced. By tradition it was expected to be the largest of any reunion class that year and caused a slight embarrassment if it did not surpass the sum donated by the previous twenty-fifth reunion class. Buz and I stayed with old pals and their wives in Eliot House, where our band of brothers had merrily resided a quarter of a century earlier. Some of the ladies, not turned on by spousal nostalgia, found the bare bones quarters sorely lacking in amenities.

The twenty-fifth reunion is also the occasion to review the career report cards of your fellow classmates, as recorded in the Class Report. Tony Lewis, the *New York Times* columnist, and George Plimpton, whose amusing books described his cameo appearances in professional sports and other unlikely endeavors, were our two high-profile achievers in attendance. Our classmate New York Senator Robert Kennedy, a presidential candidate in 1968, had been tragically killed by an assassin after winning the California Democratic primary that year.

According to the class poll, former President John F. Kennedy was the most admired public figure of the last twenty years. Yet fifty-three percent of the class had voted for Richard Nixon over George McGovern just the year before. I voted with the majority of the class on several key issues of public policy. Our poll revealed that seventy-three percent of our class believed that the United States should not have become militarily involved in Vietnam, and eighty-three percent of us favored tougher federal gun control laws and freedom of choice for women.

I have attended a number of Harvard commencements, sometimes note-worthy for significant speakers and speeches. Once I was a Marshal, attired in top hat and cutaway, assigned to usher and oversee a section of the large audience assembled in the big open-air amphitheatre between Memorial Church and Widener Library. Marshals were equipped with little white batons decorated with crimson ribbons, for what purpose I had no idea.

The proceedings progressed smoothly to the time for President Derek Bok to award the honorary degrees. The Shah of Iran, the most illustrious person scheduled to receive a degree that year, stepped forward and the Chief Marshal began to read the citation extolling the Shah's "enlightened leadership" of his nation and so forth. Suddenly, all hell broke loose in my section of the assembly. Dozens of wild-eyed Iranian students came rac-ing down the aisle where I was stationed, waving their arms and scream-ing "Down with the Shah!" I, with my little baton, was apparently the only official between this angry mob and the leader of Iran and the other startled dignitaries on the podium. The students paid no heed to my commands to halt as they rushed by. Fortunately, they were more noisy than aggressive, and veered off before reaching the podium into a side aisle and the arms of the Cambridge police. The ceremony proceeded and the Shah received his honorary degree without further interruption.

I had read from time to time about the lavish lifestyle of the Shah of Iran and his family in St. Moritz, the Riviera, and elsewhere, but thought no more about him until four years later when I visited Tehran for an urban planning conference. The economic divide between the high-living royals and their upper class cronies and the rest of the population was evident as we traveled about. The newspapers trumpeted praise over the accomplishments of the Shah and his regime with no hint of dissent, apparently a well-controlled press.

However, the Shah's acclaimed steps to modernize and westernize Iran had alienated the fundamentalist Muslim clerics. There had been street demonstrations and rumors of revolutionary plots brewing in the bazaars. A little more than a year after our visit the Shah's government was over-thrown, and he was forced to flee. The U.S.-hating Ayatollah Khomeini took over, and an angry crowd of Iranian students seized fifty-five American Embassy personnel and held them hostage. Had some of the stu-dents who charged down my aisle at the Harvard commencement returned home to become revolutionary activists in Iran? Maybe.

Over the years George Plimpton returned to several of our Harvard class reunions, and at our fiftieth he was as witty as ever. One evening the class attended a concert at the Boston Pops, and there was George, a back row member of the orchestra playing the triangle. He did not see much action, but when his moment came, he struck the instrument with authority. Later he gave a short talk about the challenge one faced in playing the triangle well. The instrument was by no means as simple to play as it appeared. For example, one must be careful not to drop the small baton at the crucial moment in the score calling for its ringing tone.

Based on our responses to the fifty-fifth reunion questionnaire, over the last decade our class had bucked the conventional belief that people become more conservative in their views as they grow older. On key political and social questions we had taken a more centrist or liberal viewpoint. Two thirds of the respondents had voted for Al Gore in the 2000 election. (Maybe Gore got extra credit for having gone to Harvard and roomed with Tommy Lee Jones.) Most of us supported the U.S. military action in Afghanistan in response to 9/11, but were opposed to the unilateral invasion of Iraq and concerned about the erosion of civil liberties led by Attorney General Ashcroft. Most of us were worried about the general tenor of our foreign relations. We believed we should work through the United Nations in preventing aggression around the world, while recognizing that every country has the right to defend itself when threatened by imminent attack. An overwhelming ninety-one percent believed that we should end the Cuban trade embargo.

Many feared the social consequences of the widening disparity of income among Americans, and were dismayed at the large number of Americans without health insurance and the poor performance of so many public schools in educating our children. Sixty-nine percent opposed the Bush tax cuts. A surprising fifty-eight percent favored the legalization of marijuana, up from thirty-eight percent twenty-five years earlier. I would only support the legal use of marijuana when prescribed by doctors for medical use. On the other issues I agreed with the mainstream views of my classmates.

A nice line I heard at one Harvard commencement was delivered by Father Hesburgh of Notre Dame, the chief speaker that year. Harvard is the best endowed university in the world, thanks to well-organized and persistent fund-raising campaigns and the generosity of affluent alumni. As the heavens opened up and rain came pouring down on the huge throng assembled outdoors in the amphitheatre to observe the exercises, Father Hesburgh quipped, "I have always heard that Harvard knew how to soak the rich."

In 1974 when Buz and I ended our second stay in Washington we returned to Long Island and moved into my mother's old home in Laurel Hollow, not far from where we had lived earlier. Back home again our girls attended East Woods School, Ned was at Harvard, and I was commuting once again to J.P. Morgan at 23 Wall Street. I had decided to switch from international banking to another job that would make use of my experience at HUD.

The Reckless
Lenders

My new position at the bank was president of Morgan Community Development Corporation, a subsidiary financing the construction of apartments for low or moderate income tenants in buildings ranging from high-rises to attached town houses. Most were in the Midwest, where my favorite developer was Tom Brademas in Mishawaka, Indiana. We invested in three of his projects which were part of a community center with shops, restaurants, and a theatre in reclaimed buildings on the site of an old brewery.

Morgan provided equity financing under federal programs offering tax incentives to encourage investments in affordable housing. Two of our investments were in New York City – one in a housing development in the South Bronx, the other in Bedford Stuyvesant in Brooklyn. I felt a bit lonely returning on the subway to Manhattan after inspecting our project in BedStuy. Sitting in my Brooks Brothers suit and clutching my brown leather attaché case, I became the object of icy scrutiny. I was the only Caucasian in sight during several stops on the crowded train, and felt mildly relieved when a Puerto Rican fellow finally boarded our car. Street crimes were a good deal more common in the city in those days before the Giuliani era of law and order.

My experience in financing housing and urban development led to participation in the work of related organizations – including the Regional Plan Association, the Visiting Committee to the Harvard School of Design, and the New York City Community Preservation Corporation, where I was a member of the mortgage loan committee. The corporation made loans to rehabilitate apartment buildings in the poorer neighborhoods of the city – buildings that needed this help just to keep going. Many run-down buildings – in fact entire neighborhoods – were teetering on the brink of abandonment by their landlords. When that happened the buildings deteriorated rapidly, and the tenants were forced to flee from vandals, thieves, and arsonists.

Some real estate conferences were a bore, such as developers' conventions in Miami Beach and Las Vegas, two unappealing towns. Others were fascinating, such as foreign junkets with old friends in the International New Towns Congress. I thought Tehran was a depressing city, and was happy to return to the Western-style comfort and tranquility of the Intercontinental Hotel after moving about through its overwhelming traffic congestion in the noisy streets. The people seemed sullen and joyless and no more than barely tolerant of foreign visitors, unless you were interested in buying a rug. Dusty gray appeared to be Tehran's dominant color, unrelieved by verdant parks with gardens and fountains – a city totally lacking in charm.

On the other hand, Buz and I thought that Budapest was loaded with it, when we attended a conference there. The city, sitting astride the Danube spanned with graceful bridges, was filled with handsome buildings and parks, art galleries and museums, and great restaurants featuring Hungarian goulash, fine wines, and gypsy violin players. The people seemed happy and glad to welcome foreign tourists. Despite the communist regime there was a vibrant and growing unofficial private sector of small enterprises in 1979, surely a sign of changes to come.

Jim Rouse was also a member of the American delegation at the Budapest New Towns Conference, and the delegates from some dozen countries listened intently to the views of this foremost urban visionary. After our trip I wrote an article for the Morgan Guaranty Survey about the severe housing problems facing the poor and homeless in New York, and suggested steps to help overcome them – measures that would be useful in big cities throughout the country with large concentrations of poor families. I was pleased to receive Jim's complimentary appraisal of my article: "A thoughtful, clear, rational, and important set of proposals for making the present system better."

Another one of my tasks was assisting the Morgan unit developing and selling properties acquired through the bank's foreclosures on bad real estate loans. An optimistic outlook and the desire to borrow as much as possible are natural attributes of real estate developers, but it is curious how commercial developments – office buildings, shopping malls, apartments, hotels, and the like – have repeatedly over-stimulated the largesse of bankers, to their deep regret later on. Perhaps a special gratification in joining in the creation of handsome, modern edifices ignites their enthusiasm, and the high returns on construction loans have certainly been enticing.

Morgan and other banks had gone overboard in financing such projects, and the overbuilding and resulting torrent of bad loans left bankers scrambling to sell all kinds of foreclosed properties. I was one of the ones working away to shape up and sell undeveloped land in Lexington, Kentucky, a resort near New Smyrna Beach, a gated community outside Richmond, the Galeria condo tower in Manhattan's East Sixties, and more. A new group of young loan officers would make the same mistakes a decade later. History shows that bankers often have short memories; they do not heed the words of George Santayana: "Those who cannot remember the past are condemned to repeat it."

The principles of sound lending are indeed constant; only people and circumstances change. Twenty years later at the invitation of Jai-Hoon Yang, a retired Morgan economist, I would join a panel at The United

Nations Training and Research Institute to give a talk on "The Global Economic Crises From Thailand to Brazil: Lessons Yet to Be Learned." The title of my paper was "Money Panics and the Bankers." The audience was made up of U.N. delegates and staff interested in studying the causes of a series of financial crises that had rocked economies around the world, and possible steps to avoid these catastrophes in the future. The sponsors wanted a banker's viewpoint presented along with those of the other speakers – a Third World ambassador, an economist, and a professor of international relations – and with twenty-five years of international finance and banking under my belt I was happy to oblige.

Starting in Thailand in 1997, followed by South Korea and Indonesia, financial collapses had triggered huge currency and stock market sell-offs and hundreds of billions of dollars in bad loans. These in turn had caused suffering and hardship in East Asia and buffeted financial markets world-wide. A little over a year later Russia devalued the ruble and defaulted on its debts, and before long the global investors' panic spread to Latin America and other emerging markets.

I noted in my presentation that the East Asian countries had been loaded down with short-term foreign currency loans – a financial time bomb, easily detonated. When panic strikes, countries burdened with foreign debt whose repayment prospects are suspect are prime candidates for capital flight, as frightened investors and lenders head for the exits. In East Asia (as in Wall Street in the 1990s), good economic news first produced optimism, and then irrational exuberance, among investors and lenders, who threw caution to the winds in their chase after high returns. When the financial bubble burst, their rush to withdraw their funds was just as precipitous.

This sudden reversal of capital inflows, accompanied by a plunging currency, is a debilitating blow to a developing, debt-burdened country. Banks worried about incurring additional losses clamp down on lending and the ensuing liquidity shortage depresses business everywhere. Investor confidence, the bedrock of financial stability, evaporates, and the ensuing panic quickly gathers momentum and spreads to other vulnerable markets. It's the same psychology that drives an old-fashioned bank run, only on a global scale.

There was no single villain to blame for these financial crises. Along with corrupt or inefficient governments and businesses, overreaching investors were a big part of the problem. Investors and lenders are still motivated by the same greed and fears as their predecessors who speculated and lost in the Dutch tulip mania crisis in 1638. Yet the bankers, especially those from the advanced industrial nations – North America, Europe, and Japan, who are supposed to be expert, experienced, and prudent lenders – bear a heavy responsibility for their role in fomenting these financial debacles. In fact, banks unwittingly assume the role of an enabler when they make loans in amounts well beyond the capacity of borrowers to repay, and I have never known a Third World country (or a real estate developer) that was not eager to borrow all the funds that it could lay its hands on. Reckless lending by international banks was a major cause of the East Asian financial crisis with its devastating economic impact.

A World Bank report stated that the imprudent financial practices in Asian countries were aggravated by "undisciplined foreign lending which led to too much money chasing foreign investments." U.S. Treasury Secretary Robert Rubin observed that many international investors, including major banks, had not "assembled the appropriate expertise and knowledge" about the markets where they were lending and investing large sums.

Reckless international bank lending to Russia before its financial collapse in 1998 contributed to the disastrous aftermath, as well as the panicky reaction among investors in emerging markets which came to focus on Brazil. In addition to its huge budget deficit and overvalued currency, Brazil, like the Asian countries and Russia, was heavily dependent on short-term foreign bank loans. They were soon cut back, and capital fled the country to safer havens.

In my talk I also traced the history of other financial debacles aided and abetted by bankers that had occurred in my lifetime. I described the Crash of 1929, which the bankers fueled by providing billions of dollars of broker loans with cash margins as low as 10%. As the Great Depression deepened, over five thousand banks were forced to shut down and hundreds of thousands of depositors lost their lifetime savings in the biggest banking meltdown in American history. The biggest onslaught of failures by savings institutions and banks after the Great Depression occurred during the 1980s, brought on by reckless real estate lending. Why do banks, every ten years or so, lend too much money to real estate developers with the inevitable consequence of overbuilding, bad loans, and even bank failures? Rash lending with catastrophic consequences happens everywhere.

I discussed various actions that individual countries and the International Monetary Fund could take to avoid or alleviate financial panics in the future. However, only the bankers themselves can take the steps to cure overly aggressive lending. It is up to them to adhere to the lending discipline that requires adequate loan diversification, a thorough credit analysis of borrowers, and reasoned economic and exchange rate judgements. Don't count on it. Memories fade, but greed is constant.

Win Some,
Lose Some

Morgan Community Development Corporation was a small, specialized unit well outside of Morgan's mainstream banking business. I chose this job when I returned to Morgan because I did not plan to pursue a banking career much longer. I hoped to go back into government service, and MCDC seemed to be a good platform from which to work toward this goal. Only this time I chose the political route: I wanted to run for Congress, which meant winning the Republican nomination to be the party's candidate for the House of Representatives from my Long Island district in 1980. I knew it was a long shot. Election opportunities for first-time aspiring candidates are like windows that can open and close quickly. The trick was to pry the window open in the first place.

The Republican party had dominated Nassau County politics for decades, having controlled the county legislature since 1917. Arguably, the Nassau County Republican Committee ran the most powerful political machine in the country – controlling jobs, contracts, donations, and the selection and support of candidates for office. Along with the financial contributions of contractors and other firms doing business with the county, donations to the Committee from public employees funded the Committee's war chest. County workers were asked to contribute about one percent of their salary to the Committee, and it was advisable for the worker to cooperate to ensure his employment prospects with the County. Employees often made their donations by buying tickets to Republican cocktail receptions and dinners. The Committee stamp of approval and support was absolutely essential for any Republican aspiring to run for public office – judgeships, town, county, or state legislatures, or the U.S. Congress. Without the Committee's blessing, forget it.

Former Senator Alfonse D'Amato was a prominent alumnus of this Nassau County Republican machine, which during the 1970s was headed by Joseph Margiotta, a tough, savvy former state assemblyman. Joe ran a tight ship. He had formed an executive committee comprising hundreds of members whose duty was to get out the vote at primaries and elections to back the County Committee's hand-picked candidates. With the customary low voter turnout at primaries, twenty percent or fewer of registered voters, the County Committee's choice of candidate was a shoo-in. The chances of beating the Democratic candidate in the general election were very also good: Registered Republicans outnumbered Democrats three to two in the county.

Back home in Long Island I was ready to put my foot in the door at ground level, as a way to get involved and known in the Republican organization. So when my friend John Perkins, the executive committee-man in our area, decided to resign, at my request he recommended me to the County Committee to be his replacement. I sent them a résumé and letter expressing my eagerness to participate in their important work.

There are times in life when it's wisest to forego declaring your affili-ation with Harvard. For example, I never raised the subject with the guys in my barracks at Navy boot camp. The Harvard identification has been known to turn some people off – including President Richard Nixon, who made disparaging remarks about Harvard men in government even as he appointed Henry Kissinger to be Secretary of State. Shortly after I had dis-patched my letter to the County Committee I received a telephone call from Louis Sposato, a Margiotta lieutenant at Republican headquarters. The top ranks of the Nassau Republican hierarchy were largely filled by gentlemen of Italian heritage. After confirming my interest in the position Sposato posed the following question: "Harvard boy, ain't you, Ted?"

I mumbled a "Yes."

"Well," said Sposato, "I'll talk to Joe," which turned out to be the last word I received regarding my bid to become a district committeeman for the Nassau County Republican Committee. Although I did not abandon my quest to become a Congressman, this rejection turned out to be prophetic.

I raised money for the party by selling tickets to Republican fund-raising receptions and then showed up. The ones held in catering halls attended by hordes of local government workers were dreary affairs. The ones held in private homes for smaller groups to meet election candidates were more interesting. I made calls on several local Republican leaders seeking their advice regarding my candidacy. They appeared to like my credentials, always ending the conversation with, "If you're the one Margiotta picks, we'll back you all the way."

Leonard W. Hall was the grand old man of Nassau Republican poli-tics, a charming and much admired gentleman. Now retired, Hall had been a longtime Congressman from the area and chairman of the Republican National Committee during the Eisenhower administration. I called on him at his home near Oyster Bay, where in much earlier times his father had been the coachman for Theodore Roosevelt. Hall gave me a friendly welcome as I admired his marvelous collection of ornamental elephants carved from various woods, marble, and other materials that friends from all over had given him when he was "Mr. Republican." Unfortunately, Hall reported, he and Margiotta had had a falling out years before. They were not on good terms and any recommendation from him would be useless.

It was time to beard the lion in his den, so I made an appointment to see my state senator from Oyster Bay, Ralph Marino, at the Republican headquarters in Westbury. After hearing my pitch he replied, "Well, you'd better talk to Joe" and took me into Margiotta's office. Margiotta, who resembled the stereotype political boss depicted in Hollywood films with porky jowls and narrow crafty eyes, greeted me courteously. I emphasized my HUD experience in the Nixon administration and added that I was prepared to raise a significant sum to help finance a first-class Congressional campaign. When Margiotta heard that I was an officer at J.P. Morgan, he advised me to check in with Mortimer Gleason, who, before retiring, had handled the bank's business with municipal and state agencies. Mort was a Long Island resident and longtime confidant of the Nassau County Republican Committee.

Mort and I had a couple of friendly lunches and his message was loud and clear: In so many words, I was not the kind of candidate that the Committee wanted to back for elective office. People of my background (meaning Ivy League, North Shore country club WASPs) could always obtain a political appointment. The Committee preferred to award election opportunities to up-and-coming middle class Long Island guys hand-picked (and presumably controlled) by the Committee. Gregory Carmen, a Long Island attorney, would be the Republican Committee's candidate in the next Congressional race in 1980. So be it.

I hosted a lunch for Greg at the bank with some Wall Street Republicans and gave a meet-the-candidate party for him at our house in Laurel Hollow. Greg was a bright and personable candidate, and in November he handily won the election for the Third Congressional District seat in the House of Representatives. I continued to touch base with Gleason, but it was clear that I was not going to break into the Margiotta-controlled circle of promising political prospects. My political hopes were dashed, and I didn't feel like uprooting my family to another county or state where the going might be easier.

The road to Congress in my Congressional district took some ironic and unexpected turns later on. In a redistricting action in 1982 John LeBoutillier, another Republican Congressman from Long Island, was chosen by the Republicans to run for reelection in my newly configured district. Apparently the Committee did not frown on all white-shoe Harvard men, as LeBoutillier was a Harvard grad from a socially prominent family. He was also a very conservative sitting Congressman at a time when Reagan conservatism was flowering in Washington. Furthermore, in a *New York Times* article he had praised "a more rigid, tight, hierarchical political system . . . 'machine politics' with a boss at the top and a disciplined organization beneath him." No wonder Margiotta and the Republican Committee liked him. He was their kind of guy.

John LeBoutillier was also an unusual Harvard alumnus who had written a book entitled *Harvard Hates America*, in which he had heaped scorn on his Alma Mater. Later on in Congress the right-wing Representative would heap scorn on the Democratic party and personally insult

Speaker of the House Tip O'Neill. The debate that I attended between him and his Democratic opponent at that time confirmed my impression that he was a brash young man. Most other voters in our district felt the same way on election day, and we elected Bob Mrazek, the popular Democratic candidate from Huntington, to be our new Congressman.

Joe Margiotta had his own troubles in 1982. He was found guilty of taking kickbacks from insurance brokers used by the county, and went to prison. In 1985, following an investigation of corruption charges against the Nassau County Republican Committee during the 1970s when Margiotta was chairman, a federal jury found the Committee guilty of pressuring county workers to kick back one percent of their salaries to the party organization in order to receive promotions and raises.

I would not have fitted in well with this crowd, and they knew it, too. While disappointed at flunking out in elective politics, I was pleased to receive recognition of another kind soon after. At the annual meeting of The Children's Aid Society in 1981 I was elected president of the board of trustees. And the residents of Laurel Hollow elected me to eight two-year terms as a trustee of the Village. Perhaps everything works out for the best. . . .

Fifty Years Later

In 1976 New York celebrated the bicentennial of Independence Day, and I celebrated my fiftieth birthday, reaching an age equal to twenty-five percent of the span of years since the official birth of our nation. Either America was a very young country or I was getting old.

On the evening before the grand celebration in New York Harbor we joined our pals the Jewetts at the New York Yacht Club. The bar was thronged with blue-blazered, brass-buttoned yachtsmen downing Absolut martinis or Dewar's on the rocks. Commodores and sailors from Larchmont, Indian Head, Seawanhaka and other yacht clubs around Long Island Sound swapped sea stories punctuated by hearty laughter. In private clubs and bars and in the streets good humor and a new, if fleeting, camaraderie swept over the city's residents on the eve of the great event. Then the sound of marching bands heralded the approach of a big parade coming up Sixth Avenue, and the bar emptied out onto 44th Street as the yachtsmen rushed to join the cheering crowd watching the parade. A band of kilted bagpipers approached playing "Danny Boy," and its members, unexpectedly, turned out to be all Puerto Ricans. Only in New York. A scrawny Hispanic gentleman, his breath redolent of less than fine wine, staggered up to one of the upstanding yacht club members and declared: "Today we all Americans together, Sir." The yachtsman nodded condescendingly.

The Bicentennial festivities had aroused the patriotic sentiments of millions of New Yorkers, united in the special celebration of their country's birthday. Joyful straphangers exchanged greetings on our subway ride downtown to view the events and even broke into a chorus of "God Bless America." The main attraction was the parade of tall ships from all over the world sailing majestically down the Hudson River, which we viewed from a Staten Island ferryboat that several country clubs had chartered. For me the most impressive sight was New York Harbor itself, carpeted with craft of every size and design from a Navy aircraft carrier with President Ford on board to the smallest outboard. It was a glorious day in the Big Apple.

Later we joined the Jewetts in their Aquasport for a trip around Manhattan. The tall ships had docked, and their crews swarmed ashore to visit bars and meet girls in the finest maritime tradition. New Yorkers were ready to give them a warm welcome and a good time. Just south of the George Washington Bridge a lonely ship rode morosely at anchor. We cruised in for a closer look. A couple of dozen pale and forlorn faces stared back at us, before an angry looking officer signaled us to be on our way. The Cold War was still very cold, and the Soviet captain would not think of letting his crew disembark. He must have reasoned that the temptations for his men to defect were too great, and indeed they were. I felt sorry for the Russian crew members, who could well imagine the good times that their fellow sailors from the rest of the world were enjoying ashore.

A decade later our gang embarked on another ferryboat frolic in New York Harbor to watch the fireworks display honoring the centennial of the Statue of Liberty. This happy evening was enlivened by a singular shipboard incident. After a convivial happy hour and buffet the celebrating crowd surged up on deck to the vessel's starboard side to get the best view of the fabulous pyrotechnics, centering on the Statue of Liberty and Battery Park.

Apparently the vessel's resultant list to starboard drained the water out of all the toilets in the ladies' rest rooms on the port side. Following the grand display, scores of men and women were ready to answer nature's call and headed for the rest rooms. Beer and wine had flowed freely throughout the joyous evening. However, the ladies were stymied, their toilets completely inoperative under circumstances that called for urgent action. Inhibitions were abandoned as en masse they invaded the men's room with its rows of urinals and stalls. The men, startled at the unexpected confrontation, were still gentlemen, and after all, Miss Liberty, in whose honor they had assembled that evening, was a lady. Good humor and pragmatism quickly converted the men's room to unisex use with the obvious division of facilities, and the good ship docked without further incident.

While I was not a member of the New York Yacht Club, friends invited us to their social events from time to time. After joining one of the crews for a race on the Sound we attended a NYYC dinner dance at Seawanhaka in Oyster Bay. It was Saturday night and most of the sailors and their girls were either partying in the bar or doing the Watusi out on the dance floor. At some affairs it's wisest to make official announcements before opening the bar. Commodore Irving Pratt chose instead to announce halfway through dinner that motorboats and their crews were officially welcome to join the annual NYYC cruise and attend its social events, and rapped on his water glass for attention. His message, a historic civil rights breakthrough for motor yachts (which some crusty old salts referred to as "stink-pots"), largely fell on deaf ears.

Some years later Buz and I cruised into Newport with the Jewetts on *Buz Bomb II*, my Sabreline trawler, and attended a huge party at the New York Yacht Club headquarters to kick off their annual cruise. I was tremendously impressed by how well disciplined the several hundred yachtsmen were in observing the official dress code – the ubiquitous dark blue blazer with brass buttons and the club necktie. In fact there was only one fellow out of uniform wearing a light blue sport jacket – me. I do not

With my favorite girls at the Beach.

Our family (and three friends) at home in Laurel Hollow, Long Island.

Ned's graduation at Harvard with his sisters and my Uncle Corliss, 1976. Ned's daughter Emily will be the first member of the fifth generation of the family to attend Harvard.

carry an extensive wardrobe in my thirty-four-foot boat.

On winter holidays we usually headed for the ski slopes. Tragedy can strike suddenly and unexpectedly even in an idyllic spot like Vail, where we took our girls skiing on spring break in 1976. We usually took the Lion's Head gondola to the top on the first run and then switched over to use a nearby chair lift on the main slope. We were riding up on this lift when disaster hit the gondola line. A frayed cable caused two gondola cars carrying skiers up the mountain to plunge one hundred twenty-five feet to the ground below, killing four people and badly injuring eight others. We watched in shock and sorrow as the ski patrol took away the victims, and with great care and skill removed the other skiers from the cars dangling from the ruptured cable. "There but for the grace of God . . ." ran through my mind.

In skiing either too much or too little snow can spoil your holiday. On one family sojourn in Alta the snowfall was so overwhelming that for three days no one was permitted to leave the lodge for fear of being obliterated by avalanches. Another time when I was trapped behind some slow skiers on a narrow trail down the mountain at Sugarbush, I veered off onto a snow-covered hillside which appeared to offer an easy bypass to the traffic. It was March and the melting snow on the inviting slope, it turned out, was cosmetic, only about an inch thick.

Traveling at a good clip, my skis came to a screeching halt on the muddy surface just beneath the thin snow cover, and I pitched forward, landing heavily on my left shoulder. Crunch! The ski patrol appeared and escorted my toboggan slide down the mountain. I was really hurting, so the local doctor gave me a shot of morphine to ease the pain on the ambulance ride to the hospital in Burlington. The painkiller went to work, and quickly transported me to Cloud Nine. The ambulance attendant asked me about starting a new business, and I never stopped talking for the next two hours, surely boring the poor fellow to death. The x-rays indicated immediate surgery, which required the insertion of a four-prong staple into my left shoulder to hold things together. The surgeon did a fine job and the shoulder has never given me any trouble. Thereafter, whenever I told anyone about the stainless steel addition to my anatomy, the most frequent reaction was, "Gee, Ted. I'll bet you set off alarms when you go through the metal detector at the airport." I don't. Some asked, "Does it enable you to forecast changes in the weather?" It doesn't do that either.

At St. John's Church of Cold Spring Harbor my good friend David Clark was the exemplary senior warden, and I was the junior warden during my dozen years on the vestry. At vestry meetings we attended to the business side of the church's activities; on Sundays we passed the plate and counted the offering afterwards. I was in charge of the St. John's Memorial Cemetery and normally began my reports at vestry meetings by announcing that "Everything remains peaceful at the Cemetery."

Our leader and the heart and soul of the church was Carleton Lee, our well-loved pastor. I have always looked forward to the sermon at church, that part of the service when the minister can present some fresh and thought-provoking ideas that will motivate his flock. Carleton's sermons achieved that end. Because they were relevant to the events and problems that families faced in everyday life, they were helpful to us.

Watching the Sunday gatekeepers in action always afforded a few amusing moments as the service began. Stationing themselves in the two or three seats nearest the aisle, they firmly held their ground, never sliding over in the pew to make room for new arrivals. So the latecomers, smiling apologetically, squeezed and stumbled by them to reach the empty seats. "Whoops, so sorry," was the weekly refrain.

I must confess to being somewhat ambivalent about taking Communion on winter Sundays when the sounds of coughing and sneezing, and not the voice of the turtle dove, are heard throughout the land. On the other hand, everyone is inspired by singing great hymns in praise of God. It is a pity when sometimes the hymns that the pastor selects leave the congregation standing mute and barely mouthing the words. Not all hymns in the hymnal are suitable for congregate singing; some are unappealing in melody and very difficult to sing. But what a joyful sight and sound it is to hear the congregation in full voice, joined by the soaring descant of the white-robed choir, singing one of the stirring hymns they know and love.

Different folks have different reasons for attending and supporting their church. Certainly the worship of God through the guidance of the church can bring great comfort and lift the spirits of the faithful, especially those in need. And certainly the Sunday church service at St. John's is a happy social occasion among neighbors with its coffee hours, special celebrations, and wonderful Sunday School. For me the two most important biblical teachings are to "love thy neighbor" and praise God "not only with our lips but in our lives." I believe that the most important role of the church is to inspire people to be better neighbors in the fullest sense of that commandment. St. John's Church has done that job well in our community, and when Carleton retired, Churchill Pinder continued the good work.

When Carleton asked me to give the sermon one summer Sunday, I was dumbfounded. I reminded him that I was not a student of religion or the Bible, "What can I possibly talk about?" I asked.

"Oh, I know you'll find something appropriate that you're comfortable with," he replied.

As I later told the congregation, "I did not volunteer for this assignment. I was drafted, and when the commander-in-chief of St. John's Church, that is the earthbound one, asks you to serve, you do it."

My great grandfather Thomas Lamont had been an active Methodist minister in the last half of the nineteenth century, a country parson who served in a score of small towns in the Hudson River Valley. Grandfather had written a charming little book about growing up in those days entitled *My Boyhood in a Parsonage*. I knew there were files of his father's old letters and sermons in a trunk in the attic of my house, so following Carleton's request I hurried up to see if I could uncover some promising sermon material. Unfortunately, the handwritten sermons of the parson, written for his eyes only, were completely illegible. However, the family letters, diaries, and Grandfather's book gave a very good picture of the life of a country parson in the late 1800s, which formed the heart of my sermon at St. John's. Here are a few extracts.

> *There are many stories that I could tell about life at the parsonage, such as the Donation parties when the members of the parish brought all kinds of food – milk, pies, cakes, and so on to the parsonage to make up the shortfall in payment of the parson's salary and then proceeded to gobble up much of what they had brought. Should we bring back that practice, Carleton?*
>
> *In those days the church practiced a stern and austere brand of Methodism, and the Lamonts were as fervent in their fundamentalism and temperance as their sternest parishioners. One had to constantly guard against the scheming of the Evil One to lure good people astray. Dancing and card playing were forbidden. Rum was a demon, and Reverend Lamont participated in scores of temperance meetings over the years to excoriate Satan and his devils. The fire and brimstone mode of preaching was popular, and Great Grandmother's elderly Uncle Henry was a master of the style. Uncle Henry had been a Methodist circuit riding parson and lived with the Lamonts for a few years at the end of his life after his wife died.*
>
> *My grandfather recalled in his book that one winter evening when he and his sister dutifully went to prayer meeting, most of the young people were out skating on the frozen Hudson River. Uncle Henry, invited by Reverend Lamont to give the prayer, promptly fell down on his knees and raised his voice.*
>
> *"O Lord," he declared, "there are a lot of sinful folk out there a-cavorting on the river, and, O Lord, I want Thee to cast Thine eye down upon them and call them back to their rightful duties to Thy worship. I do not suggest that the ice be broken in twain and these sinners submerged in the waters, as Pharaoh's Egyptian hosts were overwhelmed by the Red Sea in their pursuit of Moses and the Israelites. No, God. I believe that justice should be tempered with mercy. But I do say, O Lord, if necessary, smite each one a mighty blow and turn his face to the shore. Otherwise, dear Lord, they will*

surely get committed to the Devil. Save them, unworthy as they may be, from the clutches of the Evil One. Thou knowest as well as I what strength the minions of Hell can wield over weak creatures. Only Thou canst overcome that dread adversary. Do Thou show these misguided children the error of their ways. We rely on Thee, O Lord, to do as I have asked. Amen!"

I concluded my sermon by recalling that, according to my grandfather, many sermons of his father, whose style was more thoughtful than evangelical, often came back to one beautiful thought: "God is the Light of the World, quickening both seed time and harvest, and the spirit of man; All of our well-being and happiness, our kindly impulses, and our generous deeds are kindled by the radiance of that Light."

Every summer since 1921 the Lamonts of Sky Farm, North Haven, had hosted the Pulpit Harbor Tea in late August for members of the yacht club and assorted guests. The tea party, held on the big lawn overlooking Penobscot Bay, followed the annual sailboat race from the Fox Islands Thoroughfare around the Crabtree Point Monument and down the north shore to Pulpit Harbor. Two to three hundred summer residents, young and old, normally attended; the party was a major end-of-the-season social event.

In later years there was an added attraction: The Casino chose the occasion to present prizes to the winners of the various sailboat races held during the summer, and proud parents attended to applaud their offspring as they stepped forward to receive their silver cups and other trophies. The sailors and guests consumed hundreds of cookies, brownies, and watercress sandwiches, and there were ice cream cones for the kids. The most popular beverage by far was not tea, but cocoa, topped by generous dollops of rich whipped cream. For many, Sky Farm cocoa was the culinary *pièce de résistance* of the affair, and cocoa aficionados praised its outstanding qualities of smoothness and taste.

When Mother died in 1972 it had fallen to Buz to carry on the Pulpit Harbor Tea tradition, a big job any year and especially so the first time out. She took it in stride, and, as she has done every year thereafter, organized and assembled her task force to purchase supplies, create flower arrangements, and prepare and serve all the goodies to the hungry crowd. On the morning of the big day she was satisfied that everything was in readiness for her first Pulpit Harbor Tea, although one nagging question remained unresolved. Mother's cook had departed without leaving any instructions or formula for creating the dozen or so gallons of the celebrated cocoa. So Buz could only hope that she had produced the right blend of two different cocoa powders, chocolate syrup, sugar, and milk.

The most distinguished resident of North Haven was Senator Leverett

Saltonstall, a former governor and the patriarch of one of the first families of Massachusetts. The senator was very popular, renowned for his friendly and courtly charm. Buz and her ladies stood by nervously as the senator sipped a cup of hot cocoa. A slight frown crossed his craggy face; "It's okay, but not quite what it used to be."

"A little too sweet?" asked Buz.

"I think so," replied the senator.

Back to the drawing board, and then the same scene one year later. This time the suspense was as thick as a Penobscot Bay fog as the senator lifted a cup of cocoa to his lips. Long pause. "Now that's more like it," declared the senator, and the sun broke through the clouds of fog, lighting up smiling faces all around the cocoa pouring table.

Our 1976 Christmas letter began as follows:

"Algebraic problem – The U.S.A. reached an age this year equal to four times that of the head of the household (X) and eight times the length of his marriage to (Y). Identify X and Y."

We celebrated our twenty-fifth wedding anniversary on a warm June day chez Lamont in Laurel Hollow. Along with our local friends most of our wedding party made the scene, which featured songs, toasts, and even a short documentary produced by T. Jewett entitled "This Is Your Life." I paid tribute to the lady of the house and "the smartest move that I have ever made. Buz is the rock in our family." Helena and Kim were prospering at East Woods School, apparently majoring in field hockey and brownie making. The same school had given Ned a good start, and he was now a senior at Harvard. Except for some conventional mid-life problems – like career frustrations, teenage daughters coming home too late, and a golf game stuck at mediocre – life was sweet. We were a very happy clan thanks mainly to Buz, the best mate, friend, and partner that I could have. I was one lucky guy.

The Grand Tour

The following June Buz and I and our girls crossed the ocean on the *Queen Elizabeth II* to visit England. I concluded after our voyage that I preferred flying to sitting in a deck chair staring out at the gray Atlantic and eating too much. The highlights of our trip were viewing the Druids' mysterious handiwork at Stonehenge, Salisbury Cathedral with its magnificent soaring spire, walking through the green hills of the Cotswolds with fleecy white sheep grazing on the hillsides and fleecy white clouds in the blue sky overhead, and strolling about little towns with names like Lower Slaughter and Upper Swell. What a glorious time to be in England!

British friends invited us to watch the crew races at Henley, where we sipped champagne with ladies in wide-brimmed sun hats and gentlemen in pink rowing club jackets. The U.S. Tennis Open at the Arthur Ashe stadium in Flushing cannot compete in style with Wimbledon, where tradition is loyally observed. Players wear all-white costumes; strawberries with Devonshire cream instead of Nathan's hot dogs and pizzas are served in the concession garden; and the contestants bow and curtsy to the very proper dukes and duchesses who present the prizes. We had a grand time at Henley and Wimbledon, where in some ways the days of "My Fair Lady" did not seem so long ago.

Our girls enjoyed seeing the sights in London – the changing of the guard at Buckingham Palace, the Tower of London, and so forth. However, in looking back we now recognize that our young teenagers had quite different interests from those of their parents when traveling abroad.

I am a history buff and love to visit old palaces, castles, and cathedrals. When we had taken Ned to England in 1967, we dragged him off to view the Elgin Marbles at the British Museum when Carnaby Street, the commercial center of rock culture, was the place that really appealed to him. A decade later Helena was keen to meet the local boys whether on tours of stately homes and gardens or at the local disco. It's enlightening for tourists to meet the citizens of the countries that they visit, and from Romeo and Juliet to Archie and Veronica teenagers have sought out each other's company. My own teenage memories are funny and sweet.

Buz and I had attended the 1976 Olympic Games in Montreal for a few days with our friends Charlie and Shirley Ames, and enjoyed the festive holiday atmosphere of the city filled with thousands of spectators from all over the world. Attendees were allocated a selection of tickets to various sporting competitions. Some were better than others; we did not rank water polo as a great spectator sport.

Four years later we joined the Scott Buzbys for the Winter Olympic games in Lake Placid, where Scott, a Goodyear executive, had arranged for us to stay at the *Sports Illustrated* lodge. It was a large and deluxe timbered complex built by some business tycoon earlier in the century. Very good duty. We joined the other American spectators in exuberantly cheering on the U.S. hockey team as it defeated the Czechs. The team then defeated the Russians in a historic upset a few days later to win the gold medal.

I returned home with a sizable collection of pins and medals from the various national teams at the Olympics. The athletes enjoyed pin trading with their peers from other countries, a friendly exchange of Olympic souvenirs unimpeded by language barriers, and soon the spectators got into the act. Our currency was Goodyear and *Sports Illustrated* pins, supplied by the companies to their guests. They were of only moderate value in the pin market. One gave up two Goodyear or *SI* pins for one Russian badge featuring a group of smiling Matryoshka dolls or one Chinese pin with the image of a cuddly panda.

That spring we joined a group organized by our friend and neighbor Bob Jay to do the grand tour of Egypt, a major world class tourist attraction since Herodotus ventured up the Nile and chronicled his travels some two dozen centuries ago. I was enthralled by the splendors of ancient Egypt. It was absolutely mind-boggling to view the artifacts, buildings, and paintings of a civilization flourishing more than four thousand years ago, revealed largely through the burial customs in those ancient times. The early Egyptians believed that when they died they entered into an eternal afterlife. Accordingly, in preparation for the hereafter they filled the solidly built tombs and pyramids for their departed kings with all kinds of decorative and useful objects and vivid pictures of life in those times, which, thanks to the dry desert climate, have been preserved for century after century.

The remains of some other early civilizations have not fared so well. Buz and I have twice toured the Mayan ruins in the tropical surroundings of the Yucatan. Forests and vegetation had long ago overgrown the palaces and temples of Chichén Itzá, Palenque, and other abandoned Mayan centers, which in their rediscovery excavations had to be laboriously carved out of the consuming jungle. The verdant growth and dampness had damaged or destroyed buildings and artifacts of far more youthful vintage than the antiquities of ancient Egypt.

In Egypt our group followed the well-traveled route of armies of tourists before us (including Napoleon's). Buz and I had our photograph taken in front of the massive Sphinx. We took a camel ride at Giza and explored the Great Pyramid of Cheops, whose inner burial chamber is not a place to visit if you suffer from claustrophobia. At Luxor we marveled at the Temple of Karnak (I couldn't help thinking of Johnny Carson's comic role as the all-knowing wizard), and explored the ancient royal tombs in the Valley of the Tombs of the Kings and Queens. We had seen exhibits at New York's Metropolitan Museum and the Cairo Museum of artifacts from the tomb of Tutankhamen, including the beautiful sold gold mask covering the head of the young pharaoh in his golden coffin. The discovery of Tutankhamen's tomb in 1922 had been the most momentous event in Egyptian archeology in modern times. It was an exciting moment when our turn came to climb down into the tomb itself and view the royal burial chambers with their vivid murals of life in Egypt some three thousand years ago.

Next we cruised upriver to Aswan. Graceful feluccas glided by our passenger boat as we steamed along the great river that plays such a crucial role in the life of the nation and its people who live in the Delta and Valley of the Nile, within a few miles of its banks. In some places, upstream from towns and cities, life along the river banks still resembled scenes from biblical times.

I had a special interest in viewing the High Dam at Aswan, having researched the plans for its construction at the World Bank back in the 1950s. In the twists and turns of Cold War politics the Russians had ended up building the dam. The Nile provides the lifeblood of Egyptian agriculture, and the completion of the towering High Dam in 1970 brought the river's annual flood under proper control for the first time in history. In addition, the new dam generated electric power to light Egyptian homes, many for the first time, and run its industries, providing huge social and economic benefits to the developing nation.

From Aswan we flew south to Abu Simbel, site of the magnificent temple of Ramses II with its four giant statues hewn from solid rock guarding the entrance. When the High Dam was built the entire temple and statues had been cut free and lifted hydraulically to high ground to save them from submersion in the newly formed great lake behind the dam – truly a dazzling engineering feat. Alexandria, once headquarters for the beguiling Cleopatra, was our last stop in Egypt, and who but the beautiful Elizabeth Taylor could have so fittingly played the role of the Queen of Egypt on film? Claudette Colbert, perhaps? (They both did.)

Our tour had sped forward at the rapid pace dictated by our itinerary, firmly prodded along by Peter, our professional guide. "Please place your bags outside your room by 6 a.m." was almost a daily instruction in preparation for the next leg of the journey. Everyone in our group stayed cool, and one member deserves special commendation for his monumental patience and forbearance. Bill Driscoll's bag never caught up with him from the time we left Heathrow to fly to Cairo. When we were in Luxor, his bag was in Cairo; when we were in Aswan, Bill's bag had made it to Luxor, and so on. Bill remained calm throughout. Our Egyptian tour was the most awe-inspiring and fascinating excursion that I have ever taken.

That same year, 1980, was our year for exploring great rivers. In

September Buz and I visited her mother's Alsatian relatives in Strasbourg, and then boarded a tour boat to cruise down the Rhine to Rotterdam along with some fifty other passengers. Heidelberg and the other castle towns were charming, the weather was benign, and all the passengers were in fine spirits until the captain made a most unwelcome announcement. "Due to technical difficulties" our Rhine River cruise would terminate at Cologne instead of continuing on to Rotterdam, the official destination.

All the passengers had signed on and paid for the full shipboard cruise from Strasbourg to Rotterdam, and the prospect of bus transportation with a lowly box lunch replacing the last leg of the voyage was very disturbing. Then our Greek waiter in the dining room quietly informed us of the real reason the cruise was ending ahead of schedule. There was nothing wrong with the engines; there were no "technical difficulties." The German cruise operators simply wanted to take advantage of a very profitable piece of business: The company that manufactures Eau de Cologne in Cologne had chartered the vessel to take its executives and some clients on an outing.

Word of the cruise line's duplicity spread rapidly among the passengers, and disappointment soon turned to anger. Tourists from all over – Australia, Japan, Brazil, and other distant places – had for many months looked forward to cruising down the Rhine to Rotterdam. Now the German cruise line managers had suddenly and without consultation shortened the scenic voyage. These executives and the captain quickly became the object of irate and disparaging remarks. Diplomacy was not one of the captain's attributes, and, despite our requests, he refused to meet with the passengers or offer any further explanation for curtailing the cruise. He had decided that silence was the best tactic.

Upset and frustrated at the turn of events I decided to try another way to communicate with the stonewalling captain in a final effort to reverse his decision. I drafted a petition from the passengers to the captain protesting the sudden curtailment of the cruise, pointing out that such action violated the terms of the tour plan that we had purchased from our travel agencies, and threatening legal action if he persisted in this "theft of service" (a term that I had heard lawyers use in legal complaints by commuters against the Long Island Rail Road).

A sense of history stirred my imagination about the justness of our cause and my role in leading it. Down through the ages, ordinary citizens have petitioned higher authorities, be they captains or kings, to cease their repressive or tyrannical rule. Our colonial forefathers had sought just such relief from George III. The passengers rallied to my flag, gathered in the main salon, formed a line, and, one by one, signed the petition. My signature was large and bold, just like John Hancock's. I then formally presented the petition to the purser with our request for a prompt reply. (The captain had declined our invitation to attend the meeting.)

Later that evening we received the captain's response over the public address system. "Please have your bags ready and be prepared to disembark at Cologne at 10 a.m. tomorrow. The buses will be at the dock to take you to Rotterdam." As the crew loaded our bags onto the buses, porters were wheeling crates of champagne and wine up the gangway. Others were unloading a caterer's truck crammed with gourmet dishes for the dining pleasure of the Cologne executives and their party. We ate our boring box lunches in a field by the highway to Rotterdam.

In Holland Buz and I explored the canals near Amsterdam with a Dutch friend in his cabin cruiser, then drove to Paris, via Brussels and Bruges, and flew home. I immediately registered a complaint with my travel agent about the shabby treatment that we had received on the Rhine River cruise. We each received a refund of $200, compensation that did not soften our bitter memories, and, I am sure, those of the other passengers. German tourism would do well to avoid that kind of public relations blunder.

I trust that our unfortunate experience was an extremely rare occurrence. On another European river cruise some years later everything went smoothly according to plan. We boarded the *River Cloud* at Nuremburg and cruised down the Danube to Budapest, touring riverside castles and towns en route. In Vienna we watched the Lipizzaner stallions go through their elegant paces, and attended a Viennese waltz concert in the Liechtenstein Palace. It's entirely appropriate that poetic license be extended to composers like Johann Strauss; I never thought the Danube would actually be blue anyway.

The Joys
of Midtown

After I left J.P. Morgan in 1980, I rented office space in George O'Neill's suite of offices at 30 Rockefeller Plaza, the RCA Building. After fifteen years in the shadowed, all-business canyons of Wall Street, it was a joy to be located in the bustling and lighthearted center of midtown Manhattan. In the winter skaters did their figure eights, or just happily glided around in circles, in the Rockefeller Center skating rink under the watchful contemplation of the huge golden statue of Prometheus. Tourists thronged the inviting open plazas to gaze at the enormous Christmas tree that is lit up each holiday season with much fanfare. Others rested on the steps of St. Patrick's Cathedral across Fifth Avenue, or peered into the lavishly decorated store windows along the avenue, expressing their wonderment in many tongues.

In warmer weather, mimes and street musicians performed for the swarms of visitors and office workers stretching their legs at lunchtime. At lunch I often strolled downtown to the Harvard Club just off Fifth Avenue on 44th Street, stopping to browse at Barnes & Noble or Scribner's. In the summer I sometimes walked uptown to the zoo to dine al fresco on a park bench. The midtown stretch of Fifth Avenue, handsome and joyful, was dressed in its finest and eager to greet the city's visitors from all over the world.

Thirty Rockefeller Plaza was the seat of the Rockefeller family offices, and I knew one family member well – Abby O'Neill. My parents had sold their house in Oyster Bay Cove to George and Abby many years before, and they were old friends and neighbors. I also had had fleeting encounters with several of Abby's prominent uncles. I had briefly met David Rockefeller a few times at charity events before I moved into my new office and started working out at the Cardio Fitness Center in the nearby McGraw Hill building. David, just retired as chairman of the Chase Manhattan Bank, now operated out of the Rockefeller family offices and also exercised at the Fitness Center. So did Bryant Gumbel, who came over to work out after the "Today Show," which he co-anchored from the NBC studio in Rockefeller Center. The young female physical therapists quite understandably paid more attention to Bryant than to Rockefeller and Lamont, offering to massage his stiff neck, helping him do stretching exercises, and so forth.

One morning I was getting dressed in the locker room when David Rockefeller came in, accompanied by John, the manager of the Fitness Center. John was a young man, very macho, built like Arnold

Schwarzenegger and exuding self-confidence. At the time the locker room was being remodeled. Some walls had been torn down, and building materials and debris were scattered about. David remonstrated in his well-bred manner, "What a mess! Do you expect to get it all fixed up again soon?"

John threw an arm over the shoulders of the former chairman of Chase, renowned civic leader and confidant of presidents and prime ministers, and replied, "Oh David, you and I are both in management. You know how long these construction jobs can drag on."

The French have long laid claim to *"égalité* and *fraternité,"* but it is the Americans who practice it. In addressing each other we have moved away from using the traditional designation of "Mr." or "Mrs." to greeting people informally by their first name – at social occasions and to a large extent in the workplace. Even at J.P. Morgan, still an institution with an Old School atmosphere in the sixties, generally everybody above the rank of assistant treasurer addressed the CEO by his first name. "Sure, Pat, I'll take care of it," would have been the normal response to a request by Ellmore Patterson, the Morgan CEO for a number of years. During my grandfather's era at J.P. Morgan, however, only a few senior partners would dare to address J.P. Morgan as "Jack." He was "Mr. Morgan" to everyone else. Circumstances do vary with time and place: The folks in Long Island who perform services – the plumber, electrician, and so forth – address us as "Mr." or "Mrs." Yet on the island of North Haven in Maine the local tradesmen, proud Downeast Yankees, call us "Ted" and "Buz," which is fine by me.

Earlier when I was on a business visit to Little Rock, where HUD had assisted in financing a new town, I had called on Governor Winthrop Rockefeller at his ranch on Petit Jean Mountain and had a pleasant conversation about new community development in Arkansas. However, the real heavyweight politician among the Rockefeller brothers was Governor Nelson Rockefeller, a four-term governor of New York and later Vice President under President Jerry Ford.

In 1968 I joined a small group to discuss campaign fund-raising at Governor Rockefeller's elegant Fifth Avenue apartment. The governor was planning to seek the Republican presidential nomination. I had long been interested in politics and public affairs and was a "Rockefeller Republican," the term designating the moderate branch of the party that was imperiled by the growing ascendancy of the conservative right wing. I must confess that privately I felt that donating funds to Nelson Rockefeller was tantamount to "carrying coals to Newcastle," a feeling that was confirmed when I spotted the Picassos and other masterpieces from Nelson's extensive art collection adorning his walls. The governor turned on his famous upbeat charisma, and I was only slightly distracted to observe, as he sat opposite me, that his short black socks left exposed

Arnold Palmer and friends at a Boys and Girls Club convention in Orlando, one of their annual meetings in different cities that we attended.

Awarding Children's Aid Society college scholarships.

Retiring as president of C.A.S. with Nicholas Scoppetta, my successor, and Phillip Coltoff, CEO. I remained active as chairman of the board.

Sketch of four recent C.A.S. presidents: Nicholas Scoppetta, Charlton Phelps, Ted Lamont, and John Griswold.

an eye-catching amount of bare leg below his trousers. However, I doubt that this sartorial gaffe was a factor in his defeat by Richard Nixon in the contest to become the Republican nominee for President.

I spent a couple of years in the O'Neill office working on various pro bono publico and investment projects. Exeter's latest capital campaign was under way, and I joined the team soliciting major gifts, working once again with the trustees and Steve Kurtz and Dan Stuckey, P.E.A.'s new principal and vice principal.

In 1981 I was elected president of the board of trustees of The Children's Aid Society after serving as a trustee since 1964. I presided at monthly board meetings and attended various committee meetings, staff conferences and inspection tours of our neighborhood centers and summer camps. While the board oversaw all the activities of the Society, the management and staff naturally had primary responsibility for operations and initiating new programs. My job was made easy because C.A.S. already had excellent management in place. The Society is fortunate that Phil Coltoff, the chief executive, chose a career in social work. He is bright and personable and would have been a star in business or politics, had he chosen to go down another road. The Society is also very lucky to have Phil's deputy, Pete Moses, who has so ably carried out the agency's operations.

My main contribution to program development at C.A.S. was to push for new and better programs for adolescents – high school boys and girls. From Head Start on up we did a good job in educating and motivating youngsters. But our good work was all in vain if, as teenagers, they hit the streets and got into all the kinds of trouble that lay waiting to tempt young people. One part of our special effort with high school students was our C.A.S. College Scholarship Program, and scores of young people have attended college with our scholarship aid. Another part was our Work Readiness Program. For a number of years I visited Columbia Business School each fall to recruit volunteer participants for this program. These Columbia students, as well as older volunteers, spoke to groups of teenagers at our Harlem centers about different careers and how to prepare for them, plus some pretty basic but badly needed advice – such as how to apply for a job, or the importance of a neat appearance and being punctual. I spoke to the kids about a career in banking, but the best role models in addressing these teenagers were the young men and women from Columbia Business School.

I also recruited half a dozen friends to beef up the Society's board of trustees, able and energetic people that I knew would make important contributions to the agency's work. One was our longtime friend Truda Jewett, who became an active trustee and later left the board to become the Society's associate executive director in charge of the Development Office. I have never known a more effective fund-raiser anywhere than my good friend "T."

People taking early retirement often become consultants in their former business, and, following the practice, I presented myself as a financial consultant. In 1981 a mutual friend introduced me to Tony duPont, the founder and CEO of duPont Aerospace Co., Inc. – a small Los Angeles engineering company that had designed the DP-2, a thirty-passenger twin-engine commercial jet. Tony's career spanned twenty-five years in aircraft design and development. This former Pan American World airways pilot had later become a senior executive at Douglas Aircraft in designing commercial jets.

Tony now planned to acquire a plant to manufacture the DP-2 and needed to raise at least $12 million in equity plus substantial debt to finance the new venture. Tony wanted me to become the vice chairman of his company with the responsibility of raising the needed capital. Start-up projects inherently bear a greater risk of failure than operating enterprises, and I had seen many fall by the wayside in the past. Nevertheless, I was intrigued by the project, especially the apparently large market demand for a plane with the DP-2's characteristics, and signed on.

The DP-2 would have a transcontinental cruising range at a top speed of 545 knots, faster than all the current airliners with the exception of the Concorde. While the plane could be used efficiently to serve the commuter market, we anticipated that its most effective use would be in providing non-stop service on longer routes whose passenger density was too low to justify a normal frequency of service by the larger hundred-plus passenger airliners. There were innumerable routes, city pairs, that the DP-2 could efficiently serve. From New York to Albuquerque, Reno, Palm Springs, or Lexington, Kentucky, were examples. No more flying to a hub city to change planes for the next leg of the journey. The time had come to provide fast non-stop jet service to hundreds of towns across the country, and we had the plane to do the job.

Finding a suitable manufacturing site did not appear to be a problem. Local officials in Wilmington, San Diego, Suffolk County (Long Island), and New Bedford were eager for the business and employment that a big new enterprise would bring to the area. At our meeting at the State House in Boston Governor Edward King told us, "I'll do anything that's legal to get you guys to locate your plant in New Bedford."

However, raising private capital for such a project was another story. Launching a new model aircraft successfully is a high-risk venture even for established manufacturers with experienced and skilled workers, deep pockets, and ready access to credit and government assistance. The danger of huge production cost overruns, delays in FAA certification, and other unforeseen problems were all too real, and the small DP-2 team starting from scratch didn't have the gravitas to impress outside investors. I heard this constant refrain from the dozens of investment firms and venture capitalists that I met with. DuPont Aerospace would have to link up with an established manufacturer to launch the DP-2.

We presented the project to Grumman, the Long Island aircraft manufacturer, but they didn't bite. Tony decided not to seek another partner in the aircraft business. He didn't want to relinquish a substantial equity interest, probably the majority, and feared losing management control of the project. He now contemplated a West Coast manufacturing site, and raising equity through investment by wealthy individuals in a venture capital partnership that would generate huge tax losses in the early years. Questioning this approach, because I believed our best bet was to try to link up with an established aircraft manufacturer, I no longer felt I could be helpful and bowed out. The DP-2 never took off.

When I returned to Morgan in 1974 after my tour of duty with HUD, I did not rejoin the board of the State Street Research mutual fund. As an officer of a bank with a large investment department I did not want to risk being perceived as holding conflicting interests in my dual roles. But after leaving the bank in 1980, I returned to the board of State Street. Its management company was acquired by Metropolitan Life a few years later. In the burgeoning mutual fund market that developed over the next decade, I ended up on the boards of some twenty funds managed by State Street. Each fund was tailored to reflect a particular investment characteristic – growth, value, big cap, little cap, government bonds, and so forth. As board members we now reviewed marketing strategies and new initiatives to compete successfully in the booming mutual fund market as well as investment performance. State Street even started up a special fund for professional athletes whose compensation was turning them into multi-millionaires, hiring Derek Sanderson, the former Boston Bruins hockey star, to promote the fund.

In hindsight, our board paid too little attention to the expenses of managing the funds that were paid for by the shareholders whom we represented. In the soaring stock markets of the 1980s and 1990s, fund performance was our central focus, and these costs, as long as they were competitive with their peer funds, took a back seat in the board's oversight duties. While the market value of the funds increased substantially during these years – into the hundreds of millions and billions of dollars in varying cases – the expense ratios, contrary to our expectations, edged steadily upwards too. Whatever happened to the economies of scale? State Street management's reply was that this advisory fee income was absolutely needed to compensate and hold their highly talented stock pickers and marketing staff. Yet the State Street Investment Trust, the flagship stock fund (which incidentally performed better than many comparable funds) had lagged the S&P 500 Index over the years, while the index funds, which matched the market, incurred substantially lower costs.

In addition to the advisory fee and certain operating expenses, the expense ratio included a so-called 12-b1 fee for marketing the funds, mainly compensation to brokers. State Street management believed that these fees, ranging up to 1%, were absolutely essential to grow the funds, and the board, with some reluctance, bought their argument each year. When I retired from the board in 1998, the expense ratio for major classes of stock of the Investment Trust was 1.60%. However, by 2003 the ratio had climbed to 1.90%, wiping out any income available for dividends to shareholders. Furthermore, individual new shareholders paid sales charges, up front or deferred, of up to 5.75%, all in all not a very good deal unless one was getting really outstanding results.

I also joined the board of Sun Life Assurance Company of New York, invited by a friend who was a Sun Life executive. The New York company was a wholly owned subsidiary of Sun Life of Canada, the big Canadian insurance company. My directorship was a bit of a sinecure. State law required that insurance companies operating in New York be incorporated in the state with New York citizens serving as the outside directors on the board. At the State Street funds, my fellow directors and I were responsible for serving and protecting the interests of thousands of shareholders. At Sun Life there was only one shareholder – the parent company, which didn't really need my advice. From time to time at board meetings I asked if Sun Life was complying fully with the regulations of the New York State Insurance Department. At least I would do my duty as a New York citizen on the company's board of directors.

My good friend and neighbor Frank Hawley had teamed up with John Foster, a former Morgan investment officer, to manage a series of venture capital partnerships. I thought Frank was a very smart businessman and signed on as an investor in several of the partnerships as they were launched from time to time. The Foster management firm did very well by their investors, following a strategy of consolidating a number of small enterprises in the same business into one organization, building it up, and then going public or selling it to a large company. Many of the investments were in the health care field.

All of the Foster partners assembled each year for the annual meeting at the River Club in New York. After the meeting and cocktails, we sat down to a gala dinner, after which master of ceremonies John Foster introduced an unusual form of after-dinner entertainment for the gathering of businessmen, dowagers, bankers, hotshot financiers, and wealthy young heiresses and divorcées. According to John's program it was time for his guests to regale the group with their best risqué or raunchy jokes and stories, and he went around the table urging each person to contribute to the evening's entertainment.

My turn came after the previous speaker had told an amusing story about a skinny Chinese prostitute. Well, when in Rome, do as the

Romans do, so somewhat reluctantly I stood up and told a tale I had picked up about the exchange that took place in the men's room of the House of Commons between Sir Winston Churchill and Labor prime minister Clement Atlee, whom Sir Winston had once described as "a sheep in sheep's clothing." The punch line is key in these exercises, and I had a good one.

Susan, my secretary in the O'Neill office, was cheerful, able, and the mother of two little girls. Before her marriage she had been a secretary in the J.P. Morgan investment department. After fathering two babies Susan's no-good husband had taken off leaving her alone and destitute with two infants to look after. He simply disappeared and abandoned his family without any financial support. Susan, who had to stay home and look after her little ones, went on welfare to provide for her family. There are some five million mothers and children on welfare in the country, and while there are undoubtedly some who abuse the system, many welfare mothers, like Susan, simply need a helping hand to get them through a bad patch.

Moreover, with so many young mothers at work nowadays the availability of child day care centers for working mothers is absolutely essential. Susan was delighted to earn enough to leave welfare and go back to work when her girls were old enough to go to a day care center, where she dropped them off each morning before coming to the office.

Susan's personal life also took a happy turn when she fell in love and became engaged to Peter, a young man in training at the New York Police Academy. When we attended their wedding, I was surprised to see that Peter was a fairly small fellow. Susan had chosen a towering bouffant hair style for her wedding day, which accentuated her husband's small stature as they stood together at the altar making their vows.

A few weeks later I asked Susan how Peter's career as a police officer was progressing. "Great," she replied, "except for one thing. At the Academy they taught him some physical arm holds to use if necessary when arresting a criminal, and sometimes he practices them on me. You know, Mr. Lamont, I can break free every time!"

A Change of Pace

In 1983 I embarked on a new career: I decided to write a biography of my grandfather – *The Ambassador From Wall Street, The Story of Thomas W. Lamont, J.P. Morgan's Chief Executive*. The best place to work on a book was at home, where, with few distractions, I could do my research and writing surrounded by the books and papers that I had gathered.

The idea for the project had come to me when I explored the contents of a row of boxes in the attic of our house in Laurel Hollow, in which Grandmother Lamont had lived at the end of her life. The boxes were filled with bundles of old family letters. They were handwritten in ink on rag bond paper mainly from the late 1800s, during Lamont's youth, when his father had been a Methodist minister guiding parishes in small towns in the Hudson River Valley. I would write the biography of the country parson's son who came to lead J.P. Morgan & Co. for more than two decades, when the powerful bank was at the pinnacle of domestic and international finance. Lamont had been in the middle of economic and political history-making from World War I to World War II. Another title that I considered was *From Methodist Parsonage to Morgan Partnership*. It was a great story, and nobody had written it yet.

I was twenty-one when my grandfather died; my contacts with him had been limited to large family gatherings like Christmas at Palisades or picnics in Maine. We were on different intellectual tracks. In those days I turned to the sports page while he read his friend Walter Lippmann's column in the *New York Herald Tribune* or the editorial page of the *New York Times*, which might be running his latest letter to the editor. Nevertheless, I had some special credentials to write about Lamont's life and career – my first-hand knowledge of the family, a private collection of family letters, and my own career including twenty-three years with the World Bank and J.P. Morgan & Co. I knew the family and the business. So I went to work with my ball point pen and yellow legal pad.

My new lifestyle gave us more time to smell the roses. We returned to Alpine skiing, usually with a joyful group of Cold Spring Harbor neighbors, visiting places that we had skied forty years earlier as students – Zermatt, Klosters, and Gstaad, from where I reported to friends at home that "The Palace Hotel is no Vermont ski lodge." On our first evening in steep-sloped Val d'Isère, our group invited a few of the mountain guides to have a drink. The next day one of them was lost in an avalanche while leading a group of young French hotshot skiers in a restricted area. It was shocking and saddening news. We stuck carefully to the pistes after that.

Once again Bob Jay, our local tour leader, organized a great excursion – a raft trip down the middle fork of the Salmon River in Idaho. Bouncing downstream through the swift whitewater rapids was great sport. Beaching the rafts in the afternoon at a new riverbank campsite always triggered a mass exodus somewhat like a mini Oklahoma Land Rush. Each couple rushed ashore to stake a property claim on the spot where they wanted to pitch their tent, sometimes engendering friendly confrontations. Some folks liked the riverfront; others preferred to be near the latrine tent; and still others liked to be as far away from everyone else as possible. I have always liked shorefront property.

As a member of The Pilgrims, the premier American–British friendship society, I have often heard distinguished officials and diplomats at Pilgrims dinners praise the "special relationship" that binds our two nations together. I am an Anglophile. I love the green rolling countryside and the little market towns with venerable churches. I enjoy the rich literary heritage of writers and poets such as Charles Dickens, Jane Austen, William Wordsworth, and John Masefield, who, with his lady, often visited and traveled with my grandparents Tom and Florence Lamont. The Lamonts' favorite poem by Masefield was "Sea Fever," with its classic opening lines:

> *I must go down to the sea again, to the lonely sea and the sky,*
> *And all I want is a tall ship and a star to steer her by.*

Poets in earlier times wrote lines that had rhythm and rhymed and flowed smoothly to paint a picture or tell a story, a style abandoned by modern poets whose free verse in the *Harvard* magazine or *The New Yorker* is a weak substitute. What poem can be more sublime than "The Daffodils," by Wordsworth, which I learned by heart as a schoolboy and sometimes recite to show off at dinner parties.

On our visits to England during the eighties, Buz and I touched base with our hospitable American friends Martha and Vic Kenyon, who were living in London at the time. They once lent us their car for a tour to Coventry, Chester, and the Lake District, where we visited Dove Cottage, the former home of Wordsworth. We strolled along Hadrian's Wall and viewed the beautiful cathedrals at Durham and York. At Canterbury Cathedral we found the plaque with its inscription by John Masefield honoring Thomas W. Lamont for his generous gift after the war for the repair and restoration of the cathedral. German bombs had slightly damaged it and destroyed its library during the war.

We knew it could have been much worse. Dietrich Proske, a good friend and Oyster Bay neighbor, had been a Luftwaffe bomber pilot in the war. Dietrich was a modest fellow who never talked about the war, but late one evening after a party when the men were exchanging war stories, he told the following tale. He had gone to school in England, and he loved the country and its people. Nevertheless, as a patriotic German, he felt duty bound to fight for his country when war broke out and became a Luftwaffe pilot. On one mission he was ordered to bomb Canterbury Cathedral, a blow intended by Hitler and Goering to weaken British morale. Dietrich couldn't do it, and, claiming that the cloud cover was too thick to see the cathedral, dropped his bombs on other targets. So the ancient cathedral, cherished by the whole Christian world, survived.

Trips to England mostly start or end in London and for me London has always seemed much more than simply a great international metropolis. It is the city of Charles Dickens, Sherlock Holmes, and Winston Churchill, filled with an abiding sense of history; nor has the British Museum lost its charm. The royal family's palaces and other regal trappings, as well as their personal affairs, have long intrigued the public in Britain and abroad. Queen Elizabeth and I are the same age, and I have always admired her pluck and dignity in coping with the carryings-on of the royal offspring. I would guess that lots of parents nowadays can understand and sympathize with the Queen over the troubles that she has endured.

Driving out from the center of London near Marble Arch the first time was absolutely nerve-wracking, but in time we got used to driving on the "wrong side" of the road. On our next trip we headed west through Dorset, Devon, and Cornwall, then north to Bristol and Bath and back to London via the Cotswolds and Oxford. Touring the West Country happily reminded us of pastoral and drawing room scenes in nineteenth-century English novels and Masterpiece Theatre on TV. We became big fans of stately manor houses, sumptuous gardens, and forests of blooming rhododendrons. At Pencarrow, a Georgian country house in Cornwall, the tour guide invited me to play a tune on the same piano used by Arthur Sullivan when he composed "Iolanthe" while staying at the house. I obliged with a chorus of "Danny Boy." We also visited Shakespeare's home town of Stratford-on-Avon. It was a major tourist attraction, although many have held that the celebrated actor and playwright did not write his own plays. The real author, according to some, was probably Edward de Vere, the Earl of Oxford, a true nobleman who chose to conceal his identity. No matter who wrote Shakespeare's plays, they were the work of a genius.

The Kenyons joined us in another jaunt – first to Portsmouth, where we viewed the restored warship *Mary Rose*, the flower of Henry VIII's navy that had lain sunken at the bottom of the harbor for some four centuries. The top-heavy vessel had capsized, so the story goes, when all her sailors rushed to one side to wave good-bye to their sweethearts on shore as the ship embarked on her maiden cruise to attack the Spanish fleet.

Taking the car ferry to Cherbourg, we toured Normandy and the D-Day beaches, where the assault to liberate Europe from the Nazis began on June 6, 1944. As a supply officer for the Ninth Air Force my father had been stationed in Normandy a month later. At the Normandy American Cemetery, long rows of small white crosses, more than nine thousand, marked the last resting place of American soldiers from every state in the Union who were killed in the Normandy invasion. It was an overwhelmingly moving place.

After ascending Mont St. Michel in Brittany, Buz and I toured the châteaux in the Loire Valley. We noted how well the French nobility in the seventeenth and eighteenth centuries lived (as long as one doesn't mind using lavishly decorated chamber pots instead of modern indoor plumbing) compared to everyone else. Surely the ingredients for a good revolution were all in place.

Another Kenyon–Lamont excursion took us to Morocco. "Casablanca" may be the greatest movie of all time, but we found it a boring city. However, Marrakesh was colorfully exotic and the Mamounia Hotel was a model of luxurious splendor, with prices to match. The Royal Moroccan Golf Club was a bit run-down, but boasted the best caddies anywhere. Wherever your shot landed, even in the lush foliage bordering the fairways, it always found its way to a perfect fairway lie by the time that you got to it. In the bustling bazaar we succumbed to the constant salesmanship and bought a rug. That's what tourists do in Morocco.

In a small town on the edge of the Sahara Desert an American girl walked, somewhat stiffly, into the hotel bar where we were having a drink. She seemed eager for companionship and to tell her tale of woe. She was a travel magazine writer and member of an American tour group that had signed up for a camel safari in the desert. Coming from California, they had arrived at the departure point only to learn that the French guides and chef had gone on strike. "Not to worry," said the chief Arab camel driver. "We'll take you on a lovely tour. We don't need those French guys." The group discussed it and agreed; they had come a very long way to go home empty-handed. Mounting their camels they rode off into the desert.

"To sum it up," the girl continued, "It was an absolutely ghastly experience." The food was horrible, being the fare that Arab camel drivers enjoy instead of the gourmet meals promised in the brochure. The camel saddle did not fit her anatomy causing great discomfort and lingering soreness. Sanitary arrangements were deplorable. The tents had been washed away by a freak rainstorm one night, and the tour consisted of boringly circling the same large group of desert dunes day after day.

"Wow!" I said." Are you going to tell it like it was in your article for the magazine?"

"Oh, no!" she replied. "I could never do that. This tour is supposed to be a deluxe and romantic adventure."

Back home not long afterwards I attended a Boys and Girls Clubs benefit dinner at which Bob Hope was the honored guest and speaker. When I was introduced to him, I told him that his movie "The Road to Morocco" had really identified the little North African country for millions of Americans: Whenever I told friends I'd just returned from Morocco, they invariably replied, "So you were off on 'The Road to Morocco!' Did you see Bob Hope? And how about Dorothy Lamour?" "Hey! That's a good one, feller," responded Bob.

Virtually everybody tends to lie or shade the truth about certain subjects – from extracurricular love affairs to the performance of their new car. I don't remember anyone ever confessing that they had purchased a "lemon" and would never buy that model again. Likewise, I have rarely heard anyone admit that they had had a really lousy vacation – that their choice of travel tour or resort had been a big mistake. Our vacation with our girls to Cotton Bay on Eleuthera in the Bahamas fell resoundingly into that category, however, even with the good company of Bob and Sally Viscount and their daughter.

Cotton Bay, once a classy resort started by Pan American Airways, was now under local management and had seen its best days. Nevertheless, we were enjoying ourselves until disaster struck near the end of our holiday. Playing tennis with Bob, I lost my balance going up for an overhead, and thrust out my left arm to break my fall. I broke my left wrist instead, although I didn't know it at the time. Later during cocktails at a friend's house my wrist really began hurting, and a rum punch did nothing to relieve the pain. My hostess handed me a pill, saying, "This will fix you up," and without thinking I popped the pain killer in my mouth. A dumb move. Drugs and alcohol are a dangerous combination. Within minutes I turned glassy-eyed, and my legs turned to rubber. My friends helped me back to our cottage where I slowly recovered, although my wrist continued to hurt like the devil.

It was time to see a doctor, so we drove over about twenty-five miles of painfully bumpy road into Rock Sound. The local doc, who resembled Lionel Barrymore at the end of his long acting career, had just returned to his combination home and office from a party. Reeking of Scotch, he stated shakily, "I don't know what I can do for you, my boy."

"Just give me something to kill the pain and some kind of cast," I replied, wondering why the old fellow had decided to end his days working in this crummy little town. Had he been banned by all the stateside medical societies? The doctor then gave me a shot from a huge hypodermic needle, more suitable for ministering to Secretariat, I thought, and placed something resembling a large cardboard shoe box on my wrist, presumably to serve as a cast. Neither remedy was effective, and I spent a miserable night.

The next morning I drove into the public health clinic, where a Vietnamese doctor x-rayed the wrist, put on a proper fiberglass cast, and supplied me with enough ibuprofen for our flight home, where I went directly to North Shore Medical for repairs. I have never gone back to Eleuthera.

Murder
at the Castle

T. Jewett was a tour manager par excellence, and one spring, she came up with a brilliant holiday scheme for a dozen of us. She rented a castle, Monte Sereno, for a week on a wooded hillside near Sintra just north of Lisbon. The castle came with a cook and staff, verdant gardens, and lovely vistas from its ramparts of Estoril and the valley below. Monte Sereno was a perfect setting for good times and also for a game of "Murder," an after-dinner, lights-out, play-acting whodunit in which the murderer "strangles" his chosen victim and another player in the role of detective attempts to uncover the killer. I was appointed playwright for the evening's entertainment and created the following cast of characters. In our little drama each guest had been invited to the castle to attend an elegant candlelight dinner served by *Igor,* the family's faithful retainer, who longed to retire, if only the Duke would give him the old-age pension that he had promised.

Duke de Monte Sereno – an elderly and impoverished Portuguese aristocrat whose bloodline went back centuries. He disdained the *nouveau riche arrivistes* in Estoril and resented his wealthy American wife's wandering eye and dominating ways as she bankrolled their luxurious lifestyle. During the war the Duke had successfully aided fleeing refugees to escape the clutches of the Gestapo, and written a best-seller about his exploits, *Passage From Lisbon*, soon to be made into a movie starring Humphrey Bogart. However, he had received a mere pittance in royalties from his New York publisher, Erica, whose lame explanations about computer screw-ups were unconvincing.

Duchess de Monte Sereno, known as Leonore – the Duke's wife and widow of the multimillionaire Manhattan developer Harry Thump, whom she had loved dearly. She had vowed vengeance on the mobsters, whose demands for construction payoffs and violent threats had brought on Harry's heart attack and premature demise. She had come a long way from her days as a pom-pom girl at Peoria High School basketball games and loved being a duchess, a titled member of Portuguese nobility. However, she was increasingly restless with the quiet life preferred by her aging husband and enjoyed flirting with the tanned young men in tight pants hanging around the Estoril Casino and Bath Club. She also held periodic rendezvous with an amorous Spanish matador.

Tony Prosciuto – posing as a traveling sales representative for a pizza company, but actually a hit man for the notorious Bambino Crime Family in New York. Tony had been sent to Portugal to cut out a big piece of the

Estoril Casino action for the Mob in New York. Tony did not believe in negotiating. If there was an obstacle in his way, he removed it. Formerly he had forcefully represented the Family's interests in the corrupt building-trade unions that held up new construction projects in Manhattan until they were paid off. Darkly handsome in the Italian manner, he came naturally to chasing girls and catching them one way or another.

Bebe – a shapely jet-setting party girl. However, time and money were running out for Bebe, who had had atrocious luck as she gambled her way through the Riviera and Biarritz. She had just lost heavily playing baccarat at the Estoril Casino and was begging Jose, the Casino owner, for relief in paying off her debt to the house. The previous evening she had been seen dancing a close tango and conversing furtively with Tony at the Casino *boîte de nuit*. Bebe was far more talented in the bedroom than at the gaming tables.

Jose – the Estoril Casino owner who had built an extremely profitable business by being absolutely ruthless in collecting debts owed the Casino. The Casino also received substantial payments from other mysterious sources known only to Jose. He would like to take Fatima, who performed in his club, up to his penthouse for the night, but so far she had demurred. He was getting impatient. Furthermore, Tony's threats of physical violence, if he didn't hand over the big slice of Casino profits demanded by the Mob, made him very nervous. He was considering ways to eliminate the problem.

Fatima – the lovely *chanteuse* at the nightclub, who performed Egyptian belly dances at private parties. She was growing frightened over Jose's lecherous advances, and would like to ditch her sleazy life and elevate her station by marrying an aristocrat. Someone like the noble Duke, who caught her act and bought champagne for her at the club from time to time, would make a perfect husband, at least for the time being. Unfortunately his mean and haughty wife stood in the way.

Pedro – the handsome, well-tanned former fisherman and the owner of The Calimari, the most popular seafood restaurant in Estoril. This strapping, well-muscled man, who could physically take down any person in the room with ease, had caught Leonore's admiring eye and vice versa. But there were lots of dishes on his menu. He also frequented the nightclub to watch Fatima perform, and was furious at Jose's crude treatment of her.

Agatha – a famous British author of murder mysteries, whose seeming befuddlement was a mask for her razor sharp mind. She claimed to know a hundred ways to commit a murder that would go undetected and always seemed to arrive at the scene of a murder very shortly after it was committed. Critics praised the realism of her accounts. She was visiting Lisbon to research a new setting for her next mystery story. Agatha also possessed an encyclopedic memory for crimes and criminals and an uncanny ability to see through their current disguises.

Heinrich – a former Gestapo officer and German spy stationed in Lisbon during the war. His primary assignment had been to hunt down enemies of the Third Reich attempting to flee abroad. He had been known and feared for practicing what came to be known as "The Heinrich Maneuver," which caused his victims to disappear permanently. Now a salesman of German band instruments, he believed that cosmetic surgery had successfully concealed his earlier identity, but his face-lift was beginning to sag. If the Duke or anyone else recognized him, he would have to strike fast, just like a Panzer division in the good old days.

Ingrid – the voluptuous masseuse at the Bath Club, who would do anything her clients desired if it would help her haul in a rich husband. Her boss Jose would be a good catch, and she could take better care of him than that stupid cow Fatima. Her special massage entitled "Swedish Summer" was known to have made grown men cry out in ecstasy. In gratitude for her skills her customers sometimes confided in her quite valuable bits of information. Over time, her possession of so many secrets and intimate facts about prominent citizens had given her a unique status in the community far more influential than her apparent rank.

Ferdinand Cortez – a descendant of the famous explorer who secretly owned a sixteenth-century map showing the exact location off Caba de Roca of a sunken galleon with a cargo of precious treasure – gold, silver, and jewels. He had sought a loan from the Duke to finance retrieval of the treasure, but the Duke demanded a sixty-five percent cut and even threatened to inform the authorities about the treasure if Cortez refused. Cortez could never let this happen, and was pondering his next move. Then in a burst of indiscretion during a massage session with Ingrid, Cortez told her the location and number of the safety deposit box containing the map.

Erica – the glamorous New York publisher of *Passage From Lisbon*. Shortly after publishing the Duke's book and selling the movie rights, Erica had bought a large estate in Greenwich. She had never expected that the doddering old Duke, shut up in the family castle, would suspect that she was pocketing most of his compensation from the sales of his book. What if he blew the whistle on her? Nothing must disrupt her affair with a famous tennis star who had just won the women's championship at Wimbledon. Before she made the big time, Erica had been a crime reporter on *The Daily News*, and Tony Prosciuto looked very familiar to her.

Olga – an aging Albanian princess who was secretly a member of a militant Muslim terrorist group and would just as soon blow up the Casino or murder everyone in the room. Everybody thought she was a bit looney.

Hercule – an undercover Interpol agent assigned by the F.B.I., Scotland Yard, and French Sécurité to investigate leads regarding the large-scale laundering of drug money at the Casino. His cover was the role of an international playboy and gambler. In the course of his investigation he had uncovered the seamy side of life around Estoril, including the criminal or just plain sleazy activities of some of his fellow guests.

After dinner the party gathered in the living room where I assigned them their respective roles. Each participant then drew a playing card from a pack. Whoever drew the ace of spades would be the "murderer." The room was darkened and the game began.

For some minutes there were sounds of people shuffling and bumping about, and then a shriek and the cry of "Murder!" I turned on the lights, and there indeed was the victim lying supinely on a satin couch decorated with the Monte Sereno coat of arms. Playing the part of Hercule, and after revealing my true identity as a super sleuth, I was chosen to investigate the cold-blooded act, which I proceeded to do in my best H. Poirot manner. After interrogating all the witnesses I summoned the party together to announce my findings. While all of them had had a motive to murder, I had concluded, *sans doute*, that the murderer was none other than Igor. Once again it was the butler who had carried out the dastardly deed. One never knows what evil lurks in the heart of man.

Martha and Me

By 1979 all the kids had departed for boarding school, college, and other pursuits. After graduating from Harvard in 1976 Ned had become the editor of *The Black River Tribune*, a weekly newspaper in Ludlow, Vermont. He then became the first Lamont to be a Yale alumnus, graduating from the Yale School of Organization and Management in 1980. Just as I was a loyal Princeton Tiger for a year, Ned enthusiastically backed his school of the moment, even scoring the winning touchdown for Yale S.O.M. in a touch football game against its traditional rival, Harvard Business School.

Ned then signed on with Cablevision Systems, the rapidly expanding cable television company based in Long Island, and became a member of the Cablevision teams that won key franchises for the company in Boston and Fairfield County in southern Connecticut. Ned moved to Westport to set up the Fairfield system where Cupid's arrow struck home, uniting him with Anne Huntress. Annie was a cheerful, pretty blonde, a bright and intelligent young woman who had grown up near Milwaukee. She had gone to Stanford and was embarking on a career as a venture capitalist with Oak Investment Partners in Westport.

Following East Woods, daughter Helena attended Miss Porter's, her grandmother's old boarding school in Farmington, Connecticut. Finishing school finished *academe* for Helena. After graduation she rejected the conventional paths of her peers in order to see the world – first a visit to Athens to stay with the family of a young Greek boy she had met, and next on to Baja California to take part in a National Outdoor Leadership kayak program.

Helena then announced that she planned to join the crew of a trimaran, captained by her kayak instructor, embarking on a voyage to Tahiti. The makeup of the crew seemed a bit casual, and my research into the proposed venture made me very uneasy: Trimarans can break up in heavy seas; the course to Tahiti was across vast empty stretches of the Pacific, far from the commercial routes followed by other vessels; no help would appear promptly if they got into trouble. Helena was not an experienced sailor, and I told her that I thought that the cruise was a bad idea. Running true to form, she set sail from Mulegé with her pals.

Helena is a pretty, fair-skinned blonde. After several days at sea she came down with such a bad case of sun poisoning that the captain rowed her ashore and dropped her off with $25 in her pocket at La Paz, a forlorn little Mexican town near the tip of the peninsula. She telephoned from a dingy small hotel to report her plight. Despite living in the age of electronic banking, the money transfer from Morgan to the small Banco Nacional branch in La Paz, via Mexico City, seemed to go by Pony Express, generating more urgent calls. (I had learned earlier to be patient when doing business south of the border.)

Buz and I then flew out to La Paz to make sure that Helena was okay. She was, and now decided to stay on in La Paz and Cabo San Lucas, where she hooked up with a new friend, Alfonso, a mustachioed young Mexican teacher at the local college. When she was fully recovered they took a ferry over to the mainland and a bus down to Mexico City, where she rented a small apartment and took some Spanish language courses and a newspaper job making use of her English. Pretty American blondes were popular with Mexican youths. Helena made friends easily and was happy with her life. The *mañana* outlook on living suited her fine.

After we had left Helena in Mexico, we stopped off in Los Angeles for a few days and drove out to visit the Lamont winery and vineyards in the small town of Lamont near Bakersfield. My only connection with the winery had been that of a mail order customer for several years. The Lamont label always attracted attention at our dinner parties, and our guests seemed to enjoy the wines, although one regularly declared that their attributes were exceedingly modest and I only bought them for the label. Maybe she had a point.

We had toured the Napa Valley vineyards with their fancy wine bars and tasting rooms all geared to please the hordes of visitors. The Lamont winery was not in this league. In fact the young receptionist was frankly surprised to receive tourist visitors, but after rummaging around came up with a couple of baseball caps with the winery logo. The winery's main business was shipping its output north in huge tank trucks to be blended into some well known Napa Valley wines.

My other objective was to find out how the town came to be named Lamont, and the local postmistress filled me in. Jimmy Lamont was the homesteader who first settled in the area. I have no idea if our forebears were related, but I salute my hardy pioneering fellow clansman.

After East Woods Kim attended Emma Willard, the fine all-girls school in Troy, New York, and then went on to Connecticut College in New London. At college she majored in early childhood education and later worked as a counselor for two summers at The Children's Aid Society's summer camp for handicapped children. This kind of work is not for everyone. A lot of heart as well as skill is needed for this job and Kim did well at it. During the winter months she was a teacher in the Head Start program run by C.A.S. for the children of homeless families living in a welfare hotel in the city. Her college classmate Nick Burlingham, who had joined our crew on a Virgin Islands cruise earlier, was a welcome figure on the scene with growing frequency.

The kids usually joined us, at least briefly, at North Haven during the summer where the conversion in boat building material from wood to fiberglass was accelerating. My brother Lansing ordered the construction of the last wooden-hulled sailing dinghy in the fleet. Clearly the importance of historic preservation ranked higher on his agenda than the performance and annual maintenance of his craft, which is now lodged in our local museum.

I bought a twenty-two-foot Mako open motorboat, powered by twin fifty horsepower outboard engines – the theory being that if one collapsed you wouldn't be adrift without power at the mercy of the elements. The problem was that one or the other engine was always folding. Limping to or from picnics or cruises on one engine was frustrating and nerve-wracking, and it wounded our pride to ask for a tow. Furthermore, good outboard mechanics in Penobscot Bay were as rare as highly skilled brain surgeons; there were many more shipyard employees selling inflatable water toys and picnic coolers. At the height of the tourist season the line of patients at Dr. Fix-it's dockside waiting room in Camden was long indeed, especially when he was enjoying a lengthy lunch break.

We later moved up to a sturdy and efficient 150 hp engine and enjoyed smooth sailing, which boosted my morale and silenced the scoffers. We named our motorboat *Buz Bomb* and our new fiberglass sailing dinghy *Crazy Salt* (our favorite food seasoning before the doctors told me to lay off the salt), rejecting grander names like *Enterprise* or *Endeavor*. Only cute little names are appropriate for such small craft.

The big family event of 1983 was the marriage of Ned to Anne Huntress in St. John's Church of Cold Spring Harbor, followed by a tented reception at our home. The dance music supplied by debonair Alex Donner and his band was loud and joyful; the exotic hors d'oeuvres and dinners supplied by Martha Stewart and her well-organized crew were excellent. In 1983 Martha Stewart was still in the early stages of her dazzling career, well before she became a conglomerate and such a celebrity that the SEC decided to investigate her security transactions. Annie, who knew Martha and her business from Westport, had chosen her to cater the wedding. I had never heard of Martha Stewart, and after our first meeting I would never forget her.

I was reading a newspaper on the back lawn when Martha rolled up in a white stretch limousine to inspect the premises a week before the wedding. She was accompanied by a manservant in a white uniform and two large white-coated Samoyed dogs. She greeted us coolly, no small talk, and commenced her tour of the house and grounds in the manner of a queen who has been forced to spend the night in a small run-down castle. When Buz led her into our kitchen, there were a few moments of suspenseful silence as she looked about before announcing, without enthusiasm, "It will do."

Martha and Alex helped make the party a joyous occasion. It was an extremely warm September evening, and jackets were shed as the dancing became more frenetic. The champagne was chilled and plentiful; the swimming pool was cool and inviting; so what self-respecting band of ushers wouldn't throw the groom into the pool and jump in afterwards themselves? The marriage of one's firstborn is a milestone for all parents – a moment in time for which there is no more fitting song and lyric than "The world will always welcome lovers as time goes by."

Later on in her career Martha Stewart would forget that honesty is the best policy and pay the price for lying to government agents investigating her stock sales. She also forgot that the attempt to cover up crimes has often had devastating consequences for the perpetrator, from Nixon and the Watergate break-in to the Catholic bishops and the sex abuse scandals.

Martha's original transgression, for which, incidentally, she was not charged, was selling stock on the basis of "inside" information received from her broker. While Martha in this case knew better, this provision of the insider trading statute seems unfair for the millions of ordinary investors. The typical investor is not knowledgeable about the finer points of securities laws, such as what constitutes insider trading and how he must treat it. He trusts his broker or investment advisor, qualified professionals, to give him sound and lawful advice. When his broker calls to advise him to sell a stock and cites reasons which may, unbeknownst to the investor, be based on "inside" information, it is natural for him to accept the recommendation without further ado. If the broker is unlawfully disseminating "inside information," throw the book at him. He initiated the call and knows better. What if the client was planning to sell the stock anyway before the telephone call, but hadn't gotten around to ordering the transaction? After receiving the call he is locked into keeping the stock, because if he makes the sale then, he runs the risk of being charged with insider trading. The client who answers the telephone and innocently follows his broker's advice has done nothing wrong.

"The Ambassador" and Other Pursuits

I was progressing steadily in researching and writing *The Ambassador From Wall Street*. I also spent an inordinate amount of time trying to interest a literary agent and a publisher in my book, a common experience for many first-time authors, even Tom Clancy. While biographies of celebrity movie stars, athletes, and politicians command public attention, the story by an unknown author of a Wall Street banker who died more than forty years before was a hard sell. Despite my frustrations in finding a publisher, I enjoyed writing biography and history. I got a special kick out of digging out historical nuggets from original sources, previously undisclosed, such as some of the goings-on at the Paris Peace Conference in 1919, which Lamont attended as a member of the American delegation led by President Woodrow Wilson.

My invaluable partner in life and authorship is Buz, who took my handwritten manuscript, with arrows, balloons, and cross-outs, and typed it up on a Smith Corona word processor. (I have since learned to type, so Buz can rest easy.) It was no small feat: the book ran to 547 pages, including 22 pages of bibliography and source footnotes, and there were the usual frustrations of mechanical breakdowns, power outages, and the like.

Of all the two dozen people that I interviewed, one stood out – Franz Schneider, Jr. Franz, who died in 1993 at the age of 105, was clear-headed to the end. He had been the financial editor of the *New York Evening Post* when Lamont purchased it in 1918, and later of other newspapers before becoming a successful businessman. He was a Wall Street insider during the twenties and thirties, and had known Lamont well as both a journalist and business friend, the only person left with those unique qualifications when I was doing my research. Franz was a wonderful gentleman with a great sense of humor. He was very helpful to me.

Thomas W. Lamont's business papers at the Baker Library at Harvard Business School were my major original source for researching TWL's career. I spent many days sitting on the hard wooden chairs in the library's Manuscript and Archives section, going through some 276 boxes of files. I soon brought in a pillow to be more comfortable during my long hours of reading and scribbling. In recent years several famous authors have been found guilty of plagiarism. In the endless note-taking called for in doing historic research I can see how a few passages from other works might inadvertently slip into the text of a new book without proper attribution to the true author. I was careful to avoid this kind of sloppy mistake.

I also visited most of the places where TWL had stayed, from

Charlotteville, the tiny crossroads hamlet west of Albany where his grandmother and Lamont families had lived in the 1800s, to Cliveden, Lord and Lady Astor's palatial manor near London.

Without a publishing contract and deadline I had ample time to do other things. I continued to go into New York a couple of days a week, often to attend Children's Aid Society meetings where after serving as president I became chairman of the board. Buz and I regularly visited the C.A.S. neighborhood centers in the city and our two summer camps. At Thanksgiving we passed out turkey dinners to poor families at our Harlem centers – once in company with Frank Perdue, the poultry king who supplied the turkeys, and Mayor Ed Koch, who both resembled a couple of barnyard roosters preening for the TV camera crews.

The C.A.S. annual meetings are held in the New York City Bar Association building across 44th Street from the Harvard Club. On the day of our meeting one year, a well-publicized strike by the Harvard Club employees had just been settled after long and tense negotiations. The pickets had put away their signs and donned their crimson jackets again. In introducing Senator Patrick Moynihan, the guest speaker at our meeting, I said that he must be pleased as a former Harvard professor and an Assistant Secretary of Labor to see that the labor strife across the street at the Harvard Club had been amicably settled. I thought I was being quite clever, but you never know.

Every few years The Children's Aid Society held reunions in New York for the alumni and descendants of the Orphan Train, who had some wonderful stories to tell. For seventy-five years ending in 1929 C.A.S. transported children – abandoned or left in their care by destitute New York families – by train to midwestern states. At different stops along the way families, mainly from neighboring farms, came into town to select the children they wished to adopt. Some one hundred thousand city kids were placed and grew up in their new families, and by and large the outcomes for these children, while not perfect, were very good. The futures that these youngsters faced in the city without family and home were grim.

Art Smith was left as an infant in a basket in Gimbel's department store in 1918 and placed in city foster care. In 1922 he became an Orphan Train child, was adopted by an Iowa farm family, graduated from high school and college, fought in North Africa and Italy as a U.S. Army lieutenant in World War II, became a successful businessman, and later a very popular and able C.A.S. trustee. He and his wife Georgiana were married for sixty-plus years and have a bunch of children, grandchildren, and a great-grandchild.

Hubert Humphrey once said, "The moral test of government is how that government treats those who are in the dawn of life, the children; those who are in the twilight of life, the elderly; and those who are in the shadows of life – the sick, the needy, the handicapped." That is the mark of a civilized society. In 1988 I was elected to be a trustee and treasurer, and, later, vice president of the board of the St. Johnland Nursing Center in Kings Park, Long Island. St. Johnland is a 250-bed nursing center, with segregated sections for Alzheimer patients, head trauma, and other patients needing rehabilitation, and is currently building an adjacent 175-unit retirement community. Most patients are on Medicaid. Joan Wood and Mary Jean Weber have ably directed St. Johnland's operations during my tenure.

It is far easier to recruit strong governing boards for non-profit organizations in big cities like New York, where there is such a huge pool of talent, than out in the suburbs, where many folks are away at their jobs in the city. St. Johnland is fortunate in having such an able board. Retirees with good business experience can make important contributions on the governing boards of non-profits such as churches, hospitals, nursing homes, and youth clubs in suburban areas. There is plenty to do, besides playing golf, for retired guys with time on their hands.

The Boys and Girls Clubs of America is the national umbrella organization overseeing and assisting its many local member clubs throughout the country. BGCA is an impressive and important organization with about four million kids visiting their clubhouses and participating in their programs. As a member of its board of trustees I attended their annual conferences held in cities all over the country. The conferences, filled with organizational meetings and program seminars, were not all work and no play. In Dallas we attended a Cowboys football game. At the Orlando meeting Buz and I posed for a photograph with our hero Arnold Palmer at a cocktail reception at his Bay Hill golf club. Arnie assumed that we had played a round of golf at his club before the party. "How'd you like my course?" he inquired brightly. Buz sheepishly confessed that we had visited Epcot Center instead of playing golf. "Oh, that's nice," said Arnie, slightly crestfallen.

However, we did play golf later on at a few of the world's great courses on a trip to Scotland with three other couples, all Piping Rock Club golfers. Bill Simpson, who had left his native Scotland for the States many years before, was our leader in organizing our rounds at St. Andrews, Muirfield, and Royal Dornoch. We shared the course at Royal Dornoch with a bunch of workers from an oil platform in the North Sea who had flown in aboard a giant helicopter for a little R&R. Royal Dornoch was a great course with a relaxed and easygoing atmosphere.

The scene at St. Andrews was quite different from what we had experienced on our earlier visit. In 1967 we had casually dropped by without reserving a starting time, rented some clubs, and teed off. There were not many other golfers on the course. In the intervening years the popularity of golf had exploded around the world. On our 1984 trip Bill had made the reservations for our round at St. Andrews months before our arrival, and we had been given the precise starting time of 7:40 a.m. The first tee was surrounded by a horde of golfers with huge professional looking bags who had flown in from all over the world to play at the mecca of golf, the place where it all began. I did not spot any women golfers, and the starter confirmed my observation in telling me, "We don't have many mixed foursomes playing today, Mr. Lamont. Move your group around promptly, please." Over the public address system came the announcement, "Mr. Lamont's foursome to the first tee!"

My batting average on first tee drives is not great. Once when playing with Ted and Maru Brown at the Farmington Country Club, in Charlottesville, the starter fitted us into a tournament for Virginia golf pros. I dribbled the ball ten feet off the first tee on my opening drive, and I can still see in my mind's eye the little local caddies snickering behind their hands at my ineptitude. Knowing that I was the focus of attention at St. Andrews for scores of golfing elite assembled at the historic course, observing my every move and practice swing, a familiar wave of nervousness swept over me. I would rather have made a speech to a large crowd of bankers and have the jokes go flat than be center stage on the first tee at St. Andrews and top the ball. I swung wildly, made contact, and thank goodness got the ball up in the air and away, not so far, but away. Without looking back I picked up my tee and strode swiftly down the fairway.

My troubles at St. Andrews were not over. Central casting could not have done better in selecting a caddy for me who epitomized the real thing. He was wise and wizened looking and wearing a worn tweed cap and jacket, the traditional Scottish caddy garb, but you can't judge a book by its cover. He was clueless about distances and the finer points of the Old Course and how to "club" me. I was on my own.

Some years later Buz and I drove and golfed around Ireland with our pals Jake Underhill and Betsy Ashton. We played a half dozen courses starting at Ballybunion on the west coast, and moving north and then south, ending up at Portmarnock near Dublin. The times were peaceful in Ireland in the summer of 1995, and the pubs and restaurants in Belfast, the scene of such bitter strife in earlier years, were filled with happy folk. Sadly, the violent confrontations would return.

In my opinion, we American golfers have it easy compared to the local gentry playing those tricky seaside links courses in the British Isles, noted for their pot hole bunkers, hummocks and hills, and frequent onslaughts of wind and rain. It is very easy to lose a ball: The tall grass, gorse, and heather bordering the fairways and greens just gobble them up. Even Tiger Woods lost a ball in the "hay" at St. George's on the first hole of the British Open in 2003, with fore-caddies and spectators all about. At the Augusta National in the U.S., home of the legendary Masters tournament, the ground in the woods bordering the fairways was cleared out and covered with tanbark. When I drove a ball into the trees, it was easy enough to find and punch out. In Ireland my wandering golf shots were gone forever.

One year we flew out to Hawaii with Bill Simpson et al to see the sights and play golf at Kapalua Bay on Maui and Princeville on Kawai. On another Pacific excursion we stopped off at the big island of Hawaii, noted for its spectacular volcanic action. I have bounced errant golf balls off royal palms, desert cacti, and swimming pool patios, but never before off black lava outcroppings, which bordered the course that we played.

During the 1980s, when the Japanese economy was booming before its calamitous collapse, Japanese golfers thronged the Hawaiian courses, and Japanese tourists were everywhere. On our trip the National Park Service guide's tactful talk at the memorial site of the sunken U.S. battleship *Arizona* in Pearl Harbor did not call attention to the treacherous and inhumane nature of the air attack by the Japanese fleet without warning on December 7, 1941, killing some twenty-four hundred American sailors and soldiers. At dockside in Pearl Harbor I boarded the same 1942 model submarine that my brother had served on, now on display for tourists; it was strikingly small and cramped, almost claustrophobic, compared to today's giant nuclear subs. For the latest generation the "day of infamy" was no more than a page in a history book, or the subject of an occasional movie, and that's not altogether a bad thing. It's much more fun to enjoy the invasion of classy Japanese baseball players like Hideki Matsui and Ichiro Suzuki and my smooth-running Lexus. Now the great ocean that lies between our two nations lives up to its name.

We've played on some not so great courses, too. One stands out as a real "Billy goat pasture." In 1990 Frank and Lee Hawley introduced us to The Mill Reef Club, a sun-washed, rain-starved Caribbean island where Lord Nelson based his fleet at English Harbor in colonial times. Mill Reef is a great place to get away from the winter blahs, and we went back several times. The beach was beautiful, the water was incredibly blue, the trade winds rustled the palm trees and bougainvillea, and the nine-hole golf course was an abomination.

For starters, balls hit down the middle of the baked fairways of pebbles and sparse crabgrass often rolled away into strange places – such as coral outcroppings along the beach. I contemplated what I could do with a bulldozer and a few truckloads of topsoil. Arranging for more rain would be harder. Buz's superior golf skills deserved a club with a better golf course. So we moved on to Jupiter Island in southern Florida, which had a fine golf layout. It was also the home of one of the most popular golfers in the U.S., Australian Greg Norman, who gave an engaging talk to the club members one evening.

In many ways, Australians and Americans are much alike. Australians seem partial to our American culture and way of life, and vice versa:

Americans like the "Shark's" swashbuckling approach to golf and life; the sports-loving "Throw another shrimp on the barbie" lifestyle Down Under; Crocodile Dundee; and a host of good guy tennis aces for many years led by the great Rod Laver. In both countries the pioneering early settlement and bold exploration and development of vast continents shaped the national personality. Americans and Australians have enjoyed a far more free and open society than the class-entrenched social order of Britain from which both nations sprang. Furthermore, Australians are grateful to the U.S. for repulsing and ending the Japanese threat to their shores in World War II. Appreciating the long journey that travelers have made to visit their country, Australians are very hospitable to their foreign guests.

Geoff and Mary Ashton, one-time neighbors in Laurel Hollow before their return to Sydney, and John and Mary Pechar, whom we met on a trip to Europe, gave us a grand time in 1990 when we visited Down Under. The Pechars took us sailing on Lake Macquarie, and the Ashtons showed us about Sydney, which is built along the shoreline surrounding the huge harbor, and is surely one of the most beautiful urban settings in the world. We also spent a weekend with the Ashtons at Markdale, their lovely country home and gardens and base of their extensive sheep station deep in the bush country. I was well aware of the importance of wool exports to the Australian economy and tuned in while Geoff discussed business with his colleagues: Business was lousy, and wool stocks were piling up in government warehouses. One newspaper headline caught my eye: "Australia has 25 million excess sheep." I decided not to chime in with my own observations on raising sheep.

At the time, we were running about twenty-five sheep at Sky Farm in North Haven, for fun and definitely not for profit, and their days were numbered too. Our wool was good quality and used by local ladies to make colorful sweaters and shawls for sale. We also produced sheepskin blankets and enjoyed excellent lamb chops. There was another modest dividend. To my amazement, a check from the U.S. Department of Agriculture for several hundred dollars arrived each year, a subsidy to farmers who raised sheep and produced wool. Briefly I felt undeserving, but the feeling quickly passed and I deposited the checks. We had to end our pastoral enterprise when our friend and able caretaker, Gil Foltz, decided to head for Florida during the cold winter months.

From Adelaide we boarded a deluxe train to Alice Springs in the very geographic heart of the vast continent. The old cattle town, featured in Nevil Shute's great novel *A Town Like Alice*, is now a popular tourist attraction. We climbed to the summit of nearby Ayers Rock, a large reddish hill, sacred to the aborigines, that rises sharply from the endless plains on all sides. Our Aussie friends had never bothered to climb Ayers Rock, which indeed is the way I have treated the Statue of Liberty.

The only discordant note during our Australian tour was our

nerve-wracking flight to Markdale, about 250 miles from Sydney over dense bush country. Our group of five adults and two kids left Sydney late one Friday afternoon in the Ashtons' private plane piloted by Geoff. Weather reports to the contrary, we were soon bucking ferocious winds and driving rain buffeting our little plane about, slowing our speed over the ground and cutting visibility virtually to zero. Storms can develop suddenly in the hilly back country that we were traversing. White-knuckled at the controls, Geoff did not follow the usual practice of commercial airline pilots of reassuring passengers with soothing words like, "We're just going through a little turbulence. Nothing to worry about, folks." When Mary asked him about the plane's location, his response was an abrupt, "Don't bother me now, I'm too damn busy."

And indeed he was, steering the bouncing aircraft, calling in for information on the radio, and peering out the window for a familiar landmark. We were running well behind our ETA, and the fact that darkness was falling added to the tenseness that one could cut with a knife in the little plane's cabin. Finally we broke through the gloom, always a joyous moment when flying in bad weather, and I spotted a white church and farmhouse. "Now you know where you are," I said to Mary, pointing out the buildings.

"I've never seen that place before in my life," was the reply.

However, her husband knew where we were. With the encroaching darkness, I asked Geoff about the lights on his landing strip. "No lights," was the laconic reply. He usually flew to Markdale only during daylight hours. However, he expected that his caretaker, who should be at the landing strip waiting to pick them up in the station wagon, would turn on his headlights to light the way. He did just that, we landed safely, and all dived into a round of stiff drinks to calm our frazzled nerves. Buz and I left Markdale by automobile for Canberra after our weekend visit. Geoff Ashton is a good friend and skilled pilot. Nevertheless, I vowed never to fly in a plane piloted by a personal friend ever again. I would stick with the pros.

Family Affairs

After earning an M.A. at Columbia Teachers' College Kim became a teacher at a day care center in Boston. In 1991 she married Nicholas Burlingham at St. John's Church in Cold Spring Harbor, followed by a reception at our home in Laurel Hollow. Large contingents from East Woods School and Connecticut College, the latter attended by both bride and groom, made the party a merry affair. Nick – a big, warmhearted, and humorous guy – is a great addition to our family circle. The couple's first home was in West Hartford where Nick was a student at the University of Connecticut Law School. While Nick hit the books, Kim supervised a local day care center.

Helena continued to foster good relations south of the border in the small provincial town of Tepic, where she raised German shepherds. Apparently the considerable number of burglaries and other crimes in Mexico created a steady demand for ferocious guard dogs. She made many friends and became fluent in Spanish. Hardly anybody spoke English in Tepic.

Spanish is a very useful second language these days. Buz's fluency, acquired from growing up in Puerto Rico, has been invaluable in travel abroad as well as at home, in dealing with Spanish-speaking yardmen, cooks, and cleaning ladies. At New York City public schools where The Children's Aid Society operates she and the kids, mainly Dominican immigrant children, hit it off well in their native tongue. Now mother and daughter can break into Spanish whenever it suits them to shield their thoughts from Dad.

We visited Helena in Mexico, staying at the nearest decent accommodations – a hotel in Puerto Vallarta, a minor league beach resort on the Pacific coast. Helena and her canine operations shuttled back and forth between Florida and Mexico during the '90s. She finally settled in Palm Beach Gardens, in a house equipped with kennels and pens to accommodate her growing brood of golden retrievers – the business and breed of dog that she had now chosen to pursue. Her parents heartily welcomed her return to the States. I believe that if Helena ever wrote her memoirs about her adventures in Mexico for over a dozen years, it would be a best-seller.

Ned, with his home and office in Greenwich, had established his own company, Lamont Digital Systems, in 1984. The company provided satellite TV and computer hookups to college campuses around the country and a few community developments. Annie became a partner of Oak Investment Partners, another growing business in the booming investment climate of the '80s and '90s. In 1987 we celebrated the birth of our first grandchild, Emily, for whom another kind of career seemed promising. When she was a year old, her round, smiling face appeared on the cover of *American Baby* magazine, modeling a terry cloth beach robe and hat. In the coming years her siblings Lindsay and Teddy would complete the lineup of this upbeat family.

In 1990 Ned, a former deputy selectman of Greenwich, ran a vigorous campaign on the Democratic ticket for election to the state senate from his home town. His Republican opponent was William H. Nickerson, and the odds were heavily against Ned in solidly Republican Greenwich. He lost, but won more votes than any previous Democratic candidate for the seat. His showing was undoubtedly assisted by the campaign efforts of his parents, who handed out brochures and pot holders in shopping malls and senior citizen centers. The pot holders carried the message: "Lamont Can Handle the Hot Issues."

A few months after the election I was eating lunch at the club table in the second floor dining room of the Harvard Club in New York. Suddenly the fellow opposite me started gasping for breath, and, unable to talk, he clutched at his throat. Clearly a piece of food was blocking his windpipe. I assumed that the head waiter or some other member of the staff was trained to perform the Heimlich maneuver. Not so. Everyone stood around wondering what to do. I jumped behind the man and tried to execute the maneuver, which I had never attempted before, and failed. With hindsight I was much too gentle: You don't worry about cracking a rib in a life and death situation. I then ran downstairs to the front desk to get emergency medical assistance.

"We have an arrangement with Roosevelt Hospital, but in the heavy crosstown traffic it may take them twenty minutes to get here," was the reply.

I raced into the main dining room and told the maître d' to take me to whatever doctor was having lunch there that day. Luckily, there was a doctor at a nearby table. The doctor and I sprinted back upstairs to where the poor fellow had now collapsed over the table. The doctor, a big man, quickly went around behind the victim, wrapped his arms around his lower chest, and gave a mighty squeeze. Out popped a bit of bacon (the man had been eating a B.L.T.), and in a few minutes he had completely recovered. He thanked me profusely for coming to his aid so quickly in his life-threatening situation. I apologized for being unable to help him in my first effort and introduced myself.

"Are you related to Ned Lamont in Greenwich, by any chance?" he asked, and I replied that I was Ned's father.

"Well," said the gentleman, "I just defeated him in the state senate election in Greenwich. He ran a good campaign and is a fine guy. My name is Bill Nickerson."

There are a lot of jerks in this world, even from Harvard. Another fellow sitting at the table said to me later, "How did you dare run the risk of physically handling that person? Don't you know that if you had harmed him, he could sue you?"

My own health remained fine except for a pesky colon polyp that the doctors in one colonoscopy after another couldn't remove. I went from a Huntington, Long Island, doctor to a Memorial Sloan-Kettering doctor to a Park Avenue doctor seeking someone with the magic touch. I was told that if the Park Avenue specialist, reputed to be the best in the business, failed, surgery was the only alternative. One doesn't ignore pre-cancerous colon polyps.

The doctor gave me a tranquilizing injection, and as I was resting bare-assed on the operating table waiting for the great exploration to begin, a pretty young blond wearing a white jacket came into my view.

"Oh, by the way, Mr. Lamont," said the doctor, "Allow me to introduce Fraulein Schmidt from Stuttgart. She's taking a training course at our hospital, and I've invited her to observe my technique in this procedure. I trust that's okay with you."

"I'm glad to do my bit for medical science," I replied. "Let's just get on with it, please."

After the procedure, the doctor presented me with a wonderful Technicolor picture of my colon, which bore a striking resemblance to the Luray Caverns. Like his two predecessors, he had been unable to excise the offending polyp. Three strikes and you're out, and I was off to Sloan-Kettering for surgery.

I had just turned sixty-five, Medicare kicked in, the operation went smoothly, and I spent the next few days recovering at the hospital. My roommate was in much worse shape than I was, and I often walked down the hall with my portable IV stand to give him a little privacy when his family came to visit. No hospitals are any fun, and Sloan-Kettering, with so many cancer victims, could be a sad place for some patients and their families. I was there during the Christmas season. In the big social room on our floor a score or so of patients, many in wheelchairs, had gathered around the Christmas tree to eat cookies, sip milk punch, and listen to holiday songs. Many were in pretty poor shape, but they were determined to make the most of each day. One lady, in a burst of exuberance, stepped out of her wheelchair and danced a little jig to "Jingle Bell Rock!" It was a Christmas scene to remember.

Our family continued to flock to North Haven, like Arabs to Mecca, each summer. For those who favored peace and quiet on their summer holidays July was the month of choice. The social pace gathered speed in late August with the approach of the Labor Day exodus. Two high-spirited parties joined the Pulpit Harbor Tea as significant annual events. John and Caroline Macomber served clam chowder, corn, and lobsters to a huge throng at their lovely home, and Tom and Olive Watson offered an evening of lively square dancing in their barn.

Often notable figures, who were Watson house guests, joined the fun, and one year Walter Cronkite showed up. For our recent wedding anniversary party we had commissioned a professional entertainer to make an audio tape recording his impersonations of various celebrities extending their greetings to us. The voice of Walter Cronkite introduced the greeters we had chosen – Ronald Reagan, George Bush, Sr., and Jimmy Stewart. We had provided the impersonator with some information about ourselves and he produced a very funny tape.

While chatting with Walter at the barn dance, I told him that we had come across this very talented fellow who sold greetings tapes with an uncannily realistic impersonation of him. Walter was definitely not amused. "These guys never ask my permission," he fumed. "They run a profitable business impersonating me, and I don't even know what they're saying! Who is this fellow? I want to get to the bottom of this." I told Walter that I couldn't remember his name and quickly suggested that we join the Virginia Reel, whose lines were just forming. Walter swung his partner with gusto, and the matter of the impersonator was forgotten.

Harvard
on Land and Sea

In the course of attending Harvard events, like Visiting Committee meetings, reunions, and fund-raising dinners, I have had fleeting contacts with the presidents of Harvard over the past forty years. In keeping with American informality, Harvard presidents have always addressed me in their letters as "Dear Ted" before delivering their message about the university's needs or thanking me for past support; I assume that they follow this practice with thousands of alumni. The letters are couched in friendly and familiar terms, almost like a communication between two old friends.

However, only one of these gentlemen could actually identify me face to face, which is understandable given the hundreds of alumni that college presidents meet at different events. Maybe it was Harvard that invented the concept of the identification tag, worn on the lapel of one's suit jacket, to help its president out at large alumni meetings. It is extremely useful in enabling people to greet each other heartily. The trick is to check a fellow's name *before* saying hello. Then you can maintain direct eye contact, and he won't catch you glancing down to read the name on his tag.

Nathan Pusey had been a good friend of my father, who, with his fellow members of the Corporation, Harvard's senior governing board, selected Pusey to be president of Harvard. I was stunned by one particular conversation that I had with Nate which took place at a reception in New York after he had retired from Harvard. During the Vietnam War Harvard had banned the ROTC program for training young men and women to be military officers at the college, forcing them to travel to MIT to take the required courses. In 1993 Harvard added insult to injury by ruling that the ROTC commissioning ceremony for Harvard graduates could no longer be held on campus or even be announced in the Commencement Day publications. These wrong-headed decisions about ROTC training at Harvard were bad for the university, bad for the country, and insulting to the men and women in the armed forces past and present. Colin Powell, a distinguished general and statesman, started his military career in the C.C.N.Y. ROTC program in New York. To spurn young people who planned to join our armed forces was unpatriotic and contemptible. I was one of many alumni who were angry and ashamed of their Alma Mater's action, which surely fueled the long-standing charges of elitism at Harvard.

In our conversation I asked ex-president Pusey, "How could Harvard, its president, and governing boards ever have made such a bad decision?" Nate replied, somewhat sadly, that the faculty was all-powerful in matters relating to academic curriculum. The president and governing boards had no authority to deal with the ROTC question even though it was an issue of major significance to Harvard and the nation. Furthermore, it appeared that the faculty's decisions regarding the ROTC were influenced by political issues, such as the government's policy regarding gays in the military, rather than academic considerations. What an incredible state of affairs! Why the president and governing boards of Harvard lacked the intestinal fortitude to assume control of the ROTC program was a mystery to many Harvard alumni.

In 2005 the Harvard faculty again demonstrated a shocking lack of loyalty and concern for their university's well-being and repute. A number of members had objected to a controversial issue raised by President Lawrence Summers at an academic conference, and many more were critics of Summers' management style in his role as president of the university. Despite President Summers' prompt apology and promise to work harmoniously with the faculty in the future, the faculty quickly passed a resolution expressing no confidence in his leadership. This astounding step by the faculty, which was so embarrassing for Harvard and exasperated many alumni, was widely reported in the media.

Derek Bok, following Pusey as president, was a brilliant former dean of the Law School. He was an able leader of the university, but appeared awkward and uncomfortable in schmoozing with alumni and guests at the various gatherings he had to attend. His talks to us sounded more like academic lectures. I assume that many college presidents find this public role burdensome. Nevertheless, it goes with the territory.

On a trip to Mexico I heard a good Derek Bok story from a Mexican lady with a connection to the executive office of the president of Mexico. El Presidente was looking forward to his afternoon appointment with Bo Derek, the American actress and sex symbol, who was making a movie in Mexico City. Perhaps they would have a cool drink on the office patio, and he would pick up some interesting Hollywood gossip. His expectations were dashed when, at the appointed hour, in walked Derek Bok, the president of Harvard University and a serious man who liked to discuss weighty subjects. Mr. Bok was perplexed as to why the president seemed somewhat let down by his arrival. Undoubtedly, the president of Mexico had some words later with his appointments secretary.

Neil Rudenstine, the next president of Harvard, was an agreeable and articulate speaker. He and President Bill Clinton shared a singular attribute: Possessing pleasant built-in smiles, they hardly ever took a bad picture. I liked Rudenstine's reply to my question at a Harvard meeting in New York about the ever-increasing tuition costs at Harvard. The conventional response to this question is either, "That's why the college needs

Good times in faraway places:
the Sphinx, Stonehenge,
the Matterhorn, the Mississippi
River, the Great Wall,
and Plaza de San Marco.

your support for our scholarship program," or, "In our budget planning this year we will be rigorous in cutting all unnecessary costs." Rudenstine's answer was, "Well, sometimes you have to pay a little more for the very best."

One time I sat next to Neil at a Harvard School of Education lunch in New York. He had just returned to duty after a month or so of illness. In response to an interviewer's question Rudenstine had reeled off the names of a half dozen books he had read during his convalescence, which made for a nice story in the *New York Times* listing the books that were the current favorites of the president of Harvard. At the time I was busy promoting sales of my own book, *The Ambassador From Wall Street*, which had just been published.

I said to Rudenstine, "I wish you absolutely the best of health. But if by any chance you do get sick and a reporter asks you what books you've been reading, do me a favor and mention *The Ambassador From Wall Street*. I'd really appreciate it. I also think you'd enjoy the book!" Neil was non-committal.

As a member of the Visiting Committee to the Graduate School of Education at Harvard, I was lobbying for the school's support of an approach to public school education that The Children's Aid Society was enthusiastically backing – the community school or full-service-school concept. In New York City C.A.S. had partnered with ten public schools in Washington Heights and the Bronx where many poor Hispanic immigrant families were concentrated. When the schools officially closed at 3 p.m., C.A.S. took over and kept them open until ten o'clock in the evening, plus weekends and during the summer. After-school programs – academic and recreational – are essential in all schools and especially in cities where without them many kids will simply hit the streets and get into trouble or go home and turn on the TV. C.A.S. put in medical clinics and assigned social workers to each school as well, knowing that if children are hungry, or ill, or being abused at home, they will not succeed in the classroom. The schools became true community centers where courses in self-improvement like citizenship and parenting were offered to local residents in the evening. The community school idea, with local variations, was catching on in school districts across the country.

I described the community school program to Rudenstine that day at lunch and he seemed favorably impressed. However, he shied away from my suggestion that Harvard, if it agreed that the program had merit, might publicly back the concept as an important new way that should be considered to strengthen public education in America. He did not think it appropriate for the university to become a public advocate for this or any other particular program.

I was disappointed. It seemed to me that the country's leading institution of higher education and its highly rated graduate school, which trained hundreds of public school teachers and administrators each year, had a duty to express its views publicly on critical issues in the field of public education. Education was Harvard's business, and to avoid speaking out seemed a bit wimpy to me. Harvard's current president, Lawrence Summers, does not appear to be the sort to hold back from expressing an opinion on important issues related to the university's mission.

Harvard has long offered a full menu of enticing foreign tours to its alumni and friends, often by cruise ship. Buz and I have joined five of these cruises, sailing about the British Isles, the Baltic Sea, and the Mediterranean – from Gibraltar to Tel Aviv and Tunis to Genoa – stopping en route each day to visit historic sights and cities. The ships are not too large, seventy-five to eighty passengers; the crews are efficient and cheerful; the accommodations and dining are excellent; our fellow passengers – Harvard grads, their spouses and friends, and alumni from other institutions – are congenial. It is a luxurious way to travel. You unpack at the start and repack your bags ten days later, having seen the sights in a half dozen or so countries.

We have driven about the British Isles and Western Europe, darting from hotel to inn, packing and unpacking each day, and pondering road maps and signs in foreign languages. In Great Britain driving on the left hand side of the road is an added strain. Maybe the European Union should require all of its member countries to drive on the right. One thing is for sure: Cruising through Europe is a lot less stressful than driving.

On these cruises professors from Harvard and other experts gave lectures on the history, culture, and politics of the towns and countries that we visited and led our tours on shore along with local guides. Travel agents handled the logistics of the tours – generally, but not always, smoothly.

It had been a long, dusty bus ride from Cairo to Port Said, the seaport at the northern end of the Suez Canal, and the seventy-odd Harvard alumni and their spouses, friends, and escorts were hot and tired. The travelers, largely retirees of a certain age, eagerly looked forward to boarding their gleaming white ship, the *Aurora II*, in full view at the nearby dock, where modern bathrooms and hot showers, cool drinks, gourmet dinners, and soft beds with white sheets beckoned them.

Our tour agent presented the group's travel documents to the Egyptian army sergeant on duty at the dock. Unexpectedly, a lengthy discussion ensued and steadily became more heated. According to the sergeant our papers were not in order; some official stamp of approval was missing. The officer in charge of port departures had gone home to dinner, and the sergeant did not have the authority to waive the red tape regulation and let us board the ship. We had to remain in the buses while he tried to sort things out on the telephone. The outcome was not agreeable to the weary travelers: We were ordered to follow his jeep in our buses to the local police precinct station.

Darkness had fallen as we drove through the seedy streets of the port city, which a travel writer once described as "a foul sink." The police station and neighborhood compared unfavorably with "Fort Apache" in the South Bronx. The sergeant disappeared into the station house, and we all just sat there waiting and waiting. It was time for dinner, and hunger pangs added to everyone's physical discomfort and angry frustration.

Our situation had gone from bad to awful, and it was time to try to do something about it. It occurred to me that there were two key figures on the bus who might save the day – the only doctor on board, a psychiatrist from Silver Hill, a rehab center for substance abusers, and a professor of antiquities from Harvard. I asked them to join me on the sidewalk outside the bus to discuss my plan.

"Bill," I said to the doctor, "You should tell the Egyptian officers that in your capacity as the doctor assigned to oversee the medical needs of the group you have reviewed all the medical records of the travelers. They are quite an elderly group, and a number have high blood pressure, respiratory problems, and other ailments. Furthermore, they are now suffering from hunger and fatigue. If there was any further delay in boarding the ship, the Egyptian government would bear the responsibility for any cardiac incidents or other illnesses that members of this tour might suffer."

"Now Paul," I said to the professor, "You should identify yourself as the senior Harvard official in charge of the group. In your opinion the government's treatment of this innocent group of American tourists is absolutely outrageous. Surely the Egyptian government would not want to discourage foreign tourists from coming to Egypt by treating them in this manner. You should demand a telephone to call the American Ambassador in Cairo immediately to lodge an official protest. You could also allude to U.S. foreign aid and cooperative programs between Egypt and Harvard that could be jeopardized by this unwarranted harassment of American tourists. Surely nobody wants that outcome, and accordingly the passengers should be released to board their ship immediately."

The fellows agreed with the plan, and I asked one of the officers from the police station to join us to discuss the situation. Our performers carried out their roles with fervor, by no means entirely feigned, and a half hour later we were boarding *Aurora II*. Bureaucratic rigidity and red tape are a common Third World phenomenon.

On the same cruise we visited Jerusalem and Bethlehem. At The Church of the Nativity, a long line of tourists waited to descend a steep and winding stairway to the grotto below, where, according to tradition, Christ was born. The little cave is one of the most holy places in the world, revered by Christians, Jews, and many Muslims. A perspiring, overweight lady pierced the mood of solemnity as she eyed the narrow little stairway she had to manage, exclaiming "Boy, this better be worth it!" It was. Our group was so moved on that October morning in the small cave where our Lord was born that we spontaneously broke into singing "Silent Night."

The spiritual tranquility of the holy place would be rudely shattered some months later when the little church became the scene of a bloody confrontation between Palestinians and Jews. Even in Bethlehem the message of our Lord, "Peace on Earth, Good Will Toward Men," was consumed by the flames of hatred.

Another pleasing way to see Europe is by barge travel along its waterways. For comfort and relaxation this mode of travel is fine, but don't expect to cover much ground and see a lot if your time is limited. One autumn week we joined the Hawleys and Jack and Betty Valentine in France for a barge excursion on the Cher River, which runs through the Loire Valley châteaux country. We covered about twenty-five miles in all.

Gliding downriver through the pastoral countryside was so very peaceful that, in truth, I welcomed some completely unscheduled action that abruptly shattered the serenity of the scene. Because of an exceptional summer drought, the water level of the river was very low – so low that our craft ran aground from time to time, stirring up clouds of mud. When Captain Pierre had tried his best maneuvering techniques and failed to dislodge us, he called the lock keeper upstream to release some more water into our section of the river. After a short wait we floated off, only to repeat the process a little further downriver beyond the next lock. We enjoyed our stops along the way to visit castles and cafés and the friendly welcome we received from local residents. Barge travel was very good living in very slow motion.

Ordinary Americans and Frenchmen get along just fine, but diplomatic confrontations between our governments go back many years. Thomas W. Lamont wrestled with the French negotiators over the reparations issue at the Paris Peace Conference in 1919 and throughout the 1920s. More recently, the French strongly opposed the U.S. invasion of Iraq, and Americans indulged in a lot of silly talk about "freedom fries" and spurning brie cheese and French chardonnay. Some elitist French have resented another form of American invasion – our movies and other modern cultural symbols such as fast food restaurants.

Yet the tense relations between our governments from time to time should not diminish the friendship that exists between our peoples. While the French might shrink from George W. Bush, they love Disney World and Jerry Lewis. Buz and I happened to be in Paris during the fiftieth anniversary of D-Day when many American tourists and army veterans returned to attend the anniversary celebration. They were warmly greeted by the French in an outpouring of friendship and gratitude for the

American campaign to liberate France in 1944. In sidewalk cafés all along St. Germain des Près and the Champs Elysées, Yanks and Parisians chatted amiably and toasted each other.

A few years later we visited our friends Harold and Evelyn Tittmann in their restored old farmhouse near Manerbes in Provence, one of the charming little hill towns in the region. Driving back to Nice we spotted a McDonald's restaurant and decided to drop in for a hamburger. In Paris some residents had boycotted these American fast food emporiums, considering them to be incompatible with French custom and cuisine. Furthermore, they were shocked to hear reports that McDonald's hamburgers were being made with genetically altered beef. Apparently the folks near Nice had not received the message from Paris. Our McDonald's was filled with happy local parents and kids munching away on Big Macs and drinking Cokes. The restaurant was festooned with Halloween decorations, and in appearance could just as well have been in Omaha. Clearly the news from Paris wasn't the whole story in France, where McDonald's, with a thousand-plus restaurants, is very popular.

Club Sports

The Piping Rock Club is an old established country club in Locust Valley, Long Island – very white shoe and proper. The mandated dress code for tennis players is, naturally, all white. I've played many times on the club's grass courts, which are maintained in impeccable condition. When John McEnroe was an active player the club invited him to practice on the courts before Wimbledon, the premier international tournament, which is played on grass. One hot June day I joined the small crowd watching him hit balls with his brother, Patrick. At the end of their practice session John stripped off his sweaty polo shirt and put on a clean one.

"Do you see what he's doing – taking off his shirt!" exclaimed a senior member in a shocked voice.

"Well," I replied. "They all do it nowadays. I've even seen them take off their shirts at Wimbledon."

"I know," said the old fellow. "But *this* is The Piping Rock Club!"

We have attended the U.S. Tennis Opens since Forest Hills was their venue. After our friends Rob and Anita Stowe gave up their box in Arthur Ashe Stadium, J.P. Morgan Chase came through with seats in their corporate box. One year, after watching some tennis, Buz and I went down to the Morgan hospitality tent for lunch. On the way back to our box we ran into a local friend, Terry Parsons, an attractive, fortyish blonde. Terry's seat was way up in the "nosebleed" section on the rim of the stadium, about as far from the action as one could get. "Mind if I tag along with you guys?" she asked.

"No problem," I replied. "But we've got to get by the fellow examining tickets at the entrance to the corporate section."

After checking our tickets and observing my gray locks the attendant smiled and said, "Go on in, Dad." However, he was about to send Terry on her way.

I thought quickly and said, "You've got that right. Terry is our daughter and she's just flown in from Chicago to visit us for the weekend. It would be great if you'd let her sit with us. I know there's room in the box." The attendant thought it over a moment and replied, "Ah, go ahead in and enjoy the match." Being a bit long in the tooth has its benefits along with its drawbacks.

Golf is a great spectator sport too, both on the tube or in the gallery at tournaments, where one must scramble nimbly through the big crowds of spectators to get a good view of the action. Buz and I have attended the Masters at Augusta National, the new battleground in the feminist cause, and a handful of U.S. Opens at The Country Club, Shinnecock, and the Bethpage Black Course on Long Island. The once-exclusive country club sports of tennis and golf have soared in popularity, and, as in other pursuits, the participants are no longer all lily white. When I was a boy, Negroes were referred to as "colored people." Other designations have emerged and receded, and we have progressed all the way over the years from "colored people" to the more inclusive "people of color." In recent years three of the most powerful figures in international relations have been Kofi Annan, Colin Powell, and Condoleeza Rice, while Tiger Woods, V. J. Singh, and the Williams sisters dominated golf and women's tennis.

The huge throngs of spectators at the Bethpage tournament showed how golf has caught on with the New York sports crowd. Boisterous and good humored, not unlike the crowds at baseball and football games, they had come both to watch the world's best golfers in action and to have a high-spirited outing. At the same time they were knowledgeable about the game and spectator protocol. No one yelled "You da man!" until a second *after* the player had hit his drive. The day we attended was Phil Michelson's birthday, and as Phil and his playing partners approached the 17th green, the crowd in the grandstand broke into a chorus of "Happy Birthday" and did the "wave" as a birthday tribute to Phil. The vendors selling beer had a very good day too.

For many years we had headed west for winter ski trips, a few times to Aspen, Alta, or Sun Valley, but usually to Vail, where we rented the same house on the hill above Lion's Head for a number of years. Downhill skiing is the sport that many people give up first in their senior years. When the subject comes up, they quickly point out that they still do cross country, which is more like a walk in the park. In our seventies Buz and I abandoned our jaunts to the Rockies for skiing. We joined our kids and grandchildren skiing in Vermont a few times toward the end of March when it was warmer, and that was it for skiing. Tennis doubles and golf are the sports you can keep right on playing as time marches on, which meant heading to Florida for part of January and February, fleeing those cold winter months up north.

Our hospitable friends Dick and Martha Jackson, who had a beach house on Jupiter Island, Florida, invited us to join their house parties several times, and for some years since, we have rented houses of our own for five or six weeks each winter. Daughter Helena lived in nearby Palm Beach Gardens with her handsome golden retrievers, which loved to romp on the broad sandy beach outside our house.

The center of activity on the island is the Jupiter Island Club, which features a pretty golf course alongside the Inland Waterway with palm trees bordering the fairways, a beach club, and good tennis and dining. We like the relaxed atmosphere of the place, and with the backing of friends we joined the club.

The Jupiter Island residents, an aging group of Old Money and retired

CEOs, are congenial, sophisticated, and almost solidly Republican in their politics. To be politically correct at the club one should vote the straight Republican ticket – always – regardless of the issues or quality of the candidates. To show approval of any accomplishment of Bill or Hillary Clinton was heresy. (We were quite familiar with "country club Republicans," having been Piping Rock Club members for forty-odd years; in fact for some time I had been one of them. However, when dining at the clubs, more neutral topics than politics were usually discussed – such as the culinary skills of the new chef or, God forbid, a blow-by-blow account of somebody's winning round of golf.)

The social structure of the Jupiter Island community is three-tiered. The top class of residents is the homeowners who spend six months or so in Florida before heading north in the summer. They are the Old Guard who run the Jupiter Island Club and enjoy their local organizations – including a private restaurant called the Yacht Club, which has nothing to do with maritime activities. The Wiz Kids, a group of old guardsmen, hold their monthly luncheons with speakers at the Yacht Club, which is noted for its fine cuisine and service.

The middle category is the renters, who stay for one or two months like ourselves. And then come the short-term visitors who stay in the clubhouse rooms or cottages. Some members harbor distinct geographical preferences: The socially desirable "Upper East Side" is south of Bridge Road. The top two groups are all members of the club, and both are respectively well aware of their status vis-à-vis the groups below them. A homeowner once asked me if I was a visitor, and I replied that we planned to stay for about six weeks that year. "Oh, you're a visitor!" she replied emphatically.

At our small beach house the roar of the ocean lulls us to sleep at night and our grandchildren build sand castles in the morning. The living is so good in this pleasure-seeking community that for the first time in my life I indulged in a pedicure, hoping that none of my tennis buddies would spot me undergoing treatment in the beauty salon. However, I was assured by the pedicurist that she treated some of the community's leading citizens, and that there was really no need to draw the curtain in the alcove where she was ministering to my toes.

There was another first-time experience for me at Jupiter Island. One year Buz's brother Scott came down from Vero Beach to join us in a member-guest tournament. We made our way around the course to the 14th hole, which is a par three over water. In previous rounds I'd hit into the water, the rough, the traps, and even, but rarely, onto the green. I took out my seven wood, teed up the ball, and swung away. I couldn't follow the ball all the way, and was surprised when the caddy for the foursome in front of us, who had just left the green, started jumping up and down hollering, "Hole in one!" Wow! A hole in one is a very big deal in the golfing world (even though it is at least ninety-nine percent pure luck), and it was my first after bashing around golf courses for forty-odd years.

Then one of my partners asked, "Do you have hole-in-one insurance? You know you're going to have to treat everyone to champagne back at the clubhouse after the round." Of course I didn't, and I knew there were at least seventy-two players on the course. Rain has ruined many a golf game, but this time the drenching downpour that started as we came down the 18th fairway was manna from heaven for me. It cleared out almost the whole clubhouse crowd, who raced off for their cars and homes. I ended up buying drinks for my partners and a couple of pals. It was a kick later on to see my name inscribed on the clubhouse plaque listing the names of the members of the hole-in-one club at Jupiter Island going back some fifty years. However, my next round gave me ample reason to remain humble about my game.

Several teaching pros at Piping Rock have ministered to my golf skills, or lack thereof, with minimal impact. Certainly not their fault. Those guys were good teachers and players. Tom Nieporte and Jim Albus each won a pro tour event – the Bob Hope Classic and the Senior PGA Championship, respectively – when they were the active head professionals at the club, a unique accomplishment. At the award ceremony after his tournament in Palm Springs Bob Hope presented Tom with a big Chrysler station wagon along with his prize money. Having been informed that the Nieportes had eight children, Hope, with his trademark leer, quipped, "I don't know how you ever found time to practice, but this wagon should certainly come in handy.

Sea Stories

I proudly display the pennant of the North Haven Yacht Club on the bow of my thirty-four-foot cabin cruiser. We purchased the blue Sabreline fast trawler in 1992 and named her *Buz Bomb II*. After bouncing around Penobscot Bay in *BB I*, our Mako outboard, for twenty summers, we opted for a little more comfort in our senior years. About the same time, Buz and I gave up dinghy racing at the yacht club. Dinghies are an uncomfortable and tippy little craft, and when you slip further and further back in the fleet each race and start counting the dwindling number of boats behind you, it's time to seek another diversion.

After keeping *BB II* in Huntington Harbor and exploring the local waters for a few years, we moved her out to Greenport on the eastern end of Long Island, which opened up a whole new cruising area – Peconic Bay and Sag Harbor, Block Island and Fishers, Stonington and Watch Hill. We often invited another couple to join us or cruised in tandem with seafaring friends in their boats.

We steamed all over Long Island Sound, around the Statue of Liberty and Manhattan, and up the Connecticut and Hudson rivers. On one trip up the Hudson we cruised to Troy, hung a left, and headed west on the Erie Canal through about twenty locks to Utica before reversing direction and heading home. The countryside was unexciting, the drill in passing through lock after lock became tedious, and canal boating required operating at a slow speed. Creating the slightest wake aroused the residents on the shores of the canal and upper Hudson to vociferous protest. On the other hand, the lower half of the Hudson River, passing by Storm King Mountain and West Point, is deservedly famous for its spectacular and serene beauty. It is no wonder that so many artists fell in love with these scenes.

In taking *Buz Bomb II* on a half dozen or so round trips to North Haven and back, Buz and I stopped off in most of the good harbors en route. *BB II* can sleep two comfortably and four if you don't mind close quarters. While we have spent some nights on board at anchor, we usually headed for a marina with shore power and facilities, perhaps with a good seafood restaurant nearby – the kind of evening that appealed after eight to ten hours at sea.

Sometimes we stayed with friends in Marion, Manchester, or Edgartown. For Buz, dining at Marblehead's Eastern Yacht Club brought back bittersweet memories of her last visit to the club some fifty years earlier. She had taken a summer job as a waitress there when she was a Middlebury student and, along with her roommate, led a successful campaign for higher wages ($35 to $40 a week), shorter hours, and better meals including orange juice and ice cream. The staff also won the right to use an old tennis court they had restored – access once promised and later denied. The threat of a strike at the famous yacht club made the Boston papers, and faced with widespread public sentiment backing the waitresses and their cause, management granted their demands.

We liked nice, easygoing cruises with no excitement, but that's not always what we got. Tense situations and even near catastrophes go with the territory, as all sailors know. The first time Buz and I took *Buz Bomb II* alone to North Haven we ran into dense fog in Muscle Ridge, a passage through numerous rock-bound islands south of Rockland. I was navigating by Loran, which gave me range and bearing to our next waypoint, when suddenly the instrument went haywire and started throwing out pure gibberish. We couldn't see more than ten yards ahead but I could hear waves pounding on the nearby beaches. We had radar but no GPS in those days and I had to decide quickly what to do next. Fortunately, I had spotted another boat on our course earlier and hailed her captain on the VHF radio when he got closer. He was bound for Rockland, and, feeling immensely relieved, I followed him closely until we broke into the clear in the bay and I could head for Pulpit Harbor, our home port. It is a great moment for a captain when the fog suddenly lifts and you can see where you are going once again.

Returning *Buz Bomb II* to Long Island from Maine during the hurricane season could be tricky, too. One time a howling gale and huge waves in Massachusetts Bay drove us into Scituate harbor to seek shelter for three days. Each morning I joined the other skippers hanging around the dock, fellow unwilling captives of the foul weather. Over Dixie cups of coffee we listened to the weather reports and forecasts about when the storm might break and called homes and offices about our delayed arrivals. We finally made it home safely.

There were also unfortunate incidents that we couldn't blame on the weather. Buz steered us into trouble one time and saved us from disaster another. Near the entrance to Huntington Harbor I was below in the cabin and Buz was at the helm when I felt a sharp bump and heard a horrible scraping sound. Buz had missed a buoy and we had bounced off an underwater ledge. We continued our run into our slip in the harbor, but I could tell that we were wounded. We soon found out how grievously. When we stopped our forward motion to maneuver into the slip, the water started pouring into the engine room through the propeller shaft through-hull fitting, which had been ripped open, overwhelming the capacity of our bilge pump. Fortunately the marina staff were right at hand and came to our rescue, plugging the hole and pumping us out with a high-capacity boatyard pump. *Buz Bomb II* survived to cruise another day.

The near-disaster happened one sunny day when we were cruising along at twenty knots off Kings Point in the Sound. A forty-foot yawl was running parallel to *BB II* about thirty yards ahead. I was at the wheel and turned away for a few moments to look for a buoy with my binoculars. I did not see the sailboat suddenly tack and head directly across our bow. We were on a collision course but neither I nor the crew on the yawl, whose view was obstructed by the big mainsail, knew it. Only one person, Buz, looking out the window below in the cabin, saw the impending disaster. She blew our ship's horn frantically to get my attention. I turned and was shocked to realize we were about to smash into the sailboat just aft of amidships. I spun the wheel hard to port, and we missed the yawl's stern by a few yards as I looked down on her startled crew seated in the cockpit. Narrowly escaping a major catastrophe, I shuddered to think of what might have happened if I hadn't had an alert first mate.

Another unforeseen event occurred one afternoon when I was piloting *Buz Bomb II* into Huntington Harbor after a picnic lunch with friends in a local cove. A Suffolk County Police boat appeared out of nowhere, pulled alongside, and accused me of creating an "excessive wake" in the channel. It was more of a ripple than a wave, but you can't win an argument with a policeman. There was a heavy wind blowing across the harbor and scores of boats were moored on both sides of the channel. As I was gathering the ship's papers, the wind blew *BB II* straight toward the mass of small craft. I had to do some tricky twin-engine maneuvering to avoid hitting them – moves that apparently appeared suspiciously erratic to the marine cops. Following us into the dock they instructed me to come aboard their boat where they put me through the whole gamut of sobriety tests – walking a straight line, touching your nose with closed eyes, the Breathalyzer, and so forth. Being cold sober I passed with flying colors, but they still fined me $50 for creating wake. My only run-in with the law had taken place at sea for creating a four-inch wave.

Hotel room mini-bar prices and the fully priced billing practices of law firms have long been the butt of jokes. But boatyards, which seem to come up with endless items to charge to their hapless customers, can compete with any law firm for the inflated billing award. I have come to dread seeing the familiar envelope with the boatyard logo arrive in the morning mail.

It seems that whenever a boat's engine or equipment suffer a breakdown and need professional repair, the ensuing process resembles what humans go through in the health care merry-go-round. Your regular boatyard performs the initial diagnosis. If the proposed repair work seems questionable, too expensive, or beyond your yard's capacity, you take your boat to another yard for a second opinion, presumably one with greater expertise. If the second yard's solution doesn't work, you seek the advice of yet another "expert," running up charges at every step of the process, like $50 an hour plus materials. We humans, seeking to cure our ailments, are familiar with the escalating process of going from family doctor, to one or more specialists, to surgeon, to rehab, and so on. At least we oldsters have Medicare to pay the bills.

When my Loran stopped functioning our island electronics expert pronounced it "brain dead." I decided to seek a second opinion. The electronics man at Wayfarer, the big boatyard in Camden, the cruising capital of Penobscot Bay, fiddled with the box and pronounced it cured; it would be fine once we got out of the heavy traffic in the crowded harbor. He was wrong. The next "expert" in the Stonington, Connecticut, boatyard discovered that the Wayfarer man had punched in 2998 instead of 1998 in entering the current date in the Loran. No wonder the latitude/longitude readings were incredible.

Once we got under way with the correct date, however, the Loran was still operating erratically. I sent the box back to the factory in California for testing and repair. When the manufacturer returned it to me, he pronounced it in A-1 condition. We began a new boating season, and guess what? My Loran still produced gibberish. I told the fellow at my Long Island boatyard that the factory had checked out the box: "Look somewhere else, maybe the antenna." He installed a new antenna mast, and, lo and behold, the Loran worked perfectly. The mast, which somehow had been damaged, had been the problem all along. Most boat owners can tell similar tales of frustration.

When my starboard engine, a Cummins diesel, went kaput, my North Haven, Maine, boatyard's first move was to order a new set of injectors. The parts supplier on the mainland shipped them instead to North Haven, Connecticut, which is not known for its waterfront views. This episode was an omen of things to come. The boatyard's initial diagnosis and work, attempting several remedies, ran into four figures before the mechanic concluded that he couldn't repair the engine. It would have to be sent off-island to be completely rebuilt. J.P. Morgan was said to have counseled a young man that if he had to worry about the expense of running a yacht, he shouldn't even think of buying one. Good advice. A wise boat owner should never divide the total cost of maintaining his boat by the number of hours he actually uses it; the resulting answer is too discouraging.

All these seagoing trials have been worth it, however, many times over. Cruising about the East Coast with good friends like the Jewetts and Buzbys has been good fun, and for many years *Buz Bomb II* has sped us in comfort to the islands of Penobscot Bay for picnics, a major activity during summers in North Haven. Sometimes we visited our friends in Northeast and Winter Harbor; other times we headed south to the islands of Hurricane Sound, Matinicus, and Monhegan. The White Islands in the Sound are the traditional site for the annual Lamont clan picnic; the head count one recent year was fifty-three, including camp followers – eating, sunning, and schmoozing on the giant white granite slabs and boulders encircling the island.

On Monhegan we were told the intriguing, although questionable, tale of another visitor to the island long ago – Tisquantum, or Squanto, a notable figure in American history especially remembered at Thanksgiving. In the early years of the seventeenth century Monhegan came to be used by European fishing vessels to dry their catches of cod and other fish that they had caught in the Maine coastal waters before returning to Europe. Sometimes the ships that used the harbor had been commissioned by their owners to explore and map the coast. Many historians have believed that during the summer of 1605, when Squanto, a teenager from the Pawtuxet tribe near the present town of Plymouth on Massachusetts Bay, was visiting with friends from the Penobscot tribe in the area, he was kidnapped with four other Indians by an English exploration vessel captained by George Waymouth and taken to England.

Waymouth was employed by Sir Ferdinando Gorges, the commander of the fort at Plymouth Harbor in England, who was a member of a syndicate formed to back the exploration and colonization of New England. Gorges encouraged Squanto to learn English in order to assist British sea captains exploring the New England coast; Squanto lived comfortably and was treated well as a member of his household during the years that he spent in England before returning home, so this story goes.

In 1609 Captain John Smith returned to London from Virginia, where he had been the forceful leader in founding Jamestown two years earlier. The bold adventurer was eager to embark on another voyage of exploration to the New World, and in 1614, with the backing of a group of merchants, he set sail for New England accompanied by a second ship, captained by Thomas Hunt. According to this disputed version of Squanto's background, Smith brought Squanto with him, promising to return him to his home in Massachusetts when the mission was completed. After carefully mapping the coast from Penobscot Bay to Cape Cod, Smith was true to his word. He set Squanto free and sailed for England, leaving Captain Hunt to gather a cargo of dried fish and trade for beaver skins with the Indians.

The meager evidence for this account of Squanto's early history is suspect; furthermore, crew member James Rosier's account of Waymouth's voyage identified the five Indians kidnapped by them, and Squanto was not one of them. While the tale is probably not true, all historians agree on what happened next: The despicable Captain Hunt had a more profitable cargo in mind than fish and furs and lured Squanto and two dozen other Indians aboard his ship, took them captive, and brought them to Spain to be sold as slaves. At the slave auction in Malaga Squanto was purchased by some friars from a Catholic monastery, who taught him Christianity and gave him his freedom. Squanto was able to make his way on an English ship first to Newfoundland and then to England where he lived with an associate of Ferdinando Gorges, who recognized his value as a guide and interpreter for exploration voyages to New England. Squanto finally returned to Massachusetts in 1619, on another English ship captained by Thomas Dermer. Dermer, another gentleman explorer backed by Gorges, was well impressed by Plymouth Harbor and the surrounding area and wrote Gorges that it was the place best suited for establishing a colony in New England. As Bradford Smith points out in his biography, *Captain John Smith,* we can only speculate as to whether Gorges passed this information on to the Pilgrims when the *Mayflower* put in at old Plymouth in England en route to America. We do know that the Pilgrim leaders consulted with Captain John Smith, who also favored the Plymouth area as an attractive place for a settlement, and bought a copy of his book containing his map of the New England coast.

On our voyages in *Buz Bomb II* we have stopped off several times in Plymouth, where the Pilgrims landed in 1620. The "Plimoth Plantation" village is a realistic reproduction of the early settlement; Plymouth Rock is small and unimpressive. The Pilgrims barely survived their first winter when about fifty of them, or half their original party, died from starvation and other illnesses. When spring arrived, Samoset, a friend of Squanto from Maine who had befriended the Pilgrims, introduced Squanto to them. Samoset, who had learned some broken English from the crews of fishing vessels visiting Monhegan, now has a handsome hotel and golf course in Rockland, Maine, named after him for his good work. The Pilgrims were amazed and overjoyed at Squanto's fluency in English and willingness to help them. Squanto's own family and tribe had been wiped out by an epidemic when he was in Spain, and he became a member of the Plymouth Colony. His assistance to the struggling settlers in teaching them how to grow corn and gather food is well known to every schoolboy and girl. He also served as the colony's emissary in trading and negotiating to maintain peace with the local tribes. His aid was absolutely critical in preserving the tiny settlement during its first two years of existence.

After Squanto's death in 1622 Governor William Bradford of the Plymouth Colony, who was one of my numerous grandfathers prefixed by eight "greats," wrote that Squanto was "a special instrument sent by God for their good. . . ." It's a pity that Squanto never lived to write his memoirs. The exciting life story of the young native American, who had lived in Spain, Newfoundland, and England before welcoming the Pilgrims in English when they arrived upon our shores, would surely have become a best-seller.

Buz enjoys cruising on *Buz Bomb II* just as much as I do. I know several boating guys whose wives are unenthusiastic about life at sea and simply go along for the ride. Not Buz. When we bring *BB II* into the dock to unload passengers and picnic baskets after a full day, the first mate insists that we hose her down and clean her up. Buz keeps a very neat ship and a full inventory noting the location of everything from a pair of pliers to a ball of marlin.

BB II's below-decks engine room only provides exceedingly cramped and grimy crawl space for work on the engines. The "Black Hole of Calcutta" comes to mind whenever I make my rare descents to this unwelcome place to squirm about amongst the machinery in the bowels of the vessel. Fortunately for me, Buz has designated herself as Chief Engineer and regularly visits our engines to check on the oil, anti-freeze, bilges and the like, which leaves me free to enjoy the nice white-collar jobs like manning the helm, fiddling with the GPS, and plotting courses. I knew Buz was a super partner on land. She is also one at sea.

"The Ambassador"
Arrives

By 1993 I had almost finished writing *The Ambassador From Wall Street*, but in my search for a literary agent and publisher I was a hitless wonder. Then my friend Jack Morris, who had been a public relations officer at J.P. Morgan, introduced me to Tom Wallace, the literary agent who agreed to take on my book. In due course he negotiated a book contract with Madison Books, a small publisher in Maryland. We recruited Al Williams, my Exeter classmate and a highly respected figure in the publishing world, to edit the book, and he made a number of excellent suggestions. I joined Jed Lyons, the head of Madison Books, at the American Booksellers convention in Miami Beach to plug the forthcoming publication of "The Ambassador." Finally, after many swings and misses, I was about to become a published author.

Our initial book signing party to celebrate launching *The Ambassador From Wall Street* was to take place November 8 at the Harvard Club a few days after the first batch of books was produced. I received a copy hot off the press via FedEx and eagerly ripped open the package to view the culmination of my research and writing over the best part of the last decade. The volume had a handsome jacket featuring a reproduction of the fine portrait of Thomas W. Lamont that hangs in the Harvard Club, with quotations from John Kenneth Galbraith, the Harvard economics professor and diplomat, and some professional reviews on the back cover.

However, my joy turned to dismay when I opened the book. The frontispiece displayed a full-page picture of me, the author, instead of Thomas Lamont, the subject of the biography. It was an incredible blunder. I immediately telephoned Jed, and all the books were recalled and corrected except the copies we needed for the Harvard Club book signing. Jed handled the slip-up smoothly in his remarks at the party, pointing out that the books that people purchased would become collectors' items (like a minted coin with two heads). Most of the guests were friends, and the imperfection in the copies did not seem to slow down sales. I signed a lot of books that day as we kicked off our marketing campaign for *The Ambassador*.

The good news was that *The Ambassador From Wall Street* received complimentary book reviews. The *New York Times* called it "an affectionate and well researched biography" and noted that it "occasionally supplies a wry and insightful wit." I liked that. I had done my best to enliven the story of the life of a banker by including some lighter moments – such as playboy Mayor Jimmy Walker's abrupt exit from a bankers' evening meeting about the critical loans needed to save New York City from bankruptcy. Arriving late for the meeting at Lamont's town house, the top-hatted mayor soon took off, remarking with a smile and a wink, "Mustn't keep a lovely lady waiting, you know."

John Kenneth Galbraith said that the book "tells of one of the most influential, even powerful financial figures of his time and certainly one of the most diversely intelligent. We are greatly in debt to Edward Lamont for this literate and thoroughly interesting biography."

Publishers Weekly said, "The impressive roster of historical personages who figure on these pages testifies to Lamont's wide influence. This comprehensive, well-documented work thoroughly explores the major economic, political, and social events shaping the country during the first half of this century."

The *Exeter Bulletin* struck the same note: "Lamont's book is a great deal more than the history of Thomas W. Lamont. It is also the history of the developing economy of the United States." So did *Harvard Magazine*: "It offers fresh insight into the period between the two world wars."

BookList reported, "There are a number of individuals who have played a significant role in shaping the U.S., yet whose names are unfamiliar to most Americans. Such a person was J.P. Morgan's CEO Thomas W. Lamont, a man who advised U.S. presidents and other world leaders and helped set economic and financial policy between the two world wars. . . . His grandson Edward, himself active in international banking for nearly a quarter of a century, here offers a thorough portrait based on previously unreleased business and family correspondence. . . . Not only do we get a first hand look at history in the making, but we also get glimpses of major social and cultural personalities such as Charles Lindbergh and H. G. Wells. Recommended for banking, foreign affairs, and history collections."

The book gave glimpses of a number of other news-making friends and acquaintances as well: John Masefield, Lady Astor, Dwight Morrow, and Jan Christiaan Smuts were all close friends, and TWL worked or crossed swords with both J. P. Morgans, father and son, Woodrow Wilson, Herbert Hoover, Franklin D. Roosevelt, Mussolini, Richard Whitney, Ramsay MacDonald, William Randolph Hearst, and Walter Lippmann. As *Library Journal* put it about TWL: "He was cultivated by U.S. presidents . . . enjoyed the good life, and knew everyone worth knowing."

Naturally, I got a kick from receiving letters, and not only from friends, praising the book. I heard from bankers and businessmen who liked the business history and appreciated my presentation of complex financial subjects and transactions. I was delighted also by letters from people who said simply that my book was enjoyable reading. *The Ambassador From Wall Street* seemed to have more appeal to men than to women, so I was very pleased when one woman wrote that she knew nothing about finance but thought that *The Ambassador* was "highly readable and a good education."

The bad news was that Madison Books had no advertising budget to promote the book. We were on our own, relying on word of mouth and good friends to help us set up some fifteen book signings from Maine to Florida. The attendees at signings near home and at the Boston Athenaeum and Somerset Club in Boston seemed more intellectually attuned to the life of T. W. Lamont than elsewhere. The audience at Park Avenue's elegant Union Club were especially responsive, perhaps recognizing that TWL was once one of the city's most distinguished and civic-minded citizens, who had lived in his elegant town house just a block away on East 70th Street.

Apparently my book could appeal to readers of diverse economic and political persuasions. Shortly after speaking to these largely conservative audiences, I received an advance from a Chinese publisher to translate and publish the book in China – perhaps another sign of the dynamic changes to come in that vast and rapidly developing nation.

The folks at our book signing talk in Charleston, while gracious, seemed to have minimal interest in the life of a Wall Street banker. I tried to stimulate their enthusiasm by pointing out that Lamont had built and stayed in a winter vacation house at Yeamans Hall, an exclusive golf club just outside of Charleston – but I met with little success. And at The Moorings, a classy gated community in Vero Beach, Florida, my audience, mostly retirees, was very attentive during my talk. Afterwards, however, most of them, instead of buying books signed by the author, headed straight for the wine and cheese bar. For them the occasion was simply another happy social hour at the community clubhouse, and I was buying the wine.

I tried to spice my book talks with a few amusing episodes from Grandfather's life. In 1929 the Lamonts gave a dinner party in honor of their friends the Morrows, who had returned for the holidays from Mexico where Dwight was serving as the American ambassador. After dinner Florence Lamont organized a game of charades. One team decided to act out "Morrow" – the name of the guest of honor. Federal Judge Learned Hand played the part of Othello, the Moor, in acting out an approximation of the first syllable; lovely Faye Lippmann, the wife of Walter, the eminent newspaper columnist, played the part of Desdemona. The judge, a large man, carried out his role with considerable gusto as he "smothered" Desdemona with a pillow as she lay supine on a couch. Unwittingly he had performed too well. Poor Faye struggled to her feet, blood gushing from her nose and in great pain. A hastily summoned doctor confirmed that her nose was indeed badly broken. The distinguished Court of Appeals judge was grief stricken and mortified. "He fears that for the rest of his life his career as a United States judge will be dogged by the fact that he went to a party and broke a lady's nose," Grandfather Lamont wrote his son.

Lamont possessed a good sense of humor and a fine light touch. One New York financial editor wrote in his column, "If you were to run into him as he was coming out of the Morgan office at Broad and Wall, he would grab your arm and say, 'Walk up the street with me and help my credit and general public standing!'"

There was enough demand for *The Ambassador* to warrant a second printing, and then that Godsend to authors, Amazon.com (and to a lesser extent BarnesandNoble.com), kicked in. I suspect that most copies in recent years have been sold through Amazon, which prints a picture of the book jacket, all the professional reviews, and even those of your friends and others who submit them. There are still a hundred or so copies left, and my advice is to get on the bandwagon. You will enjoy the story of Thomas W. Lamont, J.P. Morgan's chief executive, and amaze your friends with your newly acquired knowledge of business and political history during the first half of the twentieth century.

My authorship of *The Ambassador* led to participating in several events dealing with subjects related to Lamont's career in banking and public service. One was sponsored by the Western Front Association, an international organization whose purpose was to further interest in World War I and thereby honor the memory of those who had fought and died for their countries. In the U.S., the organization held several conferences each year at which knowledgeable speakers discussed different aspects of World War I. Lanny Leggera, an Association official who had heard one of my book talks and read *The Ambassador*, invited me to be the luncheon speaker at an event in Quincy, Massachusetts.

The topic, "Financing the Entente in War and Peace," was germane. Lamont and his Morgan partners had led the financial community in floating bond issues to finance purchases by Great Britain and France of munitions and supplies before the U.S. entered the war, and to rebuild the shattered European economies after the war. In 1919 Lamont had been chosen by President Woodrow Wilson to be a member of the American delegation to the Paris Peace Conference, where the most bitterly contested issue was formulating the provisions of reparations to be paid by Germany to the Allied nations as compensation for the destruction and losses caused by the German aggression. Lamont played a major role in negotiating the original terms and the later modifications during the '20s. Reparations were important to the Allies for another reason. In their eyes their ability to repay about $10.3 billion in war loans owed the U.S. Government was directly tied to their receiving reparations payments from Germany. Lamont had also been a key player in arranging the Dawes and Young international loans to Germany during the '20s.

I also stated in my talk that I did not buy the conventional viewpoint among historians that the reparations obligation imposed on Germany was a critical factor in depressing the German economy and bringing about the rise of Adolph Hitler and the Nazis. In World War I the German army had overrun Belgium and Northern France, which suffered widespread destruction. Towns and farmlands, factories and mines – all were destroyed, and industrial and agricultural equipment and machinery were seized and shipped to Germany. Germany itself had not been invaded, however, and did not suffer physical damage at the hand of the Allies. In World War II, on the other hand, American and British bombing had devastated parts of Germany. Of course, Hitler used the Versailles Treaty and its reparations demands as a bête noire, blaming the Allies for plunging Germany into the severe economic depression of the '30s – a depression that was in fact spreading throughout all of America and Europe. A master demagogue, Hitler also falsely accused the Jews of undermining Germany's economic strength.

Germany, in the midst of a healthy economic recovery in the late 1920s, had in fact been making its reparations payments on schedule since 1924. In 1929 its reparations debt was scaled back to $9 billion, payable with interest over fifty-nine years, and the German government received the Young Loan of $300 million (following the Dawes Loan of $200 million in 1924). In recent years a growing volume of private foreign investments and credits had been flowing into Germany as foreign investors gained confidence in Germany's economy and creditworthiness. It was not until a year later, following the stock market crash of 1929, that everyone was stunned by the rapidly spreading economic depression in the U.S. and Europe. A financial panic, triggered by the collapse of Credit Anstalt, Austria's biggest private bank, spread quickly to Germany, which, borrowed to the hilt, was unable to repay its maturing obligations.

The Smoot-Hawley tariff walls, passed by the U.S. in 1930, followed by Great Britain's devaluation of sterling, triggered worldwide protectionism. World trade shrank, businesses contracted, unemployment grew, and despair spread everywhere. Germany stopped paying reparations to the Allies in 1931, having paid just $4.5 billion, much of which was financed by U.S. and foreign loans. The growing unemployment and suffering in Germany, stemming largely from the worldwide economic depression, created the environment that spawned the rise of Hitler, who became Chancellor of Germany in 1933. The reparations payments had had a relatively minor economic impact. They were not the culprit, but the false charges of the spellbinding Hitler blaming the Versailles Treaty for Germany's ills had fallen on receptive ears.

I also gave a short summary of Thomas Lamont's role in the stock market debacle of 1929 on "The Crash of 1929," an American Experience program on WNET, which I arranged to have televised in a J.P. Morgan office overlooking the New York Stock Exchange. I recalled in the interview that the market had been sinking for days before it plunged on October 24, 1929. Lamont immediately called a meeting at 23 Wall Street of the presidents of the six biggest banks, including Morgan. They all agreed to subscribe to a fund of $250 million to support the market, and TWL, as spokesman, issued rosy statements from time to time. All wishful thinking – the deluge of selling was simply overwhelming. The market slide ended in November, for the time being, almost fifty percent lower than its September high. Lamont's efforts, nevertheless, had earned him a *Time* Magazine cover picture and story. The caption under his picture read, "He Felt the Helm Respond."

In my book talks I sometimes warned my audiences to beware the month of October. Starting in 1929, six out of the ten days of the greatest stock market declines have taken place in October (and one in both September and November). October 19, 1987, witnessed the greatest single-day plunge of all – twenty-three percent. Many experts have advanced theories as to why this is so. I believe it may have to do with Halloween. It's not just the kids who run for cover from frightening demons in October, either perceived or real.

Community
Schools

After completing my six-year term as president of the board of trustees of The Children's Aid Society, I became chairman and later chairman emeritus – a title inevitably consistent with the advancing age of the recipient. Nick Scoppetta, a former deputy mayor of New York City, replaced me as president and later, continuing his public service to the city, became head of the Administration for Children's Services and after that fire commissioner. I stayed active as a C.A.S. trustee, and in the spring of 2002 presided at a board meeting at which we discussed the C.A.S. role following the terrorist attack of September 11, 2001, on the World Trade Center.

The Society had disbursed some $8 million in emergency aid to over two thousand families of victims and those thrown out of work. The generosity of donors from all over responding to the tragedy was incredible. The C.A.S. alone received about $25 million for disaster relief during the year following 9/11. Through its many sites in the city – neighborhood centers, community schools, day care centers, and health clinics – and with a staff of about nine hundred, including many experienced social workers, C.A.S. was able to move quickly and efficiently to provide urgently needed funds and services to families that were suffering.

Children's Aid has always been deeply concerned with the education of its kids and their progress in school. If children don't succeed in getting a good education, equipping them to become self-reliant contributing citizens, we are simply spinning our wheels and not getting the job done. The C.A.S. ran after-school learning programs at our neighborhood centers and at corporate offices around town, where volunteer mentors worked with the youngsters. Seeing the world of work in action was a valuable learning experience in itself for these boys and girls. To this end I became a mentor for a young man from Washington Heights, who later graduated from SUNY at New Paltz, where he did fine academically and played on the basketball team. Our first meeting was not a total success. I took him to the Oyster Bar for lunch, and he didn't take to oysters in his first exposure to them. However, I think we hit it off well, and we still exchange Christmas cards.

The C.A.S. goal of improving the academic achievement of city kids in public schools led the Society to enter into the first partnership between the New York City Board of Education and a private social agency. The C.A.S. community school program, which started in 1992, expanded steadily, and C.A.S. has now become a partner with thirteen public schools in the city. The program also became a model for a growing number of school districts around the country, some one hundred twenty by 2004, with our technical assistance center providing advice based on our own experience in New York. About one thousand schools in the U.S. and other countries (especially the United Kingdom and The Netherlands) give credit to The Children's Aid Society for introducing them to the community school concept.

The community school (sometimes referred to as full service school) concept is simple common sense. The need for after-school programs in schools is obvious, especially in a society of working moms and latch key kids, but many city public schools shut their doors at 3 p.m. The need for medical clinics and social workers at the schools to spot and treat health and personal or family problems is also self-evident. Successful education cannot take place in isolation from everything else that's taking place in a child's life.

C.A.S. also promoted the active involvement of parents in school activities, an essential attribute for good schooling everywhere. Keeping the schools open during weekends and the summer provided a healthy environment for kids to play and work, and many youngsters, often immigrant children, needed extra help with their studies during the summer in order to advance to the next grade with their classmates.

Our experience clearly demonstrated that the community school concept worked – with significantly improved academic performance in our schools, record attendance, and virtually no violence. Teacher and student morale was high. Another big plus was that the schools – open afternoons and evenings, weekends and summertime – became neighborhood centers in a large sense, serving the whole community with learning and recreational programs for young and old. C.A.S. has mainly operated its programs out of neighborhood centers, and we didn't have any in Washington Heights or the Bronx where a large number of immigrant families needed the social services that we provided. There were the school buildings, with kids in place, unused and available for use after three o'clock every day. It was a perfect match-up.

When I became a member of the Visiting Committee to the Harvard Graduate School of Education, I sponsored a series of community school conferences at Harvard attended by teachers, principals, school district administrators, and educational consultants. In my remarks kicking off the first conference I described the attributes of the community school program. The first step was to recruit a suitable partner – for example, a family welfare agency, like C.A.S., a Boys and Girls Club, or perhaps a university – to join hands with the local public schools.

At the C.A.S. community schools many students elected to stay on to attend the voluntary afternoon programs. Along with arts and crafts and sports in the school gym, teachers and volunteers followed up on the regular curriculum of studies, gave help with homework assignments, and provided individual tutoring. The after-school programs added an hour and a half of instructional time per student each day. Many children also attended the summer school "learn and play" programs. The community schools were, in fact, lengthening the school day and the school year for many students – not a bad idea.

Many teachers have noted the substantial time it takes to bring a class back to speed after the long summer vacation, an anachronism left over from the days when fathers needed their sons to work on the family farm in the summer. Many educators and government officials have been advocating a longer school year and vacations spaced to reduce the long summer recess. When Rudy Giuliani was mayor of New York, he called for increasing the school year from 180 days a year to 200, but the city budget couldn't afford it, and some in the educational establishment raised other objections. I heard one expert at a conference say that shortening the summer vacation was a bad idea, because it would injure the economy. Businesses, like fast food restaurants and landscape gardeners, needed these young people to fill summertime jobs. What an incredible misplacement of priorities! What can be more important than giving our children the best education possible to prepare them for an increasingly competitive and complex world?

For years American public school students have been scoring poorly on international tests compared to the students from other developed countries in Europe and Asia. While the absolute accuracy of national rankings may be suspect, because in some countries not all children are required to take the tests that all American kids take, the overall results are very disturbing. For example, a recent international survey in mathematics and science studies for eighth graders ranked the U.S. in nineteenth place. The American school year of 180 days is shorter than that in virtually all of these countries, whose schools remain open 200 to 220 days a year. Changing the school year in America is just one of the measures needed to strengthen public school education, but it's an important step in the right direction.

To obtain a good job in the new economy requires more skills and training than a high school education affords. As former Secretary of the Department of Education Richard W. Riley stated, "Preparation for college begins the day a child first sets foot in the schoolhouse. . . . Before- and after-school programs and summer programs help kids stay on the right track from the beginning – and pave the way to college." The Children's Aid community school program has had to rely to a large extent on private donations. We hope the day is close at hand when states and school districts throughout the country recognize the benefits of these programs and fund them from public revenues.

The community school seminars at the Harvard Graduate School of

Education, which included presentations by C.A.S. staff, highlighted a public education initiative that the school had previously ignored. I sensed that some faculty members felt that the academic responsibility of teachers did not extend beyond the classroom and the personal lives of their students were not their concern. When I was a member of the Visiting Committee to the school we did not discuss the community school concept, or reasons for the mediocre academic achievement of American students compared to that of their foreign counterparts, or revising the conventional vacation schedules, or the merits of lengthening the school day and year. Along with briefings on administrative matters and fund-raising, the program presentations at our meetings reflected the school's heavy emphasis on research and pedagogy. I was surprised that there was so little sense of urgency about considering the broader issues at one of the nation's top schools of education, especially at a time when the nation and its leaders were deploring the poor state of public education in so many parts of the country. The mission of the Harvard Graduate School of Education seemed too narrow. But there is a silver lining: Harvard has continued to hold the community school conferences which have attracted more attendees including public officials each year. This valuable strategy to strengthen public education is taking hold.

Missions Abroad

A warm spirit of camaraderie exists among the senior staff of The Children's Aid Society and the members of the board of trustees. I have been a trustee for forty years and still look forward to the meetings of our board, which take place for a couple of hours over lunch. The agendas are informative and important to the welfare of the city, and our meetings are interesting and lively as we address the business at hand. The trustees are able and sophisticated citizens from a range of backgrounds who are committed to helping the city's poor children and families enjoy a better life. They also have a good sense of humor. John Griswold, Charlton Phelps, Nick Scoppetta, Edgar Koerner, Angela Diaz, and Sheila Baird have all been outstanding leaders on the C.A.S. board. Victor Remer, Phil Coltoff, Pete Moses, and Truda Jewett on the C.A.S. staff have all been especially attentive to board relations and business. Thankfully, we're not all work and no play. There are also enjoyable social events in which trustees and volunteers participate – such as parties, benefits, and foreign trips.

Generally, groups of about twenty-five trustees, donors, senior staff, and wives sign up for each foreign excursion, which combines sightseeing with studying the child and family welfare systems and public education in the countries we visit. We call on government and private social agencies, children's hospitals, schools, and orphanages. We also check in at the U.S. Embassy for briefings on the current political and economic climate. The foreign officials we meet welcome the exchange of information about our respective programs. We have many challenges in common, including caring for the incoming flows of poor immigrant families from developing countries.

On our trip to France in 1994 we encountered a social services system far more comprehensive than our own – a range of medical and assistance programs from cradle to grave. Public education was also largely under central government control from Paris, and student academic achievement was high. Government policy called for educating immigrant children, mainly Muslims from North Africa, with little regard for their cultural and religious distinctions, aiming to make them proper French citizens as soon as possible. For example, the schools did not want the Muslim girls to wear their head scarves.

In our free time we marveled at the fabulous collection of French impressionists at the Gare d'Orsay, so handsomely converted from a railroad station into a major art museum, and were intrigued by I. M. Pei's new glass pyramid entrance to the Louvre. It was June, and what could be more sublime than picnicking with friends by a Monet-style lily pond and the blooming rose gardens at Bagatelle in the Bois de Boulogne.

Buz and I joined another group touring China in 1996, composed of Exeter alumni and friends and led by Jim Lilley, P.E.A. '45, and a former ambassador to China in the Bush "41" administration. He and his wife Sally informed our tour, which included Hong Kong and Taipei, with behind-the-scenes political and cultural insights based on their years of experience in the region. The Children's Aid Society had arranged for me to meet several government officials in charge of overseeing youth programs in China on the night of our arrival in Beijing. Ignoring our jet lag, Buz and I joined the gentlemen for dinner at a restaurant near our hotel.

Plate after plate of exotic delicacies began arriving at the table, which our hosts insisted that we sample. "You must have some Peking Duck, Mr. Lamont. It is one of our country's very special dishes." Frankly, I prefer the kind of Chinese take-out fare that we order in the U.S., like pork fried rice and beef and Chinese vegetables, but I gamely tried and praised each mysterious dish. While manipulating my chopsticks, at which I was clearly an apprentice, I endeavored to carry on a serious conversation about the common problems facing young people in our countries. In describing the work of The Children's Aid Society I informed our hosts that we served approximately 150,000 children in New York City through our neighborhood centers, community schools, summer camps, and other facilities.

"That's very interesting, Mr. Lamont," replied the Chinese official. "Actually, my colleagues and I have about 350 million youths under our jurisdiction," referring presumably to all the kids in China. Maybe he thought that he had won that round, but what his ministry actually accomplished in improving the lives of Chinese children was problematic.

A photograph of Buz and myself on the Great Wall served as our annual Christmas card that year, as we made the regular tourist rounds. China's exploding economic growth, spurred on by the rapidly expanding manufacture and export of consumer goods, was evident everywhere. A forest of construction cranes pierced the Shanghai skyline, and foreign corporate and financial executives filled the luxury hotels. Major shifts in China's economy, governance, and international relations were taking place. It was a fascinating time to visit this burgeoning global giant of a country, which is still very much a work in progress.

In contrast to the bustling activity in the handful of large modern cities in China, however, there is Third World poverty and backwardness in the hinterland, a pattern similar to that in other developing countries such as Brazil and Russia. Conditions in a hospital we visited in Guilin, when we slipped away from the official tour, were an eye-opener. The halls and rooms were grimy and damp, and the patients, lying unattended in dirty bed linens, were a sad looking lot. God forbid ending up there for treatment.

The medical director, in a stained white jacket, delivered a sales pitch about the attributes of Chinese medications made from natural ingredients, so much more healthy, he said, than the Western chemically based drugs with their dangerous side effects. Smooth snake oil salesmen have been around forever, and when the good doctor offered bottles of pills for sale that would allegedly cure all male ailments below the belt, I joined my fellow travelers in buying a bottle. P. T. Barnum was right. I took a few pills, thought better of it, and threw the rest away.

The children in the Cuban schools that our C.A.S. group visited in 1999 gave us a warm reception, with happy smiling faces all about. They seemed eager to learn despite the fact that basic teaching materials, like textbooks and pencils, were in short supply.

It was sad to contemplate the dismal future awaiting these kids in poverty-stricken Communist Cuba. The growing sentiment in the U.S. toward easing the American embargo on trade and tourism with Cuba came to a screeching halt when Castro executed some Cubans caught attempting to flee the island, and imprisoned seventy-five non-violent dissidents. Normal relations with Cuba are unlikely to return until the stubborn and brutal dictator dies. In the meantime Americans can enjoy the performances of the Cuban artists and baseball players who defect from time to time, while awaiting the day when, at long last, Cubans will again enjoy the blessings of freedom.

On our C.A.S. trip to Ireland in 2001 the country's growing prosperity after centuries of poverty was apparent everywhere. A labor pool of well-educated young people and a favorable investment climate, aided by substantial financial aid from the European Union, had attracted a flood of high-tech foreign enterprises. For the first time the country was experiencing a net inflow of migrants. The swinging scene at the bar of the Shelbourne Hotel in Dublin after work, and the many German-made cars parked outside, reflected the dynamic new Irish economy. Hundreds of happy Trinity College students and tourists thronged Grafton Street and the pubs. However, the government and the Catholic church were still catching up in dealing with social problems that had been neglected for years. Ireland's social service system lagged well behind that of most other western European countries. For many years when I was a boy I had gone to a schoolmate's apartment overlooking Fifth Avenue to watch our Irish cook march by in her emerald green uniform in the big St. Patrick's Day parade. Years later I learned what those "Free Ulster" signs were all about. Sadly, the deep-rooted anger of violent people still simmered below the surface in this seemingly contented and beautiful country in 2001.

Our next C.A.S. trip was to Italy. The beauty of Venice never ceases to delight the eye – even when the Adriatic tide is lapping at the doorstep of the Plaza de San Marco. The art treasures of Florence always inspire their viewers, despite a bit of sleaze accompanying their splendor; a newsstand near the gallery housing Michelangelo's magnificent nude figure of David sold tacky below-the-waist picture postcards of the renowned statue. On our visit to a children's hospital in Rome the doctors told us about their latest medical challenge – treating the sickly children of thousands of illegal Albanian immigrants who were steadily landing from their rickety boats on Italy's southern coasts and melding into the population.

At the end of our Children's Aid tour Buz and I joined Frank and Lee Hawley and friends at a villa that Frank had rented about twenty miles north of Sienna. We enjoyed a week of good company, wining and dining, and visits to the little hill towns of Tuscany. It's a close call, but in choosing between the two lovely regions of Tuscany and Provence in Europe, which are comparable in many ways, I prefer the scenery and hill towns of Provence. Furthermore, armed with my rusty but serviceable knowledge of French, I felt more at home there.

In 2003 our Children's Aid group visited Moscow and St. Petersburg. Moscow, the nation's powerful center of government and business, was throbbing with energy. Mercedes and other foreign-made cars and throngs of shoppers crowded the avenues and streets. St. Petersburg, celebrating its 300th anniversary, was magnificent in its finery. The much poorer parts of Russia beyond these two great cities were not on our itinerary.

From the Depression years of the '30s through World War II, the Communist Party in the U.S. had been headed by Earl R. Browder, his party's candidate for president in two elections. In Moscow I called on his grandson Bill Browder, a respected American investment consultant who advised American and European clients on Russian securities. He was cautiously bullish about Russia's conversion from Communism, and I made a small investment in a Russian cellphone company.

Buz and I marveled at the royal splendor of the Moscow Metro system and strolled about the vast expanse of Red Square. Back home, we watched a television program covering Paul McCartney's recent rock concert in the Square. Tens of thousands of Russians, young and old, were joyfully swaying together and singing "Hey, Jude" along with Sir Paul and his musical group. Even President Putin showed up. A similar scene – same maestro, same song – was the halftime highlight at the 2005 Sugar Bowl in Jacksonville. Thank goodness for the great musicians and other artists and performers who bring us all closer together.

The Russian government's scarce resources provided only minimal funding for social programs for the poor, and the non-profit sector providing such assistance was still in its infancy. The director of the government's Department of Children, Women, and Family Issues was refreshingly candid in describing the government's shortcomings in addressing the hardships facing so many poor families in Russia. We visited two orphanages, which like others throughout the country were overflowing with children abandoned by destitute parents, many of whom were alcoholics. Buz and I had a special interest in the adoption process, because we knew three families in our neighborhood who were currently engaged in adopting children from Russian orphanages. During our tour of the Hermitage we met a young couple from Dallas with a pretty little Russian girl whom they had officially adopted the day before in the final court proceeding. The little girl clung happily to her new parents. The couple had persevered through many months of the often frustrating procedure for foreign adoptions in Russia. Now, joyfully, they were bringing their new daughter home to America to meet her three older brothers.

At the end of each meeting one of our group gave a brief talk about our common problems in helping poor children and thanked our hosts for receiving us so graciously. When my turn came, I was reminded of a story told by John Lindsay, the former mayor of New York. Lindsay was scheduled to speak to a group of Russians through an interpreter and was concerned that the humor of an anecdote he planned to tell might get lost in the translation. However, when he gave his talk, the joke went over well: The Russians laughed uproariously. Lindsay remarked to the interpreter that he was delighted that the Russians enjoyed his joke so much and was a little surprised. The translator had a simple explanation: After translating the funny story into Russian, he had added, "The mayor just told a joke. Please laugh." I decided to play it straight in my remarks.

St. Petersburg in its tercentennial celebration attracted thousands of tourists, ordinary and celebrated, including former President George H. W. Bush and his wife Barbara, who showed up at the Astoria Hotel where our group was staying. The Lamonts and Bushes both had rooms on the fourth floor – the presidential suite, naturally, for the Bushes. Burly Russian security guards and cold-eyed Secret Service agents watched me warily every time I stepped off the elevator. One morning as I was waiting for the elevator to arrive, a familiar bare-legged figure clad in the hotel bathrobe stepped out into the hallway to place two suitcases outside the door of his room. It was the forty-first President of the United States of America. I must have looked surprised, because I had assumed that presidents had valets to handle these domestic tasks. Before I could wish the President "good morning," he darted back into his room.

President Bush was in fine form, chatting with the tourists as he walked through the hotel lobby. When we went by hydrofoil to Peterhof, Peter the Great's magnificent summer palace, President Bush and his entourage disembarked on an adjoining dock shortly after we arrived. Richard Abrams, a member of our group and a Yale alumnus, came up with a brilliant idea for greeting the President. As he walked by ten yards away Richard led us in a chorus of Yale's popular football song,"Boola, Boola, Eli Yale." The President laughed and gave us a thumbs up.

Thousands of Dominican immigrant children attend C.A.S. community schools and neighborhood centers, so it seemed especially fitting for a C.A.S. group to visit the Dominican Republic in 2004. In Santo Domingo we were briefed by government officials, U.S. A.I.D. and UNICEF officers, and First Lady Margarita Cedeño de Fernández – who was charming, intelligent, and beautiful. La Primera Dama could well have been a former winner of the Miss Latin America contest. I told her that the many outstanding Dominican baseball players in the U.S. served her country admirably as goodwill ambassadors. The Dominican Republic is an exceedingly poor country with rampant corruption in government, banking, and business holding back social and economic progress. Haiti, next door to the Dominican Republic on the island of Hispaniola, has long suffered from chaos and violence. It is an economic basket case, and Haitians flee across the jungle border from Haiti to the D.R. to seek a better life, just as Dominicans head for Puerto Rico and New York.

From Santo Domingo, founded in 1496 and the oldest European city in the Western Hemisphere, we drove over to Casa de Campo, the country's premier resort featuring a seaside golf course charmingly named "Teeth of the Dog." Children's Aid trips are a happy combination of work and play.

Politics

For many years following my first vote for Dwight D. Eisenhower I considered myself a moderate Republican, currently an endangered species. I was a political appointee in the Nixon administration in 1971 and voted for Republican presidential candidates (with one exception, Barry Goldwater) until 1992 when I backed Bill Clinton over George H. W. Bush in the latter's bid for a second term. While I did not agree with all the positions taken by presidents Reagan and Bush, such as their support for the Right to Life movement, I had, until then, considered them to be better qualified to lead the country than their Democratic opponents. Most voters, Republicans and Democrats, vote for the same party's candidates year after year without exception. They seem to view party affiliation in the same way that alumni feel about their college, or club members feel about their favorite social club. In many cases they inherited their political bias in their youth from their parents and have stuck with it over the years, regardless of changes in the party's direction, the issues at stake, or the quality of the candidates. There is a much smaller group of voters in each election who do not feel bound to either party in casting their ballot, and I am one of them.

By the end of George H. W. Bush's presidency in 1992 it was clear that in domestic affairs the Republican party had shifted far to the right of center. The party's dominating right wing ideology ruled the day, leaving its moderate supporters like myself out in the cold. Although I continued to vote for some Republican candidates for state and local offices, I have voted for Democratic presidential candidates since 1992.

The modern Republican domestic agenda no longer appeals to me. Its major thrusts apparently are large military expenditures and relentless tax cutting, generating huge federal deficits that will plague the country for years to come. Republicans are foot-draggers when it comes to environmental protection, universal health insurance, and needed social programs like child care for working moms – sometimes letting a bias in favor of business interfere with the public good.

I find that the labels "conservative" and "liberal" that are used to describe a person's political philosophy are often misleading. Reducing unwanted pregnancies and abortions to the absolute minimum is everyone's goal, and families, schools, and others must do a better job in counseling and educating young people. But what is conservative about a government's wish to intrude into the most personal family decisions regarding health and pregnancy? Is it conservative to deny an individual's rights to privacy in such matters? Is it conservative to dictate to doctors what they may or may not do to save a woman's life? What is conservative about running annual federal budget deficits of almost $400 billion with no end in sight under current tax and spending policies? What is conservative about starting a war with minimal military and financial assistance from other nations while giving huge tax cuts to our citizens at the same time? It's clear that the peace-keeping and reconstruction costs in Afghanistan and Iraq and our efforts to combat terrorists at home and abroad will continue to be a heavy drain on U.S. resources for years to come.

Our national debt, with its annual interest of 4-5% borne by the American taxpayers, now stands at over $7 trillion and will continue to grow rapidly under the current policies espoused by Republicans. Growing up in the Lamont household I was taught that the G.O.P. was the party of fiscal responsibility, the party that would not pile up debts for our children and grandchildren to pay off, while the Democrats were profligate spenders funding their programs by more and more taxes. However, a remarkable role reversal took place under recent Republican administrations, and a policy of "borrow and spend" became the order of the day. The George W. Bush administration made a mockery out of the federal budget process. On the other hand, the Clinton administration raised taxes, curbed the deficits, and created surpluses as the country enjoyed the longest spell of prosperity in modern times. Under the Republicans the growing number of families that have slipped below the poverty line and the tens of millions of folks without health insurance all spell trouble.

It is unrealistic to expect to reduce our large budget deficits significantly by cutting federal spending. It just won't happen. Despite the growth of the economy and tax revenues during the Reagan years, the federal deficits ballooned due to runaway Congressional spending. In recent years the Congress, under the control of a Republican majority since 1995, has embarked on another binge of uncontrolled spending. The George W. Bush administration bore a major share of blame for this lack of fiscal discipline in proposing budgets based on massive deficit financing. The President did not veto a single spending bill during his first term.

There are sound reasons why one cannot expect significant reductions in federal spending. Waging wars and the costs of reconstruction later are very expensive, especially when other countries are not making substantial contributions as they did in the Persian Gulf war when George Bush, Sr. was President. Furthermore, the discretionary programs, excluding the military, which account for only about one sixth of federal spending, are needed and popular with the American people and their congressmen on both sides of the aisle. Of course, there are moderate savings to be made if Congress and the White House had the will (lots of pork, certain agricultural subsidies, and dubious military expenditures like anti-missile systems) but there is very little scope for producing really major savings. The popular entitlement programs for the elderly,

Social Security and Medicare, now account for well over a third of federal spending – more than three times as much as entitlements for the poor like Medicaid and welfare.

Apparently, the religious right has become a significant force in the Republican party in promoting its views on banning abortions and on human sexuality. I trust that they are also heeding the many teachings of Jesus regarding caring for the poor. Those backing tax cuts for the wealthy or substituting a flat tax for the graduated income tax should take note of our Lord's views on progressive taxation –

> *And Jesus sat over against the treasury, and beheld how the people cast money into the treasury; and many that were rich cast in much.*
> *And there came a certain poor widow, and she threw in two mites, which makes a farthing.*
> *And he called unto him his disciples, and saith unto them, Verily I say unto you, That this poor widow hath cast more in than all they which have cast into the treasury:*
> *For all they did cast in of their abundance, but she of her want did cast in all that she had, even all her living.* (Mark 12:41-44)

Sustaining the level of government services necessary for a well-functioning modern civil society is not inexpensive. Most Americans believe that everyone deserves good medical care, good education for their kids, a social safety net for the elderly and poor, a strong military defense, and even roads without potholes. When the federal government cuts back on social services, the increased burden of providing them falls on state and local governments, which is where "the rubber meets the road." Most states are required by law to balance their budgets; they can't resort to unlimited borrowing like the federal government to pay their bills, and therefore face the prospect of raising state and local property taxes, never a popular measure.

Today's huge budget and international current account deficits are the Achilles Heel of our economy. If Asian and European countries were to sharply curb their purchases of billions of dollars of U.S. government bonds, our capital markets would be forced to finance our burgeoning government deficits; the weakening dollar, mounting inflationary pressures, and higher interest rates would surely slow economic growth. About forty percent of our public debt in 2004 was held abroad; we are the world's biggest debtor nation. To continue to run huge deficits would indeed be reckless and dangerous, threatening the very existence of programs that underpin our way of life. It takes guts for a politician to raise taxes – putting the welfare of the nation ahead of political ambition – and the kind of strong leadership we hope to see in the White House. More than two hundred years ago Thomas Jefferson said, "We must not let our rulers load us with perpetual debt." He was right.

My beliefs, and indeed much of my career background – the Marshall Plan and NATO, the World Bank and international finance – have led me to support a foreign policy that respects the opinions of those members of the international community that share our values, and works with them through the United Nations and other international organizations that we helped create to achieve our common goals. The world may have to live with the threat of Muslim terrorism for a long time, and we desperately need the international community on our side. We don't seek allies simply to be popular in European capitals. We badly need allies to work with us to eradicate terrorist cells around the world, to help win the hearts and minds of people in regions where terrorism breeds, and to share the costs of defeating the terrorists. As we have sadly witnessed, going it alone in Iraq (with only a handful of allies supplying very modest support) is tremendously costly. American troops bear the brunt of the casualties, and the financial costs of waging war, peace-keeping, and reconstruction are staggering.

All countries must defend themselves against threatening attacks and terrorism. However, in other circumstances the U.S. should channel its military strength to combat hostile countries through the consensus of the international community, the policy followed by presidents since World War II including George H. W. Bush in the Persian Gulf war, Bill Clinton in Bosnia and Kosovo, and George W. Bush in Afghanistan. These campaigns were strongly supported by the United Nations or NATO and achieved good results. However, the Bush administration then abandoned the policy of forging alliances backed by widespread international consensus and launched a military invasion of Iraq without the backing of the U.N. This action, reflecting a "take it or leave it," "for us or against us" attitude in diplomatic relations, alienated peoples in countries that had been our friends, inflamed the Muslim world and its terrorists, and did severe harm to America's good standing around the world.

In his book *A World Transformed* former President George H. W. Bush wrote: "Trying to eliminate Saddam would have incurred incalculable human and political costs. . . . We would have been forced to occupy Baghdad, and, in effect, rule Iraq . . . there was no visible 'exit strategy' that we could see, violating another one of our principles. Furthermore, we had been self-consciously trying to set a pattern for handling aggression in the post-Cold War world. Going in and occupying Iraq, thus unilaterally exceeding the United Nations' mandate, would have destroyed the precedent of international response to aggression that we hoped to establish. Had we gone the invasion route, the United States could conceivably still be an occupying power in a bitterly hostile land."

Confidence in our government's credibility was badly shaken when its claims about Iraq's hidden weapons of mass destruction and the threat that they presented, as well as Iraq's links to al Qaeda and 9/11, proved to be false. To start a war on the basis of flimsy or false intelligence is alarmingly reckless. No administration should view lightly the importance of preserving the people's trust in the word of their government.

Instead of leading, the Republicans built a record of snubbing or foot dragging in a number of proposed international alliances – a world court for war criminals, treaties to reduce greenhouse gases, ban land mines, restrict anti-ballistic missiles, and others. The Bush administration refused to renew the nuclear test ban treaty, rejecting the policy followed by previous presidents. It has even talked of developing a new generation of tactical nuclear weapons, a frightening prospect, at the same time that it is trying to prevent other countries from building nuclear arsenals. The Republicans' "our way or no way" foreign policy has seriously hindered initiatives to solve global problems that can only be solved through international cooperation.

However, the most frightening feature of Republican foreign policy was the Bush administration's declared intent to start "preemptive wars" when there is no threat of an attack on us, whether or not the international community supported the action. What gives Americans the moral right to invade another country on our own when there is no threat to ourselves? Such a policy creates a dangerous precedent for other countries with more aggressive agendas. Diplomacy is hard work and name-calling, such as branding certain nations as "evil," is hardly a diplomatic or productive tactic to pursue when the U.S. hopes to persuade those same governments to our point of view.

President Dwight D. Eisenhower wrote a book about his presidency whose title was *Waging Peace*. While some American presidents never served in the armed forces in wartime, Ike knew firsthand the horrors of modern warfare and believed that America should only go to war out of necessity after all other remedies have been exhausted. Ike also expressed concern about the "military-industrial complex" that generated huge ongoing expenditures for new weaponry, crowding out funding for needed civilian programs.

A war, with all its tragic and dreadful consequences – the massive killing and wounding of soldiers and innocent civilians, the destruction, carnage, and chaos – should only be started as truly the last resort to restrain a hostile nation. Moreover, we must not create breeding grounds for more and more fanatics to terrorize our people. Donald Rumsfeld reminded me eerily of Robert MacNamara, his counterpart during the Vietnam war, who also backed the wrong war for the wrong reasons.

Let's hope that we have all learned from the lessons of Vietnam and Iraq, two American wars of choice and two bad choices. When we saw the photographs of those brave young men and women on television night after night who died fighting in Iraq, I couldn't help asking, "Wasn't there a better way?"

All Americans fervently hope that a stable democratic government will emerge in Iraq to lead the Iraqi people, who have suffered so much. As the worthy effort to promote the growth of democracy around the world goes forward, surely strong moral leadership and skilled diplomacy will be the most effective tools.

Passing the Baton

With the passing years anniversaries and reunions take on big numbers. In 1995 the Lamont clan celebrated the seventy-fifth anniversary of Sky Farm at the annual Pulpit Harbor Tea. The special features were a fly-by plane towing a banner reading "Happy Birthday, Sky Farm," T-shirts emblazoned with an image of the Big House as the signature Sky Farm residence, a mammoth birthday cake portraying the same scene in yellow and green frosting, and crowds of relatives smiling happily in photograph after photograph. Our friend Jim Walker painted another colorful poster commemorating the tea, and Buz, Ada, and my niece Vicki, the most artistically creative family member, worked hard in putting the superb celebration together. Lansing, the family poet, composed and recited a special poem for the occasion.

My nephew Doug Lamont, who chose finance over a career in comedy and acting, was once again a superb MC and lead actor at Skit Night following the tea. For many years the clan and guests have gathered in our play barn on this night to perform and watch skits enacted by young and old. These short playlets, performed in high comic style, depict the summer's humorous events, such as blunders at sea, and characters who have called attention to themselves by amusing or odd conduct. As I once wrote in describing Skit Night:

> *Sky Farm has more sub-plots than TV's "Dallas,"*
> *Romance and intrigue like a soap opera serial.*
> *A warning, to you, friend, one boo-boo or foul-up,*
> *And you become juicy Skit Night material.*

It was a glorious day for the reunion, although we missed our beloved fellow clansman Corliss Lamont, who had died in April at age ninety-three. Corliss, the noted political maverick of the family, had outlived his siblings by decades and was a surrogate grandfather for many of the younger generation.

At the anniversary tea I began the practice of making short opening remarks at each Pulpit Harbor Tea about some aspect of North Haven's history. The dedicated staff of the North Haven Historical Society, which has preserved an excellent collection of genealogical and historic records about island families and events, and Lewis Haskell, the wise and witty founder and curator of the Island Museum, aided my research. I told the annual gatherings about the visits of presidents Ulysses S. Grant and

Franklin D. Roosevelt to North Haven; how the town came into possession of Winston Churchill's cigar, kept by June Hopkins at her gift store
in the same cigar box with President Grant's cigar butt; the tale of my
boyhood flight with Charles Lindbergh and his take-off with his wife
Anne from North Haven in a small seaplane on their flight to China and
Japan; and the sad story of the four North Haven island boys who enlisted
together in the Air Force in 1940 and died as Japanese prisoners of war.

Lew Haskell has a built-in twinkle in his eye and is a marvelous story-
teller. One of his best is the account of how he joined the U.S. Navy in
World War II. Like most young men then he was ready to fight for his
country when America went to war, and, having been around boats all his
life, he was eager to join the Navy. But the Navy rejected him: Lew had
flunked the Navy physical examination because of poor eyesight and a
lung condition from a childhood bout of tuberculosis. Still, he was confident he could serve the Navy ably in some capacity, and Dr. Victor
Shields, the North Haven island doctor, agreed.

"It just happens that I know Commander Brown, who is one of the
top doctors at the Portland navy base," said Shields. "We were in the same
class at medical school. In fact, he still owes me $500 (Lew guessed it was
a card-playing debt), and I have his I.O.U. right here." Shields pulled a
scrap of paper out of his desk drawer, scribbled out a message to Brown,
put it in an envelope, and handed it to Lew along with the I.O.U. "Go
back to the Portland base, arrange to see Commander Brown, and give
him this message from me. If he decides to let you join the Navy, let him
have the I.O.U."

Lew followed Shields's instructions: He met Commander Brown in
his office at the naval base and told him that he had a message from Dr.
Shields. "Oh," said the officer. "Good old Vic Shields. He's a great guy.
Let's see the message."

When he read the note his expression darkened, and he muttered
angrily under his breath. After a few moments he growled, "Well, let's
have your medical file, Haskell." Lew handed it to him, and the officer
reached for the rubber stamp and ink pad on his desk. Forcefully he
stamped the legend WAIVED next to each of Haskell's physical disabilities
listed in the file.

"Now, hand over the I.O.U.," ordered the Commander, and when
Lew gave it to him, he ripped it up into little pieces." You're in the Navy,
now, Haskell. Good luck!"

Lew became a medical corpsman, or "bed pan commander" in his
words, and served on a hospital ship bringing soldiers and marines
wounded in the fighting in the Pacific islands back to the hospitals in
Guam and Pearl Harbor. Along with the constant threat of Japanese attack,
the ship survived a fierce typhoon. And when the Korean War broke out a
few years later Lew signed up for another tour of duty in the Navy.

*Centennial celebration of the North Haven dinghy, 1987,
and heading downwind in a dinghy race.*

*Lansing, Elinor, and Ted about to embark
on another North Haven picnic.*

*A colorful gang in our Model A Ford for the
annual Community Day parade in North Haven.*

The gathering of the clan for Sky Farm's 75th birthday.

Buz, with her helpers, has put together the Pulpit Harbor Tea for more than thirty years, and I trust that the next generation will want to continue this happy summer-ending tradition. My sister Elinor Hallowell and cousin Priscilla Cunningham Lickdyke have also made a special effort to embrace and unite the whole Lamont family.

Lansing and I share the ownership of Sky Farm equally, and live in units designated by our parents. Some controversy is inherent in the joint ownership of any property like a boat or a vacation home. In the corporate world I have never seen two co-CEOs work together successfully for very long. Despite different priorities and operating styles, however, Lans and I resolve our differences well, and our families, children, and grandchildren have enjoyed each other's company for many summers.

Childe Hassam, the American impressionist, wrote about a Maine island where he once summered: "The rocks and the sea are the few things that do not change, and they are wonderfully beautiful." My brother Tommy also loved "the land where it meets the sea" – the rocky beaches festooned with brown seaweed and waving kelp at low tide; the colored lobster pots bobbing in the offshore waves; the coves and harbors with their granite piers and wooden floats; the lobster boats, racing sloops, and sailing dinghies straining at their moorings in a stiff breeze; and the soaring osprey, screaming sea gulls, and gray seals sunning on the ledges.

The long front porch of the Big House at Sky Farm affords a magnificent sweeping view of Penobscot Bay, with its chain of rockbound wooded islands in the foreground and the rolling blue hills behind Camden in the distance. On a northwest day the sparkling bay is alive with whitecaps, as sailboats of varying size and rig, including the stately old coastal schooners now on tourist cruises, enter and cross the mammoth stage.

Sunset vistas around the world provide beautiful and treasured moments – from a campsite bordering the African veldt, the Naples beachfront on the Gulf of Mexico, or a penthouse terrace overlooking the Manhattan skyline. Sunsets viewed from the Sky Farm front porch in North Haven, however, surpass all others. We watch the beauty of the scene in awe as the sun sinks behind the dark blue Camden hills. The golden western sky, against which low-lying darkening clouds show in silhouette, and the warm orange globe of the setting sun give way to deepening shades of blue and finally starry night with the twinkling lights of Camden across the bay. Reflections on the changing cloud formations from day to day bring variety to this spectacular display. Then all is still except for the chug-chug of a fisherman's boat returning from mackereling and the wash of the waves on the rocky beach below. What a sublime moment it is to be sipping a glass of wine with friends while watching this glorious scene unfold at the end of the day.

In 2004 Ned and Annie built a rambling new house on the Sky Farm property overlooking the bay. Ned at age fifty was the same age as

Grandfather Lamont when he built Sky Farm. He installed Internet access and a few other amenities that Grandfather hadn't thought of. One day I called up and was informed that Ned couldn't come to the telephone because he was in the steam room. For five generations, and counting, North Haven has been Shangri-la for the Lamont clan.

Exeter and Harvard reunions have rolled by every five or ten years, and our Exeter band of brothers enjoyed these get togethers so much that we staged mini reunions in Nantucket and Woodstock, Vermont, in between the big ones. A good group attended our sixtieth at the school in 2004 when we saluted the memory of our celebrated and talented class-mate George Plimpton, who had died the year before. George had shunned Exeter reunions, which is perhaps understandable given the circumstances of his abrupt departure as a student, until we finally talked him into attending our fiftieth. He was in fine fettle, as evidenced by his remarks as the speaker of the evening at our reunion dinner, reciting that hoary limerick linking the maturity of roses and girls.

As George's career blossomed he had moved in more rarified social circles. After his death we attended his memorial service at St. John the Divine where his friend Norman Mailer told about an incident that took place when George was playing tennis with President George H. W. Bush at Camp David one weekend. The special presidential telephone at court-side rang suddenly in the middle of their match. A Secret Service agent answered it.

"What is it now?" asked the President in an exasperated tone.

"I'm sorry, Sir," replied the agent. "The call's not for you. It's for Mr. Plimpton."

I had not seen much of George in recent years, just at the occasional party, class reunion, and – the last time – at our own fiftieth anniversary party. Buz and I celebrated the fiftieth anniversary of our wedding in Puerto Rico with 150 friends and family at Piping Rock's beach club on a warm June evening in 2001. Seating our guests at fifteen tables with opti-mum social compatibility was a major challenge given the surplus of women, a common occurrence at our age, and the last-minute additions of friends of friends, always more women, that we were obliged to include. Moving the players about in the seating plan on our dining room table to achieve the most harmonious combinations was like playing a new form of chess.

For the evening itself Puerto Rico's tropical flora were reflected in Barry Ferguson's exotic flower arrangements, and Tom Harrington's band played the bouncy melodies popular with our age group. Lansing, Elinor, the two Buzby brothers, and our five grandchildren all contributed mer-rily to the evening's entertainment. Wedding party members Perry Bartsch and Woody Kingman journeyed long distances to join the fun, as did good friends Ken and Shaunagh Robbins from Honolulu.

At our fortieth anniversary party, Buz and I had teamed together to sing the Bing Crosby–Rosemary Clooney version of "Slow Boat to China." For years I have had a Walter Mitty–like fantasy of singing before a big band, visualizing a setting like the Sands Hotel where Frank, Dean, and Sammy crooned and wisecracked before the merrymaking crowd. Buz did not share my vision and was a very good sport in performing the duet with me. At our fiftieth party my pal Austie Lyne joined me in singing "You Made Me Love You" to Buz, a favorite song harking back to our performance in the Al Jolson singing contest when we were in college.

Ned, our MC for the evening's entertainment, next introduced a spectacular unscheduled act, inviting everyone to step outside to the deck overlooking Long Island Sound. He had arranged for George Plimpton, a noted afficionado of pyrotechnics, to organize a fireworks display for the occasion. Ned had told us only that he was bringing a "mystery guest," so we were surprised and delighted when George showed up at our party; however, we had no inkling of what lay in store. George provided a witty introduction and commentary throughout the dazzling show. He had chosen the famous Grucci fireworks company to put on the display from two barges offshore, and Mrs. Grucci, the family matriarch, and her son were present to see that everything went smoothly. Madame Grucci was especially proud of the sparkling display reading "50th Anniversary" in the glorious finale of the act.

One particular incident symbolized the changing father-son relationship between Ned and me. Buz and I have long been strong supporters of sensible gun control laws like those in Canada and Europe. Several years ago we attended a Handgun Control benefit in a Manhattan restaurant featuring Jim and Sarah Brady and former President Bill Clinton. As I stood in line waiting to shake hands with the President and pondering what I might say beyond the conventional greeting, an idea popped into my head. A few months earlier Ned had been the program chairman of a dinner of the Young Presidents' Organization in Greenwich at which Bill Clinton was the after-dinner speaker. After introducing the former President, Ned had presented him with an antique golf club on behalf of the Y.P.O. as a memento of the evening, and the President had seemed delighted with the gift.

By way of introduction I told President Clinton, "We're the parents of Ned Lamont, the fellow who presented you with the golf club at the Y.P.O. dinner in Greenwich."

"Oh, what a thoughtful gift that was," said the President. "I collect old golf clubs, you know. I've got one from the king of Morocco, Jack Kennedy's putter, and some others. Your son did a fine job that evening.

I remember it well." Later in saying goodnight to us at the end of the affair the President said, "Be sure and give my best to your son, and thank him again for me." Most people, regardless of politics, agree that Bill Clinton is a very bright man loaded with charm. For my part, when I identified myself to President Clinton as the father of Ned Lamont, I had proudly passed on the baton.

For several years we have accompanied Ned, Annie, and their kids each Thanksgiving on their visit with Annie's parents, Carroll and Betsy Huntress, usually at the Huntress beachfront condo in Naples. Helena broke away from her canine operations in Palm Beach Gardens to join us. With tennis and golf, motorboating on the Inland Waterway, and good dining – including Betsy's sumptuous Thanksgiving feast – our annual Thanksgiving sojourn in South Florida is a happy family reunion.

Campus Televideo, the company of some sixty employees founded and led by Ned, is now providing satellite television to 160 university campuses and a handful of large gated communities. Annie's venture capital firm continues to thrive. Our oldest grandchild, Emily, a senior at Greenwich High School, will enter the freshman class at Harvard in September 2005. Her siblings, Lindsay and Teddy, are students at Greenwich Country Day School where we have watched them perform in class, on the stage, and at soccer games.

Helena's business of breeding, training, and selling golden retrievers continues to be the center of her life. She loves raising dogs and works very hard at it. The onslaught of hurricanes in Florida has just impelled her to move her home and business to a town outside Atlanta. Helena is a true professional in the business, and her dogs have won a score of awards in dog shows in the U.S. and Canada. Just visit her website, Bearbellagoldens.com. You will find her pups irresistible. Perhaps the dogs that were our companions over many years – shelties, collies, a yellow lab, and a beautiful golden retriever named Nugget – first ignited Helena's love for animals.

Camille, a.k.a. Kim, and Nick Burlingham still live in Stonington, Connecticut, with their two children, Caroline and Colin, where the kids attend Pine Point School. After practicing law for a few years Nick switched careers to become an executive at Columbia Air Services at nearby Groton airport. Columbia is a fixed-base operation servicing, chartering, and selling mainly corporate aircraft. Kim works part time as a supervisor at a day care center. We visit the Burlinghams for Grandparents Day at school, and they join the gang at Sky Farm for their vacation each summer.

We now have a new friend on our drives to visit the kids in Connecticut – the GPS navigation system lady in our station wagon. She is very polite in giving her oral instructions directing us to the best route to our destination. Only sometimes we disagree. For example, she persistently steers us via the Connecticut Thruway to Ned's house in Greenwich, while we prefer the Merritt Parkway. She does not give up easily when we take our route, and I find myself addressing the dashboard and telling her quite sharply to be quiet.

Our children and their families are doing well in life, and they treat their aging parents royally whenever we get together.

Love Story

One can certainly fall in love with a home, as we have with our home in Laurel Hollow, where we have lived for the last thirty years. I love the big living and dining rooms where we have entertained our friends at dinner parties and family at holiday lunches.

I like our library filled with favorite books of biography and history and a wide-screen TV, a perfect mind-stimulating mix. Outdoors I love the broad green lawns, pocket-sized meadow, enticing swimming pool, the blooming rhododendron and laurel in the spring, and verdant woods buffering us from the outside world. I love to plant impatiens in the spring and prune our shrubs and trees, and can understand the pleasure that clearing brush has brought to at least two presidents. However, along with Buz, two good friends – Jerry Sampson, a retired county police officer, and Thelma Parchment, a Brooklyn resident from Barbados – have done the heavy lifting in domestic chores.

Buz and I still get around well with a few concessions to Father Time. I have paid visits to several hospitals and belong to that group of Americans, about one out of six, that take three or more medications each day. At our Exeter reunion a friend told me he had been forced to give up crap shooting because of an injury to his shoulder. I inquired why crap shooting bothered his shoulder that much, and he replied, "I didn't say 'crap shooting'; I said 'trap shooting'." So I soon may be in the market for a hearing aid. On a recent winter sojourn in Florida Buz and I visited St. Augustine, site of the first settlement in America and another great sixteenth century Spanish fort. St. Augustine is also where Ponce de Leon searched for the Fountain of Youth. He didn't find it, and neither did I.

We went to the Kentucky Derby in 2004 with our pals, the Jewetts. It was an incredible party scene with vendors hawking Early Times mint juleps along with Cokes throughout the stands. On our visit to Ashford, a magnificent horse breeding farm in Lexington, I learned that the genealogical records of thoroughbred horses go back further than most families can track their own ancestral roots. We have been able to trace the Lamont family tree back eight generations, which is just about average for thoroughbred record keeping.

The best part of the Derby was that Smarty Jones, loved by everyone except the experts, came through for us and all his fans. I even saw a bumper sticker that read, "Smarty Jones For President." An interesting idea, but I was backing John Kerry in 2004, and Ned and I attended the

A romance for all seasons.

"All the world's a stage, and all the men and women merely players." Presenting the new members of the cast – front row: Emily Lamont, Teddy (E.M.L. II) Lamont, Colin Burlingham, Lindsay Lamont, Caroline Burlingham, Anne Lamont. Back row: Camille Burlingham, Ted, Buz, Helena, Nick Burlingham, Ned Lamont.

Buz Bomb II.

Our home in Laurel Hollow.

"The Big House" at Sky Farm.

final night of the Democratic convention in Boston when Kerry accepted his party's nomination for president. After the massive traditional balloon release at the close, potential first lady Teresa joined the high-spirited celebration in the oversold arena, batting balloons back and forth with delegates. But it was not to be. I have read that some folks felt that Kerry's campaign style was a bit prim and haughty, but he certainly didn't act that way as we watched him happily strumming a guitar with Jon Bon Jovi et al at a Radio City Music Hall gala. At another campaign event in New York Senator Kerry greeted Buz, whom he had never met before, by planting a kiss on her cheek. I wasn't surprised because I always knew that she was irresistible.

My brother Tommy once wrote, "North Haven is my Tivoli, my Mandalay, my favorite place on earth." One can certainly fall in love with a place, and summer after summer our family has relished our vacations in North Haven, even when unrelenting foul weather socked in.

When the kids were younger, those were good days to break out old home movies, some going back to the 1930s. Tactfully explaining to the children the identity of ex-spouses, abandoned sweethearts, and black sheep gone astray was a minor distraction in an exercise that always evoked warm memories of all who had gone before, as dinghy races in the Thoroughfare and family picnics to nearby islands flashed across the screen. I always thought of my parents and especially of Tommy, who has been the hero whose memory has inspired me throughout my life. Francis T. P. Plimpton, a good friend of our family, wrote a poetic memorial to Tommy, which included this verse.

> *Whatever others did, he stood erect*
> *And straight for what he thought was right, without*
> *The unsecure and qualified effect*
> *That's left by those whose faith is really doubt.*
> *And then the war, that cut across the length*
> *Of all our lives. His generation lost?*
> *Not lost but found in their awakened strength —*
> *They faced their task although they knew the cost.*
> *He chose the silent service, submarines,*
> *Where courage isn't flame, but means the test*
> *Of taut and tightened nerves against machines.*
> *And now — the restless sea, it gives him rest.*
> *He bore an honored name, but what is more*
> *He added honor to the name he bore.*

The whole family circle, young and old, was important to Tommy. His loyalty and love were reflected in his letters home – thoughtful, informed, and funny – when he was in the Navy. I like the one in which he kidded his sister Elinor about sending him a woolen scarf when he was stationed in San Diego. His character and courage, wide-ranging intellectual curiosity, and proficiency in creative writing and persuasive speech would have taken him far in life, almost certainly in public service or journalism rather than business. I have thought of him constantly and am moved to tears every time I hear the Navy hymn or "America the Beautiful" played at our Memorial Day church service. What a guy, and what a loss – the tragedy of an unfinished life that ended much too soon.

Buz has been the most important person in my life. We have been in love for more than half a century, and, more than that, she has been my best friend and partner in all the ventures we have undertaken – from books to boats and many more. She has been the perennial winner of the MVP award in our family. Along with our three children I love and honor her for being the guiding light in our family that points us down the right path by the way she leads her own life. If the definition of a saint is someone who has chosen to do kind things for other people as their purpose in life, Buz is a saint. I will always be grateful to her, along with my children, family, and friends, past and present, for their good and happy company on life's journey.